Creating Communication

EXPLORING AND EXPANDING YOUR FUNDAMENTAL COMMUNICATION SKILLS

Second Edition

Randy Fujishin

Rowman & Littlefield Publishers, Inc.
Lanham • Boulder • New York • Toronto • Plymouth, UK

ROWMAN & LITTLEFIELD PUBLISHERS, INC.

Published in the United States of America
by Rowman & Littlefield Publishers, Inc.
A wholly owned subsidiary of The Rowman & Littlefield Publishing Group, Inc.
4501 Forbes Boulevard, Suite 200, Lanham, Maryland 20706
www.rowmanlittlefield.com

Estover Road
Plymouth PL6 7PY
United Kingdom

British Library Cataloguing in Publication Information Available

Library of Congress Cataloging-in-Publication Data:

Fujishin, Randy.
    Creating communication : exploring and expanding your fundamental
communication skills / Randy Fujishin. — 2nd ed.
        p. cm.
    Includes bibliographical references and index.
    ISBN-13: 978-0-7425-5562-4 (pbk. : alk. paper)
    ISBN-10: 0-7425-5562-3 (pbk. : alk. paper)
    ISBN-13: 978-0-7425-6396-4 (electronic)
    ISBN-10: 0-7425-6396-0 (electronic)
    1. Communication. I. Title.
P90.F784 2008
153.6—dc22   2008017142

Printed in the United States of America

♾™ The paper used in this publication meets the minimum requirements of
American National Standard for Information Sciences—Permanence of Paper
for Printed Library Materials, ANSI/NISO Z39.48-1992.

For Vicky
and Our Sons

*Each one of us is an artist creating
an authentic life.*

SARAH BAN BREATHNACH

Contents

Preface

One word can change a conversation. One touch can soften an argument. One smile can invite a friendship. One angry word withheld can save a relationship. And one interaction can change your entire world.

I have witnessed hundreds of people create the beginnings to a new friendship or bring healing to an old relationship with a single word or behavior. With one statement or act, I have observed people like you and me encourage cooperation between individuals in conflict or inspire passion in an audience.

As a teacher of speech communication and as a marriage and family therapist, I have witnessed and heard the stories of how one gentle touch, one word of encouragement, one smile, or one apology improved a relationship, enhanced a job, or changed a life. Like artists, these people have created something new and exciting, bringing forth harmony, unity, and joy to their lives, as well as to the lives of others. Instead of using paint, oils, or clay, these artists use words and behavior to create their masterpieces. We are these artists—you and I.

You are an artist, playing a large role in creating loving relationships, meaningful careers, and rich, authentic lives. The way you communicate and interact with those around you determines, to a great extent, the kind of person you become. No single factor is more important in determining the nature of your relationships and the quality of your life than the communication skills you learn and develop.

I believe that with every word and behavior, you create the nature and quality of your communication within yourself and with others. Each chapter in this book addresses a specific dimension of your daily life, wherein you can create more effective, successful, and meaningful communication by implementing small, yet powerful changes in the way you speak, listen, and interact with others.

New to this second edition are sections dealing with being an ethical speaker, avoiding plagiarism, expanded discussions of visual aid usage, electronic visual aids, and note card usage. There are also new informative and persuasive sample speech outlines. I have also added sections on self-disclosure in relationships, relationship interviewing, asking questions, and self-awareness inventories. Many new opening chapter stories provide added excitement and depth to this revised edition, along with updated examples, illustrations, and anecdotes that round out this second edition of *Creating Communication*.

It is my hope that after reading this book, you will know how to create communication that will improve your personal relationships, enhance your participation and leadership in groups, develop your public speaking skills, and strengthen your interviewing abilities. By exploring new communication behaviors and expanding your creative thinking, you will become an artist of communication, creating a more productive and meaningful life.

I would like to thank my executive editor, Niels Aaboe, for giving me the opportunity to publish this second edition of *Creating Communication*. Special thanks goes to my editor, Asa Johnson, for his insightful and encouraging guidance on this project. My thanks to Paul Sanders and Steve Richmond for their friendship. And most of all, I want to thank my wife, Vicky, and our sons, Tyler and Jared. They have created a loving home that is the best place in all the world for me.

It is to Vicky and our boys that I dedicate this book.

ONE

Creating Effective Communication in Your Life

> *The highest art we create*
> *is the way we live each day.*
>
> —BALINESE SAYING

It was just another class assignment for Karen, but it changed her life.

The first homework assignment I give my communication students is to be more spacious—more accepting and nonjudgmental—in their conversational listening. I coach them to punctuate their daily conversations with periods of silence as they listen to others. Rather than verbally interrupt a speaker with judgment, advice, encouragement, or questions every twelve seconds, which seems to be the norm for my students, they are to listen without any interruptions for thirty seconds or more, whatever students feel is appropriate for the speaker, the topic, and the flow of the discussion.

"I thought this assignment would be boring—to listen so long without saying anything," Karen began. "But I tried it out on my mom last night and it was wonderful! I would normally interrupt her after a few seconds, give my opinion, and then just walk away.

"But last night was different! I let her talk for long periods of time without interrupting, just like we practiced in class. At times, I kept quiet for thirty seconds, and one or two minutes at other times. Sometimes even longer. It was so weird. But she really opened up during our talk. In fact, she talked about things I've never heard before—about Dad, her job, and how she feels about me."

"So, your mom said things she normally wouldn't tell you?" I asked.

"I think she's always wanted to say these things, but I was the one who wasn't listening," Karen admitted. "This assignment forced me to pay attention to her for a change. I feel liked I've created a whole new relationship with her."

"What a wonderful creation," I said.

"I feel like I made something really important happen."

"Almost like an artist," I chuckled.

"Yeah, like an artist of communication!" she concluded.

YOU ARE AN ARTIST OF COMMUNICATION

Whether or not you realize it, you are an artist, and your life is the canvas on which you will create your greatest work. Your most important creation will not be a painting, a sculpture, or a book. Rather, it will be the person you become during this lifetime.

Your greatest work will ultimately find its form and structure in the blending of the broad brush stokes of your family, relationships, career, and education. More important, it will be textured and imbued with the thousands upon thousands of finer, more delicate brush stokes of every word and action you paint each day on the canvas of your life.

It will be these smaller brush stokes during your everyday life—the way you treat your loved ones, the manner in which you interact with people at school, work, and in your neighborhood, and even the way you greet strangers—that will most significantly determine the kind of person you become.

As an artist of communication, you help to create the atmosphere within which your interactions with others occur. Whether it's a quick smile to a stranger, a heartfelt speech at a wedding reception, or a minute of attentive silence when a loved one is speaking, you are creating the masterpiece of your life moment by moment.

Now, you may be saying to yourself that "I'm no artist" or "Art is for those who are trained or gifted." But that's not true. We are all creative, often consciously selecting the words, behaviors, circumstances, responses, and attitudes we bring to our communication interactions with the people in our lives. Artist Edgar Whitney proclaims that "Every human being has creative powers. You were born to create. Unleash your creative energy and let it flow." Accept this gentle challenge to create more effective communication in your life and let your creative powers flow.

Every day you talk, listen, and interact with others. Most of the time, you speak and listen more out of habit than anything else, not even vaguely aware of your role in the communication process. But I'm inviting you not only to become more aware and skilled in those fundamental communication skills, but also to become more creative in the ways in which you think, speak, listen, and interact with others.

If you don't, you may be limiting your opportunities to effectively connect with people. You may even be limiting your opportunities to develop as a person.

Author Thomas Moore warns against our reluctance and maybe even our fears of becoming artists in our everyday lives: "When we leave art only to the accomplished painter and the museum, instead of fostering our own artful sensibilities in every aspect of daily life, then our lives lose opportunities for soul." Rather than being unconscious, unconcerned, or disillusioned about how you communicate with others, take up this invitation to become an artist of communication and create more effective communication in your lives.

Your acceptance, however, to create more effective communication will not necessarily guarantee success in every interaction. Human communication is much too complicated and involved. There are thousands of unconscious nonverbal behaviors involved in even a single conversation and we are usually aware of only a few of them during the course of the conversation.

The same holds true for the verbal dimension of that same conversation. The hundreds of thousands of words in our language and the millions of possible arrangements of those words are equally staggering. There is no possible way we can consciously choose the perfect words and the perfect sentences for every thought and feeling we wish to communicate.

Verbal and nonverbal communication are also governed by habit. It is easier to say hello and smile as we pass others than it is to create a unique and special greeting for each and every person. Effective communication requires that much of our interaction with others be governed by habit. Otherwise, communication would be too dense, clumsy, and overwhelming. Even if we could select the perfect words, sentences, and behaviors to communicate, there is no guarantee that the recipient of the message would interpret the words and the behaviors in the way we intended.

The process of human communication cannot be as intentional and predictable as the brush strokes on canvas or the careful shaping of clay. We cannot control the viewers' interpretation when they "see" our painting or statue. But in communication with others, you can choose to be more aware of, sensitive to, and selective of your words and behaviors. Your decision to consciously participate in the way you speak and listen to others will open the doors to more effective communication. As Karen learned, even one change in her communication behavior—listening without interrupting—created more space for her mother to share. This one change created a wonderful change in their relationship.

THE PROCESS OF COMMUNICATION

Let's begin with an examination of communication itself, for it is communication that enables us to experience our lives and share experiences with others. The late-night talks, the laughter, the gentle touches, the tears, the encouragement, and the thousands upon thousands of other communication acts all combine to create what you experience as life. Our communication with others is not a little thing. It is life itself.

All the arts we practice

are mere apprenticeship.

The big art is our life.

—M. C. RICHARDS

The importance of communication cannot be overstated. Family therapist Virginia Satir has suggested that "Once a human being has arrived on this earth, communication is the single most important factor determining what kinds of relationships he makes and what happens to him in the world." Satir continues by stating in no uncertain terms that "How he manages his survival, how he develops intimacy, and how he makes sense of his world are largely dependent upon his communication skills."

So, what exactly is communication? Let's define communication in a way that emphasizes your creative involvement in the communication process. **Communication** is the process whereby we create and exchange messages.

A Process

Any activity can be viewed as a thing or a process. A thing is static, time bound, and unchanging. A **process** is moving, continually changing, with no beginning or end. In our definition, communication is a process—something that is continually changing. Individual words, sentences, and gestures have no meaning in isolation. They make sense only when viewed as parts of an ongoing, dynamic process.

To fully understand the process of communication, we must notice how what we say and do influences and affects what the other person says and does. We must pay attention to the changes we experience and how these changes influence and affect our perception, interpretation, and interactions with others, from moment to moment, year to year, and decade to decade.

Similarly, we also need to be sensitive to the ongoing changes in those we communicate with because they are changing too. Communication is alive, and to fully appreciate it requires that we view it as a dynamic, fluid, and continually changing process.

Creating Messages

Language in any culture contains thousands if not hundreds of thousands of words to select from and arrange in endless combinations to form the basic structures of verbal communication. There are even more subtle and not-so-subtle nonverbal (or nonlanguage) communication behaviors that can be added to the mix.

It is our ability to create messages from the verbal and nonverbal dimensions of communication that truly distinguishes us from all other forms of life. Our ability to create communication not only is the most significant way humans differ from animals and plants, but it also may be one of the deepest and strongest drives within us—to express and share who we are. What more powerful and significant way to express who and what we are than by communicating our thoughts and feelings with others?

Exchanging Messages

After selecting the words, sentences, and nonverbal cues to form the thought or feeling we are attempting to communicate, we send the message to the recipient, who processes the message and gives a response in the form of feedback. The recipient's role in the communication process is also a creative process, because what he or she selectively perceives and interprets from the original message will determine the meaning of the message for him or her. The message recipient then creates a response from all the words and nonverbal behaviors available. Receiving and creating a response is just as important as creating and sending the original message.

VERBAL AND NONVERBAL COMMUNICATION

The communication process has two forms—verbal and nonverbal. Both forms usually operate together in the majority of messages you send and receive.

Verbal communication is all spoken and written communication. A mother whispering reassuring words to a child, a speaker addressing an audience of five thousand, or a sunbather reading a book on the beach is utilizing verbal communication.

Nonverbal communication is all communication that is not spoken or written. It is your body type, voice, facial expressions, gestures, movement, clothing, and touch. It is your use of distance, use of time, and the environment you create. It is your laughter, your tears, your gentle touch, your relaxed breathing, the car you drive, and the color of your pen. All these things and countless others make up your nonverbal communication.

Verbal communication and nonverbal communication enable you and me to communicate. They provide all that is necessary for the process of connecting, and it is our privilege to use them creatively, effectively, and meaningfully.

COMPONENTS OF COMMUNICATION

Even though the following seven components of communication operate almost instantaneously, we will examine them separately to more clearly understand their specific function. The seven components are source, message, receiver, encoding, channel, decoding, and context.

Source

The **source** is the originator of the message. It is the person or persons who want to communicate a message to another person or a group of people. The source of a message can be an individual speaker addressing a group, a child asking for candy, a couple sending out invitations to a family reunion, or a person writing a letter.

Message

The **message** is the idea, thought, or feeling that the source wants to communicate. This message is encoded or converted into verbal and nonverbal symbols that will most likely be understood by the receiver.

Receiver

The **receiver** is the recipient of the message. The receiver can be an individual or a group of people. Once the receiver hears the words and receives the nonverbal cues from the sender, she must interpret or decode them if communication is to occur.

Encoding

Once the source has decided on a message to communicate, he must **encode** or convert that idea, thought, or feeling into verbal and nonverbal symbols that will be most effectively understood by the receiver. This encoding process can be extremely creative because there are unlimited ways for the source to convert the idea or feeling into words and behaviors.

Consider a simple message such as "I want to see you again." The source can simply say, "I want to see you again," and smile as he says the words. He can also say, "Let's get together again," and cast a humorous glance, or he can murmur, "I need to see you again," with direct eye contact and outstretched arms. He could simply scribble a note on a napkin saying, "We need an encore," and place it gently in front of the other person. There are countless ways to encode this simple message and each one would be received and interpreted by the recipient in a slightly different way.

The important thing to remember is that you can open yourself up to the endless possibilities of selecting, arranging, and delivering messages you want to communicate. Your willingness to put greater creativity into the encoding process will enhance and deepen your communication with others.

Channel

A **channel** is the medium by which the message is communicated. The source can utilize the channels of sight, sound, touch, smell, and taste. For instance, if you want to communicate affection for another person, you can utilize a variety of channels or combination of channels. You can say, "I like you" (sound). You can give a hug (touch). You can wink an eye (sight). You can send cookies that you baked (taste). Or you can deliver a dozen roses (smell). You can creatively select the channels of communication to productively communicate your message.

Decoding

Decoding is the process of making sense out of the message received. The receiver must decipher the language and behaviors sent by the source so they will have meaning. After the receiver decodes the message, the receiver (now the source) can encode a return message and send it back to the other person.

Context

All communication occurs within a certain context. The context is made up of the physical surroundings, the occasion in which the communication occurs, the time, the number of people present, noise level, and many other variables that can influence and affect the encoding and decoding of messages. The context plays an important role in the communication process.

As you consider the effects that the context can have on communication, you might want to put your creativity to good use. Think of ways you can create a serene, healthy, and productive communication environment. Simple things like choosing a time when you both have an opportunity to meet. Making the actual physical surroundings clean, uncluttered, and peaceful. Maybe straightening up the house, buying some flowers to cheer the place up, and even putting on some soothing background music. Perhaps a drive in the country or a walk in a park will create a more relaxed context in which you can communicate more effectively. Whatever you do, remember that you can have some influence over the context in which communication occurs within your life.

MODELS OF COMMUNICATION

Models provide a concrete way to see how concepts and processes work. We'll look at three communication models that show how the various communication components interact. Although models help simplify the complex process of communication, keep in mind that they only represent reality.

Models are like words. Words are not reality. They cannot tell us everything about an object or event. For instance, the word "apple" is not an actual apple. You cannot slice or eat the word "apple" as you can a real one. The word "apple" does not tell you everything about an apple either—the smell, the coloring, the texture, the taste, the degree of ripeness, and whether or not the price sticker is still glued to the skin

Like words, these three models of communication are not reality
begin to tell us everything about the processes they are inten
However, they are extremely valuable in helping us visualize and
process of human communication.

Linear Model

One of the simplest models of communication was advanced by C. E. Shannon and W. Weaver in 1949. Their conceptualization represents a message-centered view of communication that is linear in design. This model has a source sending a message through a channel to a receiver, a process similar to a telephone. Shannon and Weaver introduced a component labeled **noise** to represent any interference to the fidelity of the message, such as physical noise from other people's loud talking or internal noise such as multiple meanings for a word contained in the message. The linear model of communication, shown below, is a "one-way" model because it fails to depict the receiver's feedback or response.

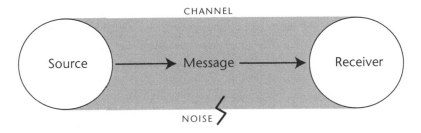

The linear model is useful for pointing out the basic elements of the communication process, but it is far too simple to describe the complexity of the process. It shows only the flow of messages from the sender to the receiver, but not the receiver's response.

Interactional Model

Communication involves more than the message transmission portrayed in the linear model. The feedback must be taken into account. **Feedback** is the process of sending information from the receiver back to the source. The source uses this feedback to adjust her message based on what the receiver communicated. The source's modification of the original message is called **adaptation.** The illustration below shows how feedback and adaptation operate in the interactional model of communication. The source sends a message to the receiver, the receiver responds with feedback, and the source adapts her message until the message is successfully communicated.

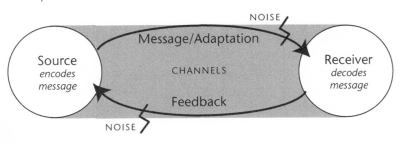

Again, this model is too simple to accurately reflect the communication process.

Transactional Model

Often, messages are sent and received simultaneously, and the "source" and "receiver" may be one or more individuals. In fact, these individuals are more accurately described as **communicators,** individuals who simultaneously send and receive messages. This is one of the primary characteristics of the transactional model of communication.

The most important idea of the transactional model is that communication operates systemically. A **system** is a collection of interdependent parts arrayed in such a way that a change in one of its components will affect changes in all the other components. In the transactional model, the various components or parts of communication are not viewed as independent of one another, but as interdependent. A change in one produces a change in all the others.

The systemic view presented in the transactional model, shown below, includes the basic components of the first two models, yet also considers the context in which communication occurs, the number of people involved, the background of those individuals, and the simultaneity of the source and receiver roles.

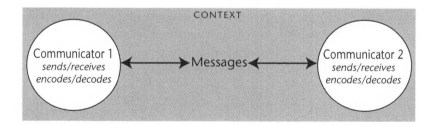

Communication never takes place in a vacuum, but in a specific **context** or environmental setting. To understand a communication event, we need to know where and under what circumstances people are communicating, because these have a major influence on the individuals involved. For example, discussing vacation plans in the comfort of your own living room with a friend would be entirely different from discussing them in the front row of a rock concert or during a funeral service.

Although communication often occurs between two people, there are many times when more than two individuals are involved. The addition of even one person to a conversation between two people can dramatically change its outcome. A speaker will have a very different speaking experience addressing an audience of five colleagues than facing an audience of five thousand. The number of people affects the communication event.

The backgrounds of the individuals involved—the cultural, psychological, physical, gender, age, and other demographic differences and similarities—influence the communication. Do the individuals speak the same language? How might gender affect communication styles and responses? Will age differences influence the interpretation of a message? What will be the effect of educational differences? What about cultural differences?

Unlike the earlier models of communication, the transactional model does not make a distinction between the source and the receiver. In reality, you are sending and receiving messages simultaneously and continually as you communicate with others. As you are speaking, you are also receiving information from the listener. You see her nodding, shifting posture, and smiling. As you are listening to her response, you are simultaneously sending messages with your diverted gaze, slouching posture, and audible yawn. This simultaneous nature of communication transactions allows you to modify or change the messages you are sending even as you speak. A change in one element of a system can bring about a change in the other elements.

The important thing to remember about the transactional model is that the individuals communicating have an impact on each other. In this respect, what and how you communicate—your choice of words and actions—can influence and change others.

Remember Karen? Her mother shared more deeply because Karen listened in a new way. Karen's perception of the event may be that her mother changed. But Karen also changed. She not only changed her listening behavior, but she also became more open to her mother, more knowledgeable of her mother's life, more accepting, and perhaps a bit more loving. The relationship changed for both women because Karen chose to create a different listening environment for her mother. Keep in mind your creative influence as you speak and listen to others.

PERCEPTION

To more fully understand communication, we must recognize the importance of perception. **Perception** is the process by which we assign meaning to a stimulus. Or put another way, perception is giving meaning to the things we see and experience. If an attractive stranger smiles at you at a party, what do you immediately think? Is the person simply being polite and acknowledging you? Recognizing you from somewhere else? Actually smiling at the person behind you? Maybe even flirting with you? Or perhaps the person is experiencing intestinal gas pains and is attempting to hide the discomfort? What's your guess? These are just a few meanings we can assign to that stimulus.

Selection

The process of perception involves our five senses. We see, hear, touch, smell, and taste. From these five senses we take in the stimuli of the world. It's from these five senses that we receive information to make sense of our lives. Because we are exposed to much more stimuli than we could ever manage, the first step in perception is to select which stimuli to attend to. In other words, we don't attend to every stimulus that is present at any given moment.

Even in the location where you're reading this book, if you were to count each stimulus in your field of vision, the number would be in the thousands, perhaps the tens of thousands. To pay attention to each stimulus at the same moment would be impossible. So you have to decide—do you select the words in this sentence or gaze at your left foot? Each selection changes your focus of vision. You can't select all the things, so you must select a few.

Interpretation

Once we have selected our perceptions, the second step is to interpret them in a way that makes sense to us. **Interpretation** is the act of assigning meaning to a stimulus. It plays a role in every communication act we encounter. Is a friend's humorous remark intended to express fondness or irritation? Does your supervisor's request for an immediate meeting with you communicate trouble or a pay raise? When an acquaintance says, "Let's do lunch," is the invitation serious or not? Almost every communication act we encounter involves some level of interpretation on our part. Let's examine some factors that influence our perception.

> *To paint beautifully, you must first see the beauty in the object you are painting.*
> —GEORGIA O'KEEFFE

Physical factors. The most obvious factors that influence our interpretation are physical. What is the condition of our five senses? Can we see accurately or do we need glasses? Can we hear sufficiently or is our hearing diminished by age? Can we smell and taste sharply or are allergies causing difficulties? Can you touch and feel with adequate sensitivity or do clothing and gloves make it hard?

The time of day affects how we physically process the sensory input. Are you more awake in the morning or late at night? Some people are most alert and attentive in the morning, while others come alive late at night.

Your general state of health can influence interpretation. When you are ill, hungry, or depressed, you see and experience a very different world than when you are healthy, well fed, and cheerful.

Age also can affect your interpretation. Older people view the world and events with a great deal more experience than do younger people. By simply having lived longer, older people have generally been through more of life's developmental stages—early adulthood, parenthood, grandparenthood, retirement. Younger people, on the other hand, usually have much more physical energy and time to play, explore, and investigate the world around them. With fewer life experiences, younger people interpret life differently.

Other physical factors are fatigue, hunger, stress, monthly biological cycles, diet, and exercise. Our bodies play an important role in our interpretation of the world.

Psychological factors. The second category of factors that influence interpretation is psychological or mental. For example, education and knowledge affect how we see the world around us. An individual who never went beyond the seventh grade sees a much different world than an individual who has completed law school. A trained botanist sees a forest far differently than does a first-grader.

Past experiences also affect how we interpret perceptions. Someone who grew up happily on a farm may view rural environments very differently than someone who grew up in New York City. A victim of robbery may be more fearful of a darkened street than someone who has never experienced a crime. An individual who grew up in a loving, stable family may have a more positive view of raising children than a person who grew up in a cold, unstable family.

Assumptions about people and the world in general influence interpretations also. A belief that people are basically good and honest, or basically untrustworthy and self-serving, will affect how we view the actions of others.

Finally, moods will influence how we interpret the things we see and experience. When we are feeling successful and competent, we see a very different world than when we are feeling sad, lonely, and depressed.

Cultural factors. A person's cultural background can affect and influence his or her interpretation of the world. Chapter 5 is devoted to intercultural communication and the role culture plays in how we communicate with those who are different from us. For now, we'll just briefly mention some cultural factors that influence perception.

Every culture has its own worldview, language, customs, rituals, artifacts, traditions, and habits. These factors not only affect how people perceive and interact with one another within a given culture, but also they influence how they interact with people of different cultures.

This present moment is filled with joy and happiness. If you are attentive, you will see it.

—THICH NHAT HANH

Culture can shape and determine how an individual sees the world. Americans interpret direct eye contact as a sign of confidence, honesty, and politeness, whereas Japanese interpret the same direct eye contact as rude and confrontational. People from Middle Eastern countries often converse within a few inches of each other's face, whereas Americans would find such closeness a violation of personal space. For Americans, the "okay" sign made with the thumb and the forefinger is a sign that everything is fine, but in many cultures it is an obscene gesture.

Position in space. The final factor that influences perception is position in space. Where we are determines how we see things. For instance, if you sit at the back of a classroom, you will perceive a very different environment than if you sit in the front row, right under the nose of the lecturer. The same holds true for adult interaction with children. You will perceive children differently if you kneel down to their eye level rather than stand over them. You even pay higher prices for better viewing positions. Think of the last concert, sporting event, or resort you attended or visited. The closer seats or the rooms with a view generally cost more.

Perception Checking

Because so many factors influence perception, what can we do to create more effective communication? **Perception checking** is a method for inviting feedback on our interpretations. Perception checking involves three steps:

1. An observation of a particular behavior.
2. Two possible interpretations of that behavior.
3. A request for clarification about how to interpret that behavior.

Many times people observe and interpret the behavior, and that's the end of it. Often their interpretations can be easily and readily corrected with a simple perception check. Here are two examples of how perception checking works:

> "I noticed you haven't been in class for the past two weeks. (observed behavior) I wasn't sure whether you've been sick (first interpretation) or were dropping the class. (second interpretation) What's up?" (request for clarification)

> "You walked right past me without saying hello. (observed behavior) It makes me curious if you're mad at me (first interpretation) or just in a hurry. (second interpretation) How are you feeling?" (request for clarification)

Often, perception checking is more to the point. You may not want to use all three steps:

> "I see you rolling your eyes at me. (observed behavior) What's the matter?" (invitation for clarification)

> "Are you certain you want to go to the movies? (request for clarification) You don't act like you're too enthusiastic." (observed behavior)

Perception checking can be a simple technique for clarifying communication behavior in a way that is not threatening or confrontational. It simply asks for clarification.

PRINCIPLES OF COMMUNICATION

Certain generally accepted truths or principles of communication are important to consider when communicating with others. These principles hold true for all people in every culture. By understanding these principles, you will experience greater communication effectiveness.

Communication Is Constant

You cannot *not* communicate. In other words, you are always communicating. Too often we think that if we are not talking, we are not communicating. You may not be communicating verbally, but your nonverbal communication is constantly displaying signs and cues that reflect what you are thinking and feeling internally. Your posture, gestures, facial expressions, clothing, use of time, and even the car you drive are just a few of the nonverbal messages that others perceive and interpret.

Even when you are speaking, your tone of voice, rate of speech, pitch, volume, pauses or lack of pauses, and vocal fillers such as "ah" and "um" are some of the nonverbal behaviors that can convey what you're thinking and feeling beneath the level of language. You're always communicating.

Communication Is Transactional

Communication can be viewed as a transaction in which the meanings of messages are negotiated between people. Unlike the earlier linear and interactional models, which view communication as primarily sending and receiving intact and unchanging messages, the transactional model considers to a greater extent the complexities of the individuals involved, the environment, and the influence the communicators have on one another.

At a deeper level, the transactional nature of communication encourages us to regard others and ourselves in a much more complex way. We can no longer view the receiver of our messages as a receptacle in which we deposit our thoughts and feelings with little or no message distortion. The transactional nature of communication creates a more other-centered awareness and sensitivity to others. No longer can we be limited to our earlier preoccupation with getting our message across. Instead, we shift our focus from self to other to participate equally in communication exchanges or transactions in which the receiver is regarded with greater sensitivity and respect.

Communication Is a Process

The Greek philosopher Heraclitus said that you never step twice into the same river. What he meant was that a river is never exactly the same as it continually twists and turns, constantly changing in depth and speed, as it flows in its journey from the snowcapped mountains to the sea hundreds of miles away.

Communication is a process like a river. It is continuous and always changing. You can begin to understand and appreciate communication only when you view the individual words, sentences, and gestures of communication as a part of an ongoing process. One sentence or gesture may hold very little meaning in and of itself. But viewed from a larger, more dynamic process perspective, the sentence or gesture takes on a different meaning. To understand the process of communication, we need to consider how our words and actions influence and affect the recipient of our message.

We, the creators of these messages, are also in process. How we perceive the world and communicate with others when we first get up in the morning can be vastly different from how we perceive and communicate during the late hours of evening. From moment to moment, like a river, we twist and turn, constantly changing the depth of our perceptions, thoughts, and feelings as we travel from morning to evening. From year to year, decade to decade, we change dramatically in our interests, beliefs, fears, and desires. What spoke to our ears and hearts in our youth may not ring true in our middle and later years. We are constantly changing.

Communication Is Irreversible

"Forget I said that." "I'm sorry I did that. Let's pretend it never happened." We have all issued statements like these in an attempt to erase or diminish the impact of an angry word or action. Even though the other person agreed to forget or dismiss the statement or behavior, the memory of a careless word or deed can last a lifetime. I'm sure you can recall a stinging criticism or hurtful act you experienced during childhood. The memory of the criticism or act can linger and haunt you many years later.

Likewise, uplifting, positive, and healing words and deeds can also be carried in the hearts and minds of others forever. I remember my father waking me before sunrise and taking me to the local café in our farming community when I was four years old. He would carry me sleepy eyed to the counter where he would plop me down on a stool and announce to the other farmers, "This is my boy!" Many a predawn breakfast at the Coyote Cafe began with his proud announcement and the other farmers' chiding chorus of "We know, Mike. We know. . . ." More than four decades have passed since those predawn breakfasts, but I'll never forget my dad's pride and love as he carried me into that café and proudly announced, "This is my boy."

Your every word and deed can leave an indelible imprint on the minds and hearts of others. Be conscious of your choices as you create messages to others.

Communication Is Learned

Research suggests that crying and laughing are interpreted similarly by peoples of all cultures. But more often than not, our communication patterns and behaviors are learned. The language we acquire, the extent of our vocabulary, the way we speak, our gestures, eye contact, our touching, and how we dress are just a few of the many examples of learned communication behavior.

Communication is also learned in a cultural context that is so pervasive and extensive that we are often unaware of it. We mistakenly assume that "our" way of communicating and expressing is the "right" way and all the other cultures are wrong. This notion of ethnocentrism is explored in chapter 5, but for now, we need only appreciate the fact that most people view their way of communicating as the "right" way.

The principle that communication is learned suggests also that communication can be unlearned and new ways of communicating acquired. This is most exciting because then we can replace our ineffective and unhealthy ways of speaking, listening, and behaving with more effective and healthy ways. Because we did not learn to communicate in effective and healthy ways does not mean we are condemned to this fate for the rest of our lives.

Communication Is Creative

The last principle of communication is that it is creative. This creativity is much broader than the creativity associated with art, music, and poetry. It is the creativity expressed in your daily communication, in the unique and special ways you communicate: When you choose to be silent. The way you listen. The times you choose to speak. The words you select from your vocabulary palette and the sentences you create. The combinations of facial expressions, gestures, movements, and postures you choose to express your thoughts and feelings. The letters you send. The telephone calls you make. The clothes you wear. The car you drive. The room you decorate. The home you live in. These are just some of the ways you create communication in your life.

> *Your life has been your art. You have set yourself to music and your days are your sonnets.*
>
> —OSCAR WILDE

Your communication and the impact it has on others does not just happen. You make it happen. You decide whether or not to return a phone call. You decide whether or not to respond to a lunch invitation. You decide whether to respond in kindness or in anger to a criticism leveled your way. You create by choosing one behavior and not another. You are always creating something in your communication life.

Do You Enlarge or Diminish Others?

I believe that we enlarge or diminish others with our communication. We heal or hurt others with our words. People go away from our interactions feeling a little better or a little worse than before.

You are free to create the words and behaviors that will ultimately enlarge or diminish the recipient of your message. No one is writing your script or coaching your movements and gestures. You are ultimately the scriptwriter, the dialogue coach, the director, and the speaker who will deliver the lines. You are given a great deal of creative latitude for how you create your messages during your life. What will you create? Will you enlarge or diminish others with your communication?

Inside you there is an artist you might not know just yet. But relax, continue reading, and gently welcome the artist within you. The highest art you will ever create lies ahead—the art of communication.

> These exercises are intended to help you explore and experiment with new ways of communicating in a variety of settings and to expand your thoughts about who you are and the communication possibilities available to you.

EXPLORING CREATIVE TASKS

1. Listen for thirty seconds or more without verbally interrupting a friend during a conversation. What changes did that create? What was your friend's response? How did you feel not interrupting as much?

2. Use perception checking in situations when another person's communication or behavior is confusing, ambiguous, or unclear. What were the results of your perception check? What changes did it create in the conversation?

3. List ten positive characteristics or traits a friend possesses. Share the list with your friend. In your opinion, was the experience enlarging or diminishing for your friend? What makes you think so? Has this conversation changed you relationship?

4. Keep a daily journal of specific instances when you were consciously aware of attempting to create more positive messages to others. What does it feel like to keep this journal? What are you learning about yourself? About others?

EXPANDING YOUR CREATIVE THINKING

1. What are some of your current creative activities or hobbies? What art forms or creative activities would you like to do in the future? What benefits do you think you would derive from them? When would you like to begin these artful activities?

2. In what specific ways could you be more positive and enlarging in your communication with loved ones and friends? With coworkers and casual acquaintances? How do you think more positive communication behaviors would change your relationships with these people?

3. What factors influence your perception and communication during a given day? When are you the most alert, positive, and energetic? Are there any specific ways you modify or improve your "view" of others? What are they? Can you think of any other ways to "see" the best in others?

4. List five specific changes that you could undertake that would make you more self-accepting, calm, and loving. Tape this list to your bedroom mirror or your car dashboard to remind yourself of your goals.

TWO

Creating Positive Communication with Yourself

> *You will talk and listen to yourself*
> *more than anyone else in your lifetime.*
> *What will your conversations be like?*
>
> —JOY BROWNE

Carlos looked tired and defeated as he sat in my office. He was currently enrolled in my public speaking class and had come to tell me he was dropping the course.

"We haven't even given our first speech, Carlos," I said.

"I know, but I guess I'm just freaked out about the whole thing."

"Are you concerned about your speech next week?"

"I guess," he said. "I just can't sleep at night since I started the class. I keep worrying about the speech."

"What kinds of things do you worry about?"

"I don't know. I'm just worried."

"No, really, what specifically do you see happening? What things do you hear yourself saying or thinking?"

"I'm thinking I'll make a mistake or forget what I'm supposed to say," Carlos said after a long pause. "They'll think I'm stupid."

WHAT DO YOU SAY TO YOURSELF?

No other individual will communicate with you more than you. What kinds of things do you say to yourself when you are facing a difficult decision, a troubling situation, or even the prospects of giving a speech? How do you talk to yourself?

If you are like most people, you give yourself a great deal of negative messages about what you are capable of accomplishing, what the future holds, and who you are. Shad Helmstetter in is book *What to Say When You Talk to Your Self* presents recent research suggesting that "77% of what we think is negative, counterproductive, and works against us." Well, the percentage of your negative thinking might not be that high, but each of us experiences moments of self-criticism, doubt, and worry many times a day.

Like Carlos, you and I are occasionally haunted by visions or voices in the dead of night. We see images that worry or frighten us. We tell ourselves things that erode our confidence, dampen our spirit, and darken our future. Like some form of silent torture, these images and thoughts keep piercing our minds, often making us want to escape, run away, or drop a course.

Yet when these visions or thoughts invade our serenity, most of us do nothing. Oh, we might attempt to wish them away, drink them away, or even drop a class or two. But we rarely confront or address them in any direct and constructive fashion. We toss and turn in the darkness and remain victims to their taunting. However, we can be more creative and dance with our demons in a new way.

CREATING NEW MESSAGES TO YOURSELF

One positive way you can deal with any negative thoughts is to use a technique called "giving equal time to the opposite." Normally when we experience a negative thought or disturbing image, we tend to remain focused on it or ruminate minute after minute.

> *Turn on your creativity and learn the craft of knowing how to open your heart. There's a light inside you.*
>
> —JUDITH JAMISON

Well, if we were to add up the minutes spent with this thought or image, the time would be considerable. To make matters worse, the longer we stay with the negative thought or image, the more anxious, worried, and terrified we become and we have created our own individual pathway to hell. Somehow we need to return home to our center, our quiet, our calmness.

"Giving equal time to the opposite" is an effective technique in bringing us back, not just to where we were before the worrying began, but often to a better place. It provides a more positive and healthy way of regarding ourselves.

The technique is simple. Fold a piece of lined binder paper in half lengthwise. On the top of the left column, mark a minus sign (–), and on the top of the right column, mark a plus sign (+). Whenever you experience a negative thought or image about a specific topic or issue, write down the negative statement or sketch a simple drawing of the negative vision you are experiencing in the left column and indicate the number of minutes you have spent with it. For instance, Carlos wrote, "I'll forget what I'm supposed to say. = 2 minutes of worry time," and he sketched out a stick figure drawing of himself looking worried.

His task in the "giving equal time to the opposite" technique is to spend an equal amount of time with the direct opposite thought and drawing. So, Carlos wrote, "I will remember my speech = 2 minutes of positive talk time," and sketched a second stick figure drawing of him smiling. For the next two minutes, he repeated the positive sentence "I will remember my speech," over and over, while looking at the drawing of him smiling while delivering his speech.

This technique may seem simplistic and even a little silly, but it forces you to consciously break your negative thought pattern and replace it with its opposite. You create the polar opposite of what you've been experiencing. From hell to paradise. It not only makes you aware of the amount of time you spend with these negative messages, it requires that you give equal time to the opposite, positive messages. This helps you to bring back balance.

My students and clients often experience great success with the "giving equal time to the opposite" technique and usually report three responses. First, they identified the specific thoughts and images that were actually bothering them. Many times, we feel upset, anxious, or worried about something, but we don't label it or give it a picture. Once a negative thought or image is named or identified, we can begin to work with it more constructively.

Second, they report that actually "giving equal time to the opposite" for a few minutes brings negative rumination to a stop, even if it is only for a few minutes. Many students and clients regard this technique as silly and impractical, but even they admit that it is difficult to hold two opposing thoughts or images simultaneously, so the technique provides some relief. Whether or not they realize it, they have created new pathways to solving old problems.

Finally, after minimal practice (usually a few attempts), they report that they can perform the "giving equal time to the opposite" technique without paper and pencil. They can use this new awareness of consciously introducing and holding more positive thoughts and images in their minds whenever those negative demons return. When you first try this technique, it may seem awkward or difficult, but keep at it. It's worth your effort.

By the way, Carlos didn't drop his public speaking course. Although initially skeptical and reluctant to try the "giving equal time to the opposite" technique, he found it helpful, not only in public speaking, but also in his social life and at work. At the end of the course, Carlos visited me again in my office and announced proudly that he had just been offered a promotion at work.

"Well, your hard work really paid off," I congratulated him.

"Hard work, and my pep talks to myself," he added. "Since taking your class, I listen to what I say to myself. If it's negative, I give 'equal time to the opposite'. Even when I don't believe what I'm saying, it makes a difference. At least I'm not spending the time worrying about so much negative stuff. I'm more positive now."

Creating new messages can help you change your self-concept and your life, just like Carlos did.

YOUR SELF-CONCEPT

Your **self-concept** is the subjective view you hold of yourself as a person. It is the sum total of your perceptions regarding your physical features, cultural background, emotional states, roles, talents, beliefs, values, likes and dislikes, achievements, and failures. The primary determinant of whom you will talk with, what you will say, how you will listen, and how you will interact is your self-concept. There are two primary ways of regarding who you are—public self-concept and private self-concept.

Public Self-Concept

Our **public self-concept** is on display when we are in public or for others to see. Our public self can find its origins in the professional roles we assume. Our professions as an engineer, teacher, doctor, or prison guard can affect how we view ourselves. Often, we internalize our professional roles to the extent that we continue to function in them outside their original context. A marine drill sergeant may treat his children like boot camp recruits. A teacher may lecture her parents as if they were students. A therapist may treat her friends like clients.

Private Self-Concept

Our **private self-concept** is much more personal than our public self-concept. It can be made up of our personal psychological traits, personal beliefs and values, and most frequent emotional states. This is the self-concept that is not known to our casual acquaintances and sometimes even close friends. Many times our private self-concept consists of those aspects or characteristics that we feel distinguish us from others. For instance, ethnicity might be a primary factor in your private self-concept if everyone else at work is of a different race, as would your being quiet and introspective if others around you are loud and boisterous. Both our public and private self-concepts help determine who we think we are and thus how we communicate with others.

HOW SELF-CONCEPT DEVELOPS

We are not born with a self-concept, but the creation and development of who we are begins as soon as we take our first breaths and continues until the moment we die. There are two primary ways that our self-concept develops—reflected appraisal and social comparison.

Reflected Appraisal

Reflected appraisal means that our self-concept matches what others see in us. As early as 1902, psychologist Charles Cooley in his book *Human Nature and the Social Order* suggested that we mirror the beliefs, attitudes, and perceptions that others communicate to us in their behavior. This reflected appraisal begins at birth by the manner in which we are treated as infants. The nonverbal behaviors of our parents, siblings, extended family members, and other caregivers can create strong internal impressions on us. The manner in which we are held, fed, played with, and talked to are a few of the many ways the perceptions of others can be internalized during infancy and last a lifetime.

Before long, the content of verbal messages is added to the thousands of nonverbal messages we receive as significant people in our lives tell us who we are. How we see ourselves as lovable, valuable, and capable to a great extent is determined by the messages from these individuals.

This process of reflected appraisal continues throughout our lives. The perceptions, expectations, and evaluations of our teachers, coaches, family, and friends continue to shape our notion of who we are and what we are capable of accomplishing. **Significant others**, those individuals in our lives to whom we assign great value, such as parents, siblings, romantic partners, and mentors, play an extremely important role in shaping our self-concept.

Social Comparison

Social comparison is how we evaluate ourselves when we compare ourselves with others. We accomplish this in two ways—by superior/inferior and same/different measurements.

By comparing ourselves with others we can often feel **superior or inferior** to others. When an exam is returned in class, we can feel inferior to the other students if we receive a low score and superior if we receive a high score. Perhaps the instructor announced that we received the highest mark on the exam and we were filled with pride. Feelings of superiority or inferiority when we compare ourselves to others in educational accomplishment, economic status, physical development, or spiritual awareness can affect our self-concept.

> *Every artist started out as a beginner. Your skill level right now doesn't matter. You'll learn.*
>
> —EDGAR WINTER

The second way we use social comparison is by deciding if we are the **same or different** as others. A man who enjoys music and spends his after-work hours practicing violin may view himself as being very different from the other men at work who lift weights at the gym or work on their cars. However, if that same man were employed as a musician with the city's symphony, he would most likely see himself as very similar to his colleagues and not feel out of place.

The reference groups, those people with whom we compare ourselves as superior/inferior and same/different, can have a profound influence on our self-concept. This leads us to the primary reason why "birds of a feather flock together." We have a tendency to associate with those who are equal and similar to us. It may be an unconscious way we keep our psychological equilibrium.

Even though our self-concept begins developing at our earliest interactions with our primary caregivers and continues until the moment of death, we don't always have a conscious knowledge of and familiarity with our perceptions of self. Mostly we have some vague, abstract notion of who we are and confront the components of our self-concept only when faced with a personal crisis or a life transition. It is during those times we are invited to consider and create a much healthier, flexible, and positive self-concept.

LISTENING CREATIVELY TO YOURSELF

We are rarely alone in this culture. When we do spend a moment or two in quiet reflection, we often judge the thoughts and feelings that arise. We don't measure up to the standards established by our parents, the magazine or television advertisements, and the culture in general. It is not surprising then that we often prefer to listen to the sounds of distraction rather than consider carefully and respectfully the contents of our inner life. So we create a flood of external sights and sounds to drown the internal music of our souls.

We need a new way to listen to ourselves that is less critical, less judgmental, and more open to simply observing and maybe even enjoying what we chance upon as we survey our self-perceptions. We need to create an attitude of curiosity, understanding, and, yes, even appreciation for ourselves.

Self-Concept Inventory

To begin the process of creatively listening to yourself, complete the following statements regarding who you think you are. Don't think too much. Don't judge or evaluate. Just jot down your first impression or thought for each item and enjoy the process of seeing who you are.

1. I am _____.
2. I am _____.
3. I am _____.
4. I believe _____.
5. I think _____.
6. I am successful at _____.
7. I enjoy _____.
8. I like _____.

9. My strongest personality trait is _____.
10. People like my _____.
11. My body is _____.
12. Physically I enjoy _____.
13. Mentally I enjoy _____.
14. Spiritually I enjoy _____.
15. Most people think I am _____.
16. My parents think I am _____.
17. My siblings think I am _____.
18. When I'm alone I _____.
19. When I talk to myself I _____.
20. As a friend I _____.
21. As a listener I _____.
22. When I am in conflict with others I _____.
23. My family thinks I am _____.
24. In small groups I _____.
25. If I were asked to lead a group, I _____.
26. If I were asked to give a speech, I _____.
27. People of different cultures are _____.
28. My greatest weakness is _____.
29. I usually leave others feeling _____.
30. I want to be remembered as _____.

Review your responses to the thirty items and reflect on your thoughts and feelings. Did you learn anything new about yourself? Were you surprised by any of your responses? Did they provide insight into your current communication behavior? Which responses were you satisfied with? Which responses were you not satisfied with?

Be gentle on yourself as you consider your responses to these thirty items. There are hundreds of other traits, characteristics, skills, beliefs, and feelings that contribute to your self-concept. As your awareness of them increases, you will also increase the amount of sensitivity, care, and attention you give them. It is not necessary, initially, to judge, improve, or change those you don't like or are uncomfortable with. Instead, just notice them. After you become familiar and comfortable with them, you can create ways to change or replace them with more positive thoughts and images if you desire.

Improvement Inventory

List five communication behaviors, personal habits, personality characteristics, relationships, and anything else you can think of that you feel need improvement. Solicit input from family and friends, coworkers and neighbors. Just the mere fact you would ask others for feedback will change your relationship with them.

1. _____
2. _____
3. _____
4. _____
5. _____

If you can admit you're not perfect and there are things you can improve, the criticism or threat of criticism from others will have less impact on you. Once you can freely admit to one weakness (or all five!), you may experience a new freedom that allows you to be more open to the communication and feedback of others.

Thanksgiving Inventory

List two things you are thankful for about your physical, psychological, and spiritual self. Choose conditions or attributes you already possess, not those you are striving or hoping to achieve.

1. I'm thankful for my (physical) _____.
2. I'm thankful for my (physical) _____.
3. I'm thankful for my (psychological) _____.
4. I'm thankful for my (psychological) _____.
5. I'm thankful for my (spiritual) _____.
6. I'm thankful for my (spiritual) _____.

Did you find this inventory easy or difficult? If you found it difficult, you may need to become aware of the many wonderful things that are already working in your life. One powerful way to create more contentment in your life is to simply become more aware of the many hundreds of things that you are currently blessed with physically, psychologically, and spiritually.

Six Months to Live Inventory

Write down five things you would like to do or accomplish if you discovered you had only six months to live. Assume you will experience no physical pain until the final day of life.

1. _____
2. _____
3. _____

4. _____

5. _____

Do any of your responses surprise you? How do you feel about your responses? Do your responses involve people, places, or things? Which item would you most want to accomplish before dying? If you were going to die in six months, how would that affect your communication with others?

Hopefully these inventories have encouraged you to reflect a little more on who you are and where you're headed. To create more positive communication with yourself, it's important to get to know yourself and how you'd like to change, improve, and grow.

Four Methods for Listening to Yourself

To get to know yourself more intimately, you may need to spend more time by yourself, free from the distractions and input of your family, friends, magazines, books, newspapers, television, computer, radio, and a myriad of other sources telling you who you should be and what you should do. Try one of the following four methods for listening to yourself.

Giving voice to your thoughts. Whenever you experience a recurring thought, especially negative ones, such as "I can't do this," "I shouldn't do that," "I have to do," "I'm no good," "I'll fail," and so on, you can "give it voice" by repeating the negative thought out loud to yourself, rather than experiencing it silently in your thinking. Don't shout or yell the statement. Anyone in the room might think you have gone off the deep end. Instead, repeat the negative thought softly yet audibly to yourself and label it as negative. For example, "I'm going to fail—I'm giving myself another negative thought," or "I can't complete the assignment—I'm giving myself another negative thought."

By saying the statement out loud and labeling the statement, you are making yourself aware of your negative message. Fritz Perls, the famous Gestalt therapist, believed that "Awareness is the first step to change." Well, this simple method of making your thoughts audible to yourself can be your first step to creating positive changes in your thinking.

Sitting in silence. This involves devoting ten minutes each day to sitting in a quiet place and doing nothing. Just close your eyes and listen to your breath. You are not to read, doodle on paper, meditate on a word or phrase, or even pray. If any thoughts or images come to your mind during the ten minutes, do not attempt to evaluate, change, or get rid of them. Just watch each thought or feeling float past your awareness. Like leaves floating past you on a stream, just observe them. No attachment. No desire. No effort. Just observe and listen to your breath. There is no performing, no attaining, or no striving. Carl Rogers once noted that, "It is only when we accept ourselves the way we are that we are free to change." You deserve a ten-minute "sitting-in-silence" time each day, just to unplug from the rush and noise of your life and simply be silent, observant, and open.

Keeping a personal journal. At the end of the day, devote just five minutes before going to bed to personal journal writing. In your journal (any notebook will do), write down a sentence or brief paragraph describing your thoughts and feelings about yourself. Note any powerful or significant impressions, observations, or responses to your communication, interactions, or dealings with others or yourself. Do not judge your observations and comments. Just note them in your journal. Try to keep your entries brief and focused. Then, at the end of each week, review your journal entries and see if there are any important points, themes, or issues worth considering or exploring further. You will be surprised how recurring themes emerge or specific behaviors, thoughts, or feelings keep surfacing as you reflect on your journal entries.

Listening to your dreams. Most of us remember our sleeping dreams for a brief moment or two on waking, but the memory of them fades quickly. We usually do not attach too much importance, significance, or meaning to our dreams. But I think they can reveal much about our inner, unconscious self.

Man is above all,

he who creates.

—ANTOINE DE
SAINT-EXUPÉRY

By keeping a dream journal by your bedside and noting the content and emotions experienced in your dreams, you can expand and deepen your explorations of who you are. The purpose of recording your dreams is not necessarily to interpret or assign meaning, but rather to explore and expand your self-awareness. Many of your feelings, desires, and longings are censored by your conscious mind and require sleep and the process of dreaming to permit the parade of unconscious thoughts and images to come to the surface of your attention.

SPEAKING CREATIVELY TO YOURSELF

You may have discovered while listening to yourself that many negative, as well as positive, thoughts and ideas were swirling through your mind. The positive thoughts are fine. It's those negative thoughts that can often bring us down, interfere with our communication with others and ourselves, and in general, just make our lives miserable. Psychologist Albert Ellis in his book *New Guide to Rational Living* outlines the ten most troubling thoughts Americans have that make their lives unsatisfactory, frustrating, and depressing. He calls them our ten most irrational ideas. See if any of them are swimming around in that head of yours:

1. The idea that you should be liked/loved by everyone.
2. The idea that you should be competent, adequate, and achieving in all possible respects if you are to consider yourself worthwhile.
3. The idea that happiness is externally caused and people have little or no ability to control their sorrows and disturbances.
4. The idea that your past history is an all-important determinant to your present behavior and that because something once strongly affected your life, it should indefinitely have a similar effect.
5. The idea that there is only one right solution to a problem and it is catastrophic if this perfect solution is not found.
6. The idea that if something is or may be dangerous or fearsome, you should be terribly concerned about it and should keep dwelling on the possibility of its occurring.
7. The idea that certain people are wicked and they should always be severely blamed and punished for their villainy.
8. The idea that it is awful and catastrophic when things are not the way you would like them to be.
9. The idea that it is easier to avoid than to face certain life difficulties and self-responsibilities.
10. The idea that one should become quite upset over other people's problems and disturbances.

Ellis discovered that almost all of the psychological and emotional distress his clients were experiencing was based upon one or more of these ten irrational ideas. In fact, irrational ideas 1 and 2—the idea that one should be liked by everyone and the idea that one should be competent in all possible respects—accounted for almost 70 percent of his clients' presenting problems in therapy.

> *You create yourself by your thoughts.*
>
> —RAM DASS

To help his clients overcome these beliefs, he developed an approach to clinical psychology called Cognitive Restructuring Therapy. In this approach, irrational beliefs are identified, challenged by the therapist, and replaced with the opposite beliefs. Remember Carlos' "giving equal time to the opposite" as he confronted his public speaking fears? Well, that technique is based upon Cognitive Restructuring Therapy.

Maybe you've told yourself one or two of Ellis's ten irrational ideas. Maybe you believe one of those ideas is true for you. Well, if you do, you may want to reconsider that belief. It is not the purpose of this book to discuss Cognitive Restructuring Therapy in any detail, other than to suggest that you may want to substitute a different belief for the irrational one you are holding. Here are the ten statements presented in their opposite form. Read the list and see if any of the ideas are helpful in creating new ways of talking to yourself.

1. *You don't have to be approved of by everyone. Not everyone has to like or love you.* It is irrational to strive for universal approval or affection. No one is liked, loved, or approved of by everyone. To strive to be approved of by everyone is not a desirable goal. People who try to win the approval of everyone often sacrifice their own principles, values, and happiness. As a result, they discover only unhappiness in their attempt to win the approval of others.

2. *You do not have to be perfect or competent in everything you do.* It is irrational to desire perfection in anything. No human being is perfect. It's also irrational to desire to be competent in everything you do. There will be some activities you will achieve competency, even mastery, but no human being is competent in everything. In fact, experiencing failure can be one of the best teachers you will ever have. Failure can teach you how to improve, what to change, and when to quit.

3. *Your happiness comes from within you and you can change your feelings by changing your thinking.* Your feelings are determined by your thinking, not by external events. You can change your feelings by changing your thinking. In fact, almost all the negative feelings you will experience can be modified or eliminated by seeing the truth of these ten beliefs.

4. *Your current behavior is not determined by the past.* Human beings can unlearn old behaviors and replace them with new behaviors. Although many habitual ways of behaving and thinking can be deeply rooted and difficult to change, they can be changed with concentrated effort and focused thinking.

5. *There can be many solutions to any given problem.* It's irrational to think there is only one solution to any problem. Most likely, there are a variety of ways to solve any problem. In systems theory, the notion of equifinality states that there exist many ways to solve any problem. When solving problems, don't be limited in your thinking. Use your imagination. Let your creativity soar!

6. *Don't worry.* It's irrational to worry and be overly concerned about every little thing that can go wrong in your life. The vast majority of the things you worry about during your lifetime will never come to pass. Much of your worry is borne from fatigue and loneliness. Get enough sleep, rest, and relaxation. Develop loving relationships. It is amazing how just being rested and enjoying the support and love from family and friends can erase much of what worries you.

7. *Most people are good at heart.* When things go wrong, we often respond by looking for someone to blame and punish. We often desire to vilify and demonize those we hold responsible for our sufferings. But very few people are totally hateful, mean, or evil. The vast majority of people are basically good, hardworking, honest folks. We need to see the good and the beauty in everyone, even those people who mistreat us. In the long run, the price of blaming, hating, or seeking revenge is too high.

8. *It's okay if you don't get your way.* One of the greatest lessons we learn in life is that we don't always get what we want. Thank goodness for that! Can you imagine if you got everything you ever wished for? You would be a gluttonous, wealthy, overindulged mess! We need to get beyond ourselves and begin to be aware of and responsive to the needs of those around us. In this life, we need to move from self to others. Don't get too hung up on what you want or what you desire. Learn to think of others too.

9. *It's better to face your problems and responsibilities than to avoid them.* It is irrational to avoid or deny actual problems or responsibilities facing you. Denial of problems that pose a threat to your safety or welfare is irrational. Physical illness, relationship conflicts, and emotional distress need to be acknowledged and addressed. Anything less will only amplify the problem. The same holds true for your responsibilities. You need to keep your promises, meet your legal obligations, and carry out your duties. To avoid or deny legitimate responsibilities will only cause pain, suffering, and punishment in the long run.

10. *Let others be responsible for themselves.* It is irrational to be overly concerned about the lives of other people. Human beings need to take responsibility for their own lives. We can be responsive to others, but not responsible for them. Each person needs to live his or her own life. With the exception of infants, young children, and the elderly, most people should make their own decisions and take care of themselves. Don't get enmeshed in the lives of other people. You've got enough to take care of with yourself. This doesn't give you license to be uncaring, detached, and self-centered. It means that you let people make their own mistakes, learn from them, and go about their lives independently of your overinvolvement. As an old saying goes, "Every time you help someone, you make them a little weaker, a little more dependent upon you." Let others be responsible for themselves.

These ten beliefs constitute a much more positive and healthy way of viewing yourself and others. You may find many of these beliefs helpful in talking to yourself in a more positive way. If you discover that an irrational belief is running through your mind and causing you some distress or pain, try "giving equal time to the opposite." One of these rational beliefs may be what you need to create the beginning of a new way of thinking and behaving. Let these beliefs create a different, more positive you.

CREATING POSITIVE COMMUNICATION: THE S.E.L.F. T.A.L.K. TECHNIQUE

In addition to using these ten rational beliefs to create a healthier attitude, you can begin to counterbalance your negative thoughts with the S.E.L.F. T.A.L.K. Technique for creating more positive communication with yourself.

Each of these suggestions can help you create more positive messages to communicate to yourself and others. Your willingness to explore and experiment with even one of these eight suggestions will increase your ability to create messages that will enhance your communication.

See your put-downs

Recall that you cannot change what you cannot recognize. Learn to recognize the negative thoughts, images, and verbal statements you make to and about yourself. Use the four methods of listening creatively to yourself, which include giving voice to your thoughts, sitting in silence, personal journal writing, and listening to your dreams. Awareness is the first step to change.

Eliminate your put-downs

Block your put-downs and negative statements. When you verbally criticize yourself, eliminate or block the statement by placing your hand over your mouth. This may sound extreme, but by using a physical reminder, such as your hand, you improve your efforts at eliminating negative messages to yourself. It's almost as if your body is retraining itself to communicate in a new way. By employing a nonverbal channel of communication, such as your hand, you can actually change your verbal behavior.

List what's good about yourself

In your efforts to create more positive communication with yourself, take stock and reflect on all the good things about you. Get paper and pen and write a list of all the wonderful, positive, and beautiful things about yourself. This may feel awkward at first, but give yourself some time and keep your list going for a couple of days. As things come to you, add them to your list. You will be surprised how quickly your list will grow. Post the list on your bathroom mirror, refrigerator, or car dashboard where you can see it often. You deserve to be reminded how wonderful you are. Many times, we don't compliment or encourage ourselves because we don't have anything positive to say. Your list can be a powerful reminder. Use it to your advantage.

Find what's good about others

One of the most effective ways to see what's good in yourself is by seeing the best in others. Sounds strange, but often when we look for the best in others and compliment them about specific behaviors, traits, or accomplishments, we begin to appreciate ourselves a little more too. Our perception of the world, including ourselves, shifts from the negative to the positive. You will also discover that as you compliment others, you will receive more compliments too. Compliments beget compliments!

Talk positively to yourself

Your positive self-talk can be expressed in a number of ways. It can be silent. When you want to counter a negative thought or image, such as "I'm so stupid for making a mistake," simply think its positive opposite, "It's okay if I make mistakes," after you've had the thought. Your positive self-talk can be audible by stating the positive message out loud. For instance, you can say to yourself, "I will be relaxed and calm during the interview," as you walk into the personnel office for a job interview. Written positive self-talk is effective because it utilizes visual communication. You can write yourself an encouraging letter, compose a positive statement on an index card, or simply scribble an uplifting word on the back of your hand to remind yourself of a positive trait or attribute.

Ask others for help

An enjoyable way to create more positive communication with yourself is to elicit the help of others. You can invite or ask a good friend or family member to participate in your positive self-communication program. The person can remind you when you say or do things that are self-critical, help you think of positive things to replace your negative thoughts and images, and point out some additional strengths you didn't know about. As artist Donna Sheeves recommends, "Invent your world, surround yourself with people who love you, who encourage you, who believe in you."

Learn to be human

One of the most important things you can keep foremost in your mind as you begin to communicate more positively with yourself is that you are human. You make mistakes. You are not supposed to be perfect. It is often our preoccupation with being perfect, being approved of by everyone, and being competent in everything we attempt that gets us in trouble. We're only human. We cannot be perfect. Everyone isn't supposed to approve of us or even like us. We cannot possibly be good in everything we try.

Keep a record of your successes

The final suggestion for creating positive communication with yourself is to keep a record of your successes. It is not only important that you create more positive communication with yourself, it's beneficial to track your successes and victories so you can reinforce, remind, and celebrate your creative efforts.

Remember to listen to yourself and to use the S.E.L.F. T.A.L.K. Technique to create more positive communication with yourself. Your willingness and ability to create positive thoughts and images for yourself and others will greatly enhance your communication and relationships with others. Just like Carlos, you can create a positive message for yourself that will improve your life.

EXPLORING CREATIVE TASKS

1. List five things you would like to change or improve about your self-concept. Share your list with a close friend and ask him or her for feedback on your list. With your friend's help, brainstorm at least three different ways you can accomplish or make progress toward each of the five items you listed. What do you think of these suggestions? When would you like to begin?

2. For one day, write down all the negative self-talk messages you give yourself. Notice if there are any patterns or categories in your negative self-talk. What do you think of these messages? How do you feel about them? Which messages would you like to change? What would the new, more positive messages be?

3. Reread the ten irrational beliefs suggested by Albert Ellis. Select one of the irrational beliefs that you would like to change. Substitute the opposite, more positive belief presented in the second list of ten rational beliefs. Write this belief on two separate 3 x 5" cards and tape one to your car dashboard and the other to your bathroom mirror. Read these cards often during the day. After one week, has the statement created anything new in your thinking, feeling, or behaving?

4. For one week, use the S.E.L.F. T.A.L.K. Technique and notice how it changes your thoughts, images, and communication with yourself. Which S.E.L.F. T.A.L.K. suggestions seemed to be the most helpful or beneficial? Why?

EXPANDING YOUR CREATIVE THINKING

1. What would your life be like if you truly believed in all ten of Ellis's rational ideas? How do you think your communication behavior would change?

2. What do you think your self-concept will be like in five years? In ten years? What areas of improvement do you think you will experience? In what areas will you still have difficulty? How can you address those difficult areas?

3. What resources can you think of that could help you improve your self-concept and the ways you communicate with yourself? What experts, books, magazines, movies, or classes could contribute to improving how you see and feel about yourself?

4. What would be the most positive thing that could be said about your life if you were to die today? What would you want the most positive accomplishment of your life to be if you lived to age eighty-five? What specific activities would you have to be engaged in to accomplish this positive goal?

THREE

Creating Expressive Verbal Communication

> *He painted pictures in my mind*
> *and changed my world with his words.*
>
> —CHARLES KURALT

As I look out to the ocean, the evening lights of Pismo Beach sparkle beneath our third-floor motel room. This little seaside town is quiet now, deserted. It's October and the throngs of noisy summer tourists have long gone, and the only sound I hear is Dad's deep breathing as he sleeps in the bed behind me. I'm sitting in an overstuffed chair, gazing at the moonlit sea, as my father's words echo in my mind.

Right as Dad was falling off to sleep he told me, "Thanks for taking me on these overnight trips. Not many sons would do this . . . and, . . . I love you."

For the last ten years of his life, I took my dad on overnight trips. Once or twice a year we would just hit the road, the two of us, and journey into friendship. These overnight trips didn't just happen. I had to take time off work, make the arrangements, and say good-bye to my wife and kids for those two or three days.

At first they were a little awkward. What do father and son talk about for two or three days alone? But over the years, we began talking more and developed a deeper friendship than ever before.

During one of our overnight talks, Dad told me how Mom appreciated my taking him on "safari," as she called it, how much she appreciated my support and encouragement. He ended with, "You know, she loves you very much."

"I know," I said, then added, "but how do *you* feel about me, Dad?"

My dad smiled, paused for a moment, and then said, "I love you, Randy."

"I love you too, Dad."

That was it. It took a few seconds to say, and maybe forty years of preparation. From that moment on, we started verbally sharing our feelings a little more.

VERBAL COMMUNICATION

Verbal communication is all communication that is spoken or written. It includes the content of your conversation with a friend, an announcement over the public address system at a skating rink, a whisper in a darkened theater, the clever words on a billboard, and the words you are reading on this page. Verbal communication is powerful, and even one word can hurt or heal others.

> *You can paint*
> *a great picture*
> *on a small canvas.*
>
> —C. D. WARNER

One word can make or break your day. A simple no to our invitation to lunch can leave us feeling rejected and depressed. A maybe can leave us hanging with uncertainty and even confusion. And a yes can catapult us into a victorious state of triumph. Just one word can create different emotions within our hearts.

PRINCIPLES OF VERBAL COMMUNICATION

To get a better understanding of verbal communication, let's explore some principles that govern its usage. By understanding and considering these principles when we communicate, we can more effectively share our thoughts and feelings with others.

Language Is Symbolic

Words do not have any meaning in and of themselves. They are arbitrary symbols assigned and agreed on to represent or symbolize the things in our experience. Words can represent physical objects like galaxies, stars, trees, insects, and people. They can also express thoughts and feelings such as honesty, patriotism, grief, and love.

A word is not the thing it represents. The word "nose," for example, is a symbol that represents that part of our face between our eyes and above our mouth that we breathe through. There is nothing particularly "nose"-like about the symbol nose. It is just the word or symbol we have agreed on to represent that part of our face. To a speaker of Spanish, *nariz* would convey the same meaning, as would *nez* for a speaker of French. For a speaker of Cantonese, the word is *bidzu*. The symbol we use to represent an object, idea, or feeling is arbitrary. Language is symbolic.

Language Is Rule-Governed

Language contains three primary types of rules—syntactic, semantic, and pragmatic. **Syntactic rules** govern how we arrange words in a sentence. Using correct syntax, we would say, "I turned on the radio," instead of "The radio I turned on."

Semantic rules govern the meaning of words and how we are to interpret them. These rules let us agree that "houses" are structures we live in and "dogs" are those furry creatures who fetch sticks and bark at strangers. Without semantic rules of shared and agreed on meanings for words, communication would not be possible.

Pragmatic rules of language help us more specifically understand and interpret the meanings of words in specific contexts. For instance, the statement "I want you" can be interpreted in a variety of ways if it was spoken by a young boy choosing members of his team, whispered by a unkempt man in the shadows of a city walkway, or shouted by an angry drunk you accidentally bumped into at a bar. Pragmatic rules of language help us consider the context of the situation and our relationship with the individual who is communicating with us. Without these pragmatic rules of language, our responses to the simplest of statements could prove disastrous.

Language Is Subjective

When you read the word "artist," what image comes to mind? Do you see an old, disheveled man with brush and palette in hand, a long-haired guitarist in black leather pants and eight inch boots, or a young girl in a white, flowing dress composing poetry at her desk? Each of these images depicts an "artist" in the minds of different people. For me, the word "artist" conjures up an image of a speaker mentally outlining the main points of an impromptu speech she will soon deliver in a high school speech tournament. Maybe she's not what you had in mind when you saw the word "artist," but what some impromptu speakers produce in competitive speaking is creative and impressive art to me.

That language is subjective means that we can never assume that the interpretation of even a single word will hold the exact meaning for someone else. This requires that we will often have to negotiate the meaning of a word with those we are communicating with. By speaking and listening, paraphrasing and negotiating meanings, we participate in a process of creating shared meanings.

Words have both denotative and connotative meanings. The **denotative meaning** of a word is its dictionary meaning. For instance, the denotative meaning for the word "airplane" is "a winged vehicle capable of flight, generally heavier than air and driven by jet engines or propellers." The denotative, or dictionary, meaning for a word is clearly stated and available for everyone to look up.

On the other hand, the **connotative meaning** of a word is the emotional or attitudinal response or attachment people have to words. Although people will have the same denotative meaning for the word "airplane," their emotional or attitudinal responses to the word can vary tremendously. To an airline pilot, the word might be associated with feelings of pride, accomplishment, and security because the job holds high status and provides high income. To a student pilot, the word "airplane" might be associated with frustration, stress, and burden because lessons can be expensive, taxing, and difficult. To a survivor of an airplane crash, the word might be associated with extreme fear, panic, and dread.

When choosing words, you need to consider not only the denotative meanings of a word, but also the many connotative meanings people may associate with that word. Being creative in word selection requires that you also be sensitive to the feelings of others.

Language Defines and Limits

We use language to define and limit objects, people, thoughts, feelings, and experiences so that we may share meaning more effectively with others. Language is used to define the meaning of words. But language can simultaneously limit the meaning of our communication as well. For instance, if you ask me what my sister is like and I respond by saying, "She's a good cook," I have limited your understanding of my sister to one skill she possesses. The fact that she is a loving mother of two children, devoted wife, caring daughter, skilled tennis player, avid sports fan, and a hundred other wonderful things is not included in my one-sentence description. By my selecting only certain words to describe my sister, I have limited your understanding and appreciation of her. No matter what words I use to describe something, I reveal or communicate only one particular aspect or characteristic of her. Language, by its very nature, defines and limits the reality we communicate.

Language Lets Us Create

Language lets us create messages and words to communicate our experience to others. We can arrange the thousands of words contained in the English language in an endless variety of combinations and structures to communicate thoughts and feelings. Different combinations of words enable you to express a message in a way that reflects your mood, attitude, and personality. This is one of the joys of life—to create messages that are uniquely yours.

> *A person's right to create is irrevocable and it's open to every aspect of a person's daily life.*
>
> —SHARON McNIFF

Not only can we use words to create an endless stream of distinctly different and unique messages, we can also use language to create new words to describe new experiences. Recently, for example, the term "hip-hop" was created to describe the music of Generation X and "pentium chip" to describe a new, powerful microchip processor for computers.

Whether it's creating new syntactical arrangements of words or inventing new words altogether, our language provides us with a marvelous means of being artists of communication.

I-STATEMENTS—OWNING YOUR LANGUAGE

The basic building block of communication is the I-statement. Whenever we communicate with another person, it is important that our messages be as specific and clear as possible. To avoid confusion and ambiguity in our communication, we need to use I-statements. An I-statement allows you to own your thoughts and feelings. This ownership of your messages enables you to effectively express who you are. Here are some examples of I-statements:

> *"I* believe school is difficult."
> *"I* want to become a teacher."
> *"It's my opinion* that investing in mutual funds is wise."

Each of these I-statements shows speaker ownership. Did you notice how an I-statement does not necessarily have to contain the word "I" to qualify as an I-statement? For example, the statement "*It's my opinion* that investing in mutual funds is wise" shows ownership ("my") even though it doesn't contain the word "I."

I-statements provide several advantages. First, I-statements let the receiver of the message know who is the owner or source of the thought or idea communicated. If I-statements are not used, the ownership of the message may often be uncertain or overstated. "*Everyone* thinks that investing in mutual funds is wise" does not clearly indicate ownership. The word "everyone" is too broad to convey specific ownership.

Second, I-statements provide a target for the receiver of the message to respond to. If a speaker says, "*Everyone* thinks that investing in mutual funds is wise," the receiver may be less likely to disagree because the speaker uses the word "everyone" as the source of the message. But if the speaker states, "*I* think that investing in mutual funds is wise," the receiver is more likely to voice disagreement with an individual speaker ("I") than a collective opinion ("everyone").

Third, I-statements prevent people from speaking for others. By owning your statements, you cannot speak for others. You can only share your thoughts and feelings with I-statements. Statements such as "Dad wants you to wash the car," "My boss thinks you could work longer hours," and "My parents tell me to trust you" are examples of the speaker "talking" for others.

Last, I-statements discourage blaming others. Many times we use what is called "you-language" instead of I-statements. We send "you" messages such as "You make me upset" or "You're a grouch." These messages of condemnation often direct blame to the receiver. A speaker who uses I-statements owns more of the message rather than shifts all the blame to the receiver ("you"). Notice the shift in these same statements when I-statements are used:

> *"I get upset when you call me 'lame'."* (You make me upset.)
> *"I see you're frowning."* (You're a grouch.)

Do you see how I-statements make the tone of each statement different than when they are phrased as "you" messages? There is less of a blaming and fault-finding tone to I-statements. The emphasis is on the perceptions and feelings of the speaker and not on the receiver. Remember to own your statements when creating communication.

THE FOUR LEVELS OF COMMUNICATION

There are four levels of sharing or communication—surface talk, reporting facts, giving opinions, and sharing feelings. Each level represents a different category of information. These categories designate differing degrees of intimacy in terms of the information shared. During the course of one conversation, we can communicate at all four levels of sharing.

Surface Talk

In this first level of sharing, we keep our conversations to a minimum of disclosure. Greetings, casual acknowledgment of strangers and acquaintances, and superficial conversations with a coworker are examples of surface talk. The primary goal is to acknowledge another human being without having to provide any personal information about ourselves. Consider the following surface level remarks:

> "Nice day!"/"Yeah!"
> "How are you doing?"/"Fine. How about you?"
> "See ya!"/"Yeah, likewise."

The purpose of surface talk is not deep sharing, but rather acknowledgement of another person in a socially acceptable manner.

Reporting Facts

The next level of communication involves the sharing of factual information. Introducing yourself at a party, stating that you've been married once before, and telling your roommate that the dishes have been washed are all examples of reporting facts. The key to identifying communication at this level is that the content of the messages can be verified or proven. The following statements are examples of reporting facts:

"I am 5'8" tall."

"My sister lives in Roslyn, Washington."

"We have lunch reservations for 1:00 P.M."

Giving Opinions

Giving opinions, the third level, involves greater risk than reporting facts because you are exposing more of who you are. You are allowing others to see more of you by sharing your opinions, attitudes, and beliefs. This can be more threatening to the person sharing because there is a greater chance of disagreement, disapproval, and conflict brought about by sharing differences of opinions with others.

> To live a creative life, we must lose our fear of being wrong.
>
> —JOSEPH CHILTON PEARCE

Yet effective communication involves risk and trust. By sharing our opinions with others, we trust that they will hear our opinions, share their opinions, and discuss the differences in an atmosphere of safety and acceptance. To create more effective communication, we can choose to disagree without disliking the other person. As you disagree, you may discover that you are wrong or misinformed. But that's all part of communicating. Keep open to hearing the other side. You just may learn something. The following statements are examples of giving opinions:

"I *believe* I could write a book."

"I *think* our relationship is healthy."

"I *predict* my parents will visit us."

Sharing Feelings

The deepest level of communication is the sharing of feelings with close friends and intimates. The communication of facts and opinions presents a two-dimensional figure of who we are, but the sharing of feelings paints a three-dimensional picture of our deeper selves. It's at the sharing-feelings level that people develop and maintain their intimate relationships.

Direct feeling statements. The most basic way to communicate a feeling is by making a direct feeling statement, which is an I-statement containing a feeling word. Here are some examples:

"I feel happy."

"I'm proud of your efforts."

"I love you."

Explanation feeling statements. The second way to share a feeling is by making an explanation feeling statement. In this statement, you not only own the feeling, you also include information about the feeling. In the following examples, each statement is divided into the direct feeling statement/and the explanation for the feeling.

> "I've felt angry/ever since my license was revoked."
> "I feel so happy/now that we are talking again."

Picture feeling statements. The third way to share a feeling is by using a simile—a description that includes the words "as if" or "like." These picture feeling statements can often provide the receiver with a different way of hearing or processing your feeling statement. Here are some examples:

> "I feel *like* I'm floating on a cloud." (I feel relaxed.)
> "I feel *as if* I'm chained to this desk." (I feel restricted by my job.)

As you talk with others, try to communicate in a loving manner, no matter what depth of disclosure you decide to share. Even feedback meant to help or improve can be made in a gentle, loving fashion. I like the words of artist Michael Burrell, who says, "The secret of art is love." Create loving ways to share your thoughts and feelings with others.

SELF-DISCLOSURE

One of the most powerful ways you can create more effective communication and intimacy is to increase self-disclosure. **Self-disclosure** is volunteering information about yourself that would otherwise be unobtainable. There is no one correct way to self-disclose and no clear-cut rules that govern this process. Self-disclosure depends on a variety of factors, including the personalities of the people involved, the setting, the nature of the relationship, their individual goals, and the level of their communication skills.

The **Johari Window,** shown below, is a matrix that illustrates what is known, not known, and hidden between two people in relationship. The window is divided into four quadrants. The first quadrant, called the **open area,** represents information a person shares with another person. This includes all you disclose about things you like, opinions you hold, and feelings about a variety of topics and people.

The second quadrant, called the **secret area,** represents information a person does not share or disclose to the other person. This includes facts, opinions, and feelings you are aware of, but have declined to share with other people, so that information remains a secret to them.

	known to self	unknown to self
known to other	OPEN	BLIND
unknown to other	SECRET	UNKNOWN

The third quadrant, called the **blind area,** is information the other person knows about you, but about which you are unaware. We all have our "blind spots"—those characteristics, behaviors, or effects of our behaviors others know about us, but we do not. Your frown when you're disappointed, your snoring while you're sleeping, and your loud voice when you're excited are behaviors that are apparent to others but not to you.

The final quadrant, the **unknown area,** represents information about you neither you nor the other person knows. Let's say you don't know if you would enjoy eating Japanese food because you've never tried it. Because your friend doesn't know whether or not you would enjoy Japanese food either, Japanese food is an unknown area. Once you have eaten Japanese food, however, you will know whether or not you like it. Then that information shifts to the secret area, until you choose to share that information with your friend, when it shifts to the open area.

OPEN	BLIND
SECRET	UNKNOWN

Ideally, you and the other person will increase the size of your respective open areas as your relationship develops. There will be more and more information you will both share about yourselves, so your knowledge of each other will increase, as shown in the Johari Window to the left.

In order that you might create more effective and intimate communication with others, consider the following characteristics of self-disclosure:

1. **Disclose only information you want to share.** The most important fact to remember about disclosing to others is that you have a choice. You don't have to share things you don't want to share. You decide what is appropriate and what is not for you.
2. **Self-disclosure involves risk.** Any sharing of personal information involves some degree of risk. Be careful when you disclose. Is the individual someone you want to share this information with? Can he or she be trusted? What would be the possible consequences if this information were shared with others?
3. **Self-disclosure should be reciprocal.** You don't want to have an unbalanced relationship in which you only listen to someone else's disclosure or problems. Also, you don't want to be doing all the sharing, while the other person only listens. Pay attention to the balance of self-disclosure occurring in the relationship. Are the open areas of your respective Johari Windows roughly equal to each other?
4. **Self-disclosure should not be coerced.** Do not force others to share information they are reluctant or refuse to tell you. No relationship

should be based on coercion or manipulation. Give the other person the freedom to choose.

5. **Self-disclosure always results in deeper understanding.** The beauty of self-disclosure is that it provides a deeper understanding of others. Even if the information they share makes you feel uncomfortable or hurts your feelings, at least you know what they are really thinking or feeling. In that sense, you have a deeper understanding of their true self.

6. **Keep self-disclosure confidential.** When another person discloses confidential information to you, keep it to yourself. Don't tell others what has been shared with you in confidence. Nothing else ends disclosure more quickly than breaking confidentiality.

Self-Disclosure Topics

Now that you're familiar with the concept of self-disclosure and some of the guidelines for healthy self-disclosure, let's try it out. Select a partner—someone you feel comfortable with—and share your thoughts and feelings about the following topics. Alternate sharing about the following topics:

1. Your hobbies
2. Your favorite foods/beverages
3. Places you've traveled
4. Aspects of your daily life that satisfy/bother you
5. Your religious/spiritual views
6. Your present financial condition—income, savings, debts
7. Characteristics of yourself that make you proud
8. Details about your unhappiest moment of your life
9. Things that make you feel immature about yourself
10. The sources of strain or dissatisfaction in your love relationships
11. The person you most admire in your personal life
12. The person you most resent in your personal life
13. Your perception of your parents' relationship with one another
14. Your personal views on love
15. Your purpose in life
16. Your views on death

How was your self-disclosure experience? What topics felt comfortable sharing? What topics were you uncomfortable or reluctant to share? Why? Did the process of self-disclosure become easier as you shared more with your partner? What did you learn about yourself from this experience?

Self-disclosure can be used to create greater intimacy, connection, and understanding in a relationship. Your willingness to open up to others and share information about yourself will not only permit the other people to know you better, it will also encourage them to disclose to you also. But you need to be aware that there are differences in the way men and women communicate with one another.

GENDER DIFFERENCES IN CONVERSATIONAL STYLES

As you have most likely experienced, there are some observable differences in the conversational styles of men and women in this culture. Not to our surprise, numerous communication researchers have discovered these differences. This is not to say that every man and woman communicates in a certain predictable way. There are always exceptions to any generalization and many individuals behave outside the identified norms. But these differences are significant.

These differences are so significant that linguistics professor Deborah Tannen in her book *You Just Don't Understand* proclaims that "The communication between men and women can be like cross-cultural communication, falling prey to a clash of conversational styles." It is not so much that men and women desire to be in conflict with each other, it's just that their conversational styles are so different. Tannen adds that "Women speak and hear a language of connection and intimacy, while men speak and hear a language of status and independence."

When do these differences begin? In early childhood. Even if boys and girls grow up in the same culture, even in the same neighborhood, people talk to them differently and they expect people to talk to them differently. In other words, society expects different things from boys and girls in the way they communicate.

Anthropologists Daniel Maltz and Ruth Borker summarized research showing that boys and girls talk and interact with one another in very different ways. They discovered that boys and girls spend most of their time playing in same-sex groups. Their favorite games were different as were the ways in which they communicate when playing those games.

Girls play in small groups or in pairs and having a best friend is highly valued. In their playing and interacting, friendship and intimacy are the highest goals. Many of the games girls play, such as jump rope, hopscotch, and playing house, do not have winners and losers. The emphasis is on spending time together playing games that don't pit one girl against another. Even the way they talk to each other is geared toward others: "Let's do this" or "How about doing that?" Their playing doesn't seem to involve competition or being better than others, but instead tends to foster connection and relationship. Much time is spent sitting in groups and talking.

Boys, on the other hand, tend to play in large groups that are hierarchically structured. There is generally a leader or two and the leadership is often challenged. The leader tells the other boys what to do and how to do it, and this ability to persuade or coerce others into compliance is a sign of high status. Most of the games boys play are competitive, often with a complex set of rules and clear-cut winners and losers. There is a constant emphasis on who is strongest, fastest, and best. The language of boys is also different from that of girls. Boys say, "I'm the leader," "I'm the fastest," "Get out of here!" and "That's mine!" There is less emphasis on asking questions and more on giving orders, making declarative statements, and challenging others.

These different gender styles of interaction and talking are carried into adult-hood, when the competitive styles of men and the more cooperative styles of women continue to be the source of misunderstanding and conflict. Deborah Tannen further clarifies these conversational style differences by making the distinction between symmetrical and asymmetrical relationships.

A symmetrical relationship is one that is characterized by cooperation, equality, rapport building, acceptance, listening, questioning, empathy, exploring problems, encouragement, mutual understanding, complimenting, and negotiating. Tannen's research indicates that women most often demonstrate these behaviors in their conversational style. Women tend to invest effort in establishing rapport, asking questions, listening without interrupting, being supportive, agreeing, complimenting, and sharing feelings. Their focus is more on the quality of relationship (rather than on problem-solving or competing), equality, connection, and cooperation.

The asymmetrical relationship is characterized by lecturing, giving advice, directing, commanding, evaluating, problem solving, challenging, and competing. Tannen believes that men most typify these communication behaviors in their conversational style. Men tend to report facts and information, lecture, use more commanding language, ask fewer questions, interrupt, give advice, evaluate, challenge, and problem solve. The focus is more on reporting, lecturing, fixing, and competing.

The relationship between the speakers in an asymmetrical conversation is secondary to the task at hand or the subject being discussed. In fact, competition characterizes much of the male conversational style, in which the desire to know, to be right, and to win is foremost in the male mind. The asymmetrical relationship is brought about by the competitive nature of the male conversational style because there is often a constant jockeying for the top position, the endless struggle to win in this competitive activity of talking.

Once again, these are generalizations. Keep in mind that there are men and women who defy these characteristic ways of talking and listening. You undoubtedly know men whose top priority is relationship, cooperation, and connection, and

> *To live a full, rich life, we need to have the courage to develop our shadow—those qualities we have ignored or avoided, the masculine and the feminine.*
>
> —CARL JUNG

women who are primarily concerned about competition, giving advice, and problem solving. But most men and women maintain the conversational styles they learned in early childhood.

What do we do with all this information? Plenty! You can become aware of and appreciate the differences in conversational styles between men and women. Rather than blame, punish, or withdraw from a disagreement or argument brought about by differences in conversational styles, you may be able to create new lines of communication. Here are some suggestions to consider as you attempt to create new ways of talking and listening:

Men
Put the newspaper down when someone is talking.
Listen without interrupting, judging, or fixing.
Ask open-ended questions ("How?" "Why?" "What?").
Paraphrase to prove understanding ("Are you saying . . . ?").
Communicate agreement ("I agree . . . ," "I see your point . . . ," "You've got a valid point . . .").
Communicate empathy ("That must have felt . . . ," "I know how you feel . . .").
Encourage exploration ("What else . . . ?" "How else . . . ?" "How did that feel?").
Compliment ("I appreciate your . . . ," "I like your . . . ," "I admire the way you . . .").
Negotiate ("How can we . . . ?" "What other solutions . . . ?" "Can we live with . . . ?").
Share your perceptions (especially strengths) about your relationships.
Share your feelings.
Listen *again,* without interrupting, judging, or fixing.

Women
State your opinions more often ("I think . . . ," "I believe . . . ," "It's my opinion that . . .").
Label a transaction when interrupted ("May I speak?" "You're interrupting me").
Label a transaction when being lectured ("I believe you're lecturing me").
Invite your own participation ("Would you like to hear my opinion/feeling?" "I want to share my opinion/feeling").
Disagree ("I'm not convinced . . . ," "I have a different opinion . . . ," "I see it differently . . . ," "This is what I think . . .").
State a need ("May I state a need?" "I need . . .").

State a boundary ("No, that's not okay with me." "This is unacceptable . . .").

State a boundary with consequence ("If you continue to . . . then I'm prepared to . . .").

Give advice ("I think you should . . . ," "You might consider . . . ," "What if you . . .").

Give a command ("I want you to . . . ," "Please get me . . . ," "Don't say . . . ," "Don't do . . .").

You don't have to use all of these suggestions, or even some of them. Trying even one new behavior for a few days will make a difference in the way others interact with you and may change the way you feel about yourself.

Each of these behaviors requires some effort and risk, especially if you've never attempted the skill before. It takes a lot of hard work to create new lines of communication. Michelangelo was once asked if his art came easy to him and he responded by saying, "If people knew how hard I worked to get my mastery, it wouldn't seem so wonderful at all." So, roll up those sleeves and begin mastering one or two new ways to communicate with others. You may just create a masterpiece.

CREATING EXPRESSIVE VERBAL MESSAGES: THE C.R.E.A.T.I.V.E. TECHNIQUE

Before you try modifying your conversational style, consider the C.R.E.A.T.I.V.E. Technique for creating expressive verbal messages. These eight guidelines will serve as reminders on how to create verbal messages that will express ownership, demonstrate clarity, and establish an open communication climate for any setting.

Concrete terms, not vague language

Use specific language when speaking with others. A common mistake in communication is assuming the listener will receive the same picture in her head that you have in yours when you communicate a word. When I say, "I see a dog," you hear my sentence and decode the meaning of my words. The word "dog" is a relatively abstract, vague term. The dog you "see" in your head could be a big dog, a small dog, a shaggy dog, or a short-haired dog. You could "see" a bulldog, a collie, or a mutt. What I saw in my mind, and intended to communicate, was a German shepherd. Notice the difference between your picture and mine? Remember to use concrete, specific language to communicate more accurately with others.

Reject inferences, share observations

Observations refer to what your five senses have gathered: what you have seen with your eyes, heard with your ears, smelled with your nose, felt with your fingers, and tasted with your tongue. **Inferences,** on the other hand, go beyond what you have observed and make assumptions about what you think and feel. Notice the difference between the following observation and inference statements:

> "The two people are walking arm in arm." (observation)
> "That couple is in love." (inference)

To create more effective communication, share statements of observation and not inference.

Express ideas, not advice

Another suggestion for creating more effective verbal communication is to avoid the tendency to evaluate and give advice to others. Rather, communicate the sharing of ideas and alternatives, instead of giving advice and solutions. For example, instead of saying, "You should get a divorce" (advice), you could suggest, "There are a number of things you can do to improve your marriage, such as take a vacation, enroll in a communication class, or enter into therapy" (suggesting options). This approach lets the other person consider and decide for himself or herself. It also allows the person to save face, rather than be judged and advised by you.

Articulate about behavior, not about the person

It is important to communicate about a person's behavior rather than comment on what you imagine the person is or what the person is like. Use adverbs (relating to actions) to describe people, rather than adjectives (relating to qualities). Communicating in this way is more specific because you report behaviors rather than attempt to label the person. Notice the difference in the following statements:

> "Harvey is a loudmouth." (describes person)
> "Harvey has been talking for ten minutes." (describes behavior)

Talk about what is said, not why

Try not to guess the motive or reasoning behind what another person says. Once again, this gets us into the area of inference and assumption. Instead, focus your communication on observable information introduced by such language as what, how, when, and where. Focus your communication on *what* is said, not on *why* it may have been said. This will keep the discussion on a level that is more effectively communicated and debated, rather than entering into the domain of possible motives and questionable assumptions.

I-statement messages

Structure your messages in I-statement form. The I-statements you send to others permit you to own your thoughts and feelings, so the receiver of your messages knows whom to address. I-statements also discourage blaming, prevent people from speaking for others, and encourage more thoughtful messages.

Verbal and nonverbal messages should reinforce one another

When speaking, try to match your voice, body, and gestures with the content of your verbal message. Mixed messages—incongruent nonverbal and verbal messages—confuse the listener and interfere with clear communication. When you say, "I enjoy spending time with you," your face, voice, and body should also communicate the message with a smile, a cheerful voice, and a relaxed and open body posture.

Express messages in terms of "more or less," not "either/or"

We tend to use polar or extreme terms when communicating with others. It was either the "most wonderful" event or the "worst" event. Either she was smart or she was stupid. Rather than label extreme descriptions with "either/or" language, try to communicate in terms of degree ("more or less" language). For example, rather than saying, "Terry is the loudest person on earth" (either loudest or softest), you could restate your opinion as "Terry speaks louder than Kevin" (matter of degree) or "Terry speaks louder than I'm comfortable with hearing."

As Fyodor Dostoyevsky once observed, "Taking a new step, uttering a new word is what people fear the most." That might have been true for the "old you," but explore the idea of being different from what you used to be. Open to the possibility that there is an artist of communication inside you just waiting for the opportunity to try new things. Take new steps. Utter new words that might change a relationship . . .

"But how do *you* feel about me, Dad?"

EXPLORING CREATIVE TASKS

1. Select one person who is important to you and list three specific instances when he or she supported you, encouraged you, believed in you, or challenged you to improve. Arrange to meet with this individual and share your list with him or her. Share your feelings (level 4) about his or her contributions to your life. What happened? What did you think? How did you feel?

2. Select three people from your life (family, friends, coworkers, acquaintances) and reflect on how open or self-disclosing you are with each person. Construct a Johari Window on a piece of paper depicting your open area and secret area for each individual. Look at the three versions of the Johari Window. What are your responses to them? Is there anything you would want to change about your disclosure with any of these people? How open are they with you? How do you want each relationship to develop?

3. Select two behaviors from the gender list of suggested behaviors that you would like to try. For one week, use these two behaviors whenever you get the opportunity. Don't go overboard. Just use them whenever the chance arises. How did other people respond to your new behaviors? How did you feel using them? How did they change or modify conversations? Do you think you'll use them again? Why?

4. Meet with a friend of the opposite sex and ask for feedback about your conversational style. Are you competitive or cooperative? Do you lecture or listen? Are you focused on the relationship or more concerned about solving problems? Show your friend the gender list of communication behaviors and have him or her suggest some new behaviors for you to try out. Don't judge your friend's suggestions. Remember, you are inviting suggestions. What was this like for you? How did it feel to receive feedback on your conversational style?

EXPANDING YOUR CREATIVE THINKING

1. How has your past experience with self-disclosure influenced your current willingness and ability to open up to others? Have others violated your trust? Have people not opened up to you? How do these things influence your present behavior? Do you want to change? If so, how might you improve your self-disclosure behavior?

2. What would your "ideal" communication self look like? Take a piece of paper and draw a circle eight inches in diameter in the middle of the sheet. Next, sketch in legs, arms, and a smiling head so the circle looks like a person (well, sort of). Inside that circle write the ten most important communication skills from either gender list of behaviors that you would like to possess. Look at your finished list. Are the behaviors mostly male or female? Would you want to be in a relationship with this circle figure? Why? Why not?

3. How might your life change if you lost your ability to physically speak? How would you "talk" to others? How might that change the way you listened to others? What do you think would be the response of family, friends, coworkers, acquaintances? Think of three benefits or advantages to this condition.

4. How would your relationships with loved ones change if you were to develop more of the conversational behaviors characteristic of the opposite sex? How would that affect your self-disclosure, sense of connection, and overall satisfaction with the relationship? What would be the advantages and disadvantages of such a shift in the way you talk and listen? How do you think that would feel to you?

FOUR

Creating Supportive Nonverbal Communication

I love my coach.
She hugs me with her smile
and kisses me with her eyes.

—SHERRY, TWELVE-YEAR-OLD GYMNAST

Early morning classes are difficult for most college students and that 7:30 A.M. class was no exception. Most of my students would be at their desks, sleepy-eyed and silent when I arrived to the classroom each morning at 7:20, except for Rose. Many mornings would find her singing out under the oak tree not far from our room before class began. Her voice floated easily across the lawn and into the classroom. Rose was in her early sixties, "filling up her day" by taking a class or two at our college and "being a blessing" to everyone she met.

Rose never sat in the same desk twice, but wherever she sat, Rose smiled and nodded her head to me as I would lecture. Occasionally, she would respond softly with "Umm" or "Yes" when she agreed with something I said. She didn't enter into discussion much. In fact, Rose rarely spoke. But I began to look forward to her smile, her laughter, her kind eyes, and her hugs.

When students gave their speeches, I noticed that many of them would look to Rose's ever-present smile and knowing nod as they began their talks. During their presentations, many students would shoot a glance in Rose's direction if they forgot a line or lost their place. She would smile and nod reassuringly, almost to say, "There's nothing to worry about, child. You'll find what you need." And they would.

I think it was her hugs most of all though. She would always preface her end of class hugs with "Can I hug you?" It was awkward for me at first, but within a few weeks, I looked forward to the end of each hour. I wasn't the only one. Rose stood at the doorway and hugged many of the students as they left the room. Within a few weeks, they would silently line up to receive their hugs from Rose.

Rose was more than just another student. She blessed us with her singing, her smile, her hugs. Most of all, she blessed us with her presence.

NONVERBAL COMMUNICATION

Some of the most powerful and significant communication you will ever send and receive will not involve words at all: the first smile of a newborn child, a kiss from a child, the silent beauty of a rainbow suspended against a darkening sky, the soothing sound of rain on the roof, the embrace of a loved one, and a congratulations hug after you have given a speech. These are a few of the thousands of nonverbal experiences that will give depth and meaning to your life.

Nonverbal communication is all communication that is not spoken or written. It is expressed by actions, behaviors, and vocal qualities that accompany your verbal messages. It also includes the way you dress, your posture, your use of time, the way you distance yourself from others, your touch, the environment you create in your home and office, and the car you drive.

Nonverbal communication has a great impact and influence on the receiver's decoding or interpretation of any message. For instance, the words "Of course I love you," can be delivered in many different ways by the speaker. "Of course I love you" can be whispered with surrender, uttered with boredom, snapped with resentment, or shouted with enthusiasm. The words are the same, but the way in which the words are spoken often determines how the receiver will interpret the message.

PRINCIPLES OF NONVERBAL COMMUNICATION

Nonverbal communication and verbal communication are similar in that they are both culturally determined, but there are some characteristics that distinguish the nonverbal dimension of communication from the spoken and written word.

Nonverbal Communication Is Continuous

Verbal communication can be broken down and examined in discrete units of words and sentences. Nonverbal communication, on the other hand, cannot be easily separated into specific units such as words and sentences. Take, for example, your facial expressions. There isn't a specific unit of meaning you can easily identify or isolate, like a word or sentence. A sentence has a beginning, middle, and ending. But a face is different. The messages it can convey in even a brief period is much more complex and continuous than a word or sentence. The mouth can quickly change from a smile to a frown. The eyes can be focused one moment and diverted the next moment. The eyebrows can immediately display the changes in the facial muscles of the individual. These subtle facial changes are continuous, unlike the separate units of verbal language.

From moment to moment, your nonverbal behavior affects others, just like Rose's smile. Without a single word uttered, Rose's smile could convey support, understanding, and caring to the speakers she was listening to. You too can create an entirely different communication experience for another person by simply demonstrating your support nonverbally, without saying one word.

> *The ancestor of every beautiful action is a creative thought.*
> —FRANK VIZARRE

Nonverbal Communication Is Instantaneous

Unlike verbal language, nonverbal communication is instantaneous. When you receive disappointing news, your face, posture, and breathing can immediately reflect your physical and emotional response to that information, whereas your verbal response can take a few moments, minutes, or even years to be expressed. You can edit, modify, and censor your verbal communication, but your nonverbal communication is expressed immediately, often beneath the level of consciousness. It's communicated instantaneously, even when your words negate or deny your internal condition or reaction.

If you want to see how immediate nonverbal communication is, give another student or coworker $20 the next time you pass them in the hallway. Note how long it takes their face to change from detached indifference to surprise.

Nonverbal Communication Is More Universal

Whereas a specific language is understood and meaningful only to those who speak the language, nonverbal communication is more universally understood. If you observe two people speaking a language you don't understand, you can still derive some meaning from their gestures, posture, facial expressions, touching, tone of voice, volume, rate of speech, and body movement. If the two are smiling, whispering, and locked in an embrace, you would conclude that they liked each other, even if you didn't understand a single word of their conversation.

Specific nonverbal behaviors such as smiling, laughing, and crying appear to hold universally identical meanings for people of different cultures. In fact, there even seems to be six universally understood facial expressions of happiness, sadness, anger, surprise, fear, and disgust, according to researcher Paul Ekman.

However, nonverbal behaviors can vary in meaning from culture to culture. For instance, because two Arab men are speaking in raised voices just inches from each other does not mean they are angry; these behaviors are characteristic of their culture. Likewise, two Japanese women speaking in a low volume, avoiding direct eye contact, and standing apart from each other does not mean that their relationship is distant and cold because these behaviors are characteristic of their culture. So we need to be careful when interpreting nonverbal communication.

Nonverbal Communication Is Multichanneled

Verbal communication is usually sent in either the auditory or visual channel—words are either spoken or written. But nonverbal communication is not limited to only one channel, but can utilize all five channels. Nonverbal communication can be seen, heard, tasted, smelled, and/or felt simultaneously, like when you swim in the ocean. You can see, feel, taste, smell, and hear the ocean as you swim. This complexity and richness of nonverbal communication is testament to its influence and power in conveying messages.

Nonverbal Communication Is Emotionally Rich

Whereas words can convey or communicate the basic meaning of an object, thought, or feeling, nonverbal communication can often convey the depth, attitude, and feeling of the speaker. Nonverbal communication conveys emotions and feelings much more effectively than words. For instance, if you cancel a luncheon date with a friend, his frown, downcast eyes, and slumped shoulders convey his disappointment even if he says, "That's all right."

Our nonverbal communication also conveys the level or degree of our feelings and emotions. We can describe an experience as "happy," but the degree to which we experienced the happiness can be more accurately communicated if the word is accompanied with a faint smile, a boisterous shout, or even a cartwheel on the lawn. Our body, voice, and behavior can easily convey the degree and depth to which we feel, more than words. As philosopher Denis Diderot said, "A dance is a poem." So, use you body to create a poem the next time you want to express joy or happiness.

Nonverbal Communication Is Function Specific

What are some specific ways you can create this poem of yours? Well, here are ways you can use your hands and body to communicate more creatively. There are five primary functions or categories of nonverbal communication—emblems, illustrators, regulators, affect displays, and adaptors. **Emblems** are nonverbal gestures or movements that have direct verbal meaning or translation in a given culture. In the United States, examples of emblems are waving goodbye, blowing a kiss, and the thumbs-up gesture. **Illustrators** add to or support a verbal message, such as showing the size of the fish you caught or showing the height of a child with your hand. **Regulators** are nonverbal behaviors that regulate social interaction. Sitting next to someone to initiate a conversation, looking to someone who has not spoken during a meeting, and standing up at the end of a conversation can regulate social interaction. **Affect displays** are those less intentionally communicated nonverbal signs of emotion given by the body. Your facial expressions are some of the primary affect displays, but foot tapping, yawning, and averting your gaze may also communicate feelings such as boredom or disinterest. Finally, **adaptors** are your unintentional habitual body movements, such as playing with your hair, stroking your chin, and placing your hand over your mouth. Adaptors may serve psychological needs to sooth, reassure, and encourage.

Nonverbal Communication Is Ambiguous

No matter what pop psychology books promise, it is impossible to "read anyone like a book." Nonverbal communication is far too complex and ambiguous. The meaning of any one particular nonverbal behavior can be interpreted in so many different ways.

A woman at a party standing with arms tightly folded across her chest is not necessarily communicating her unwillingness to interact with others as some books might suggest. Her folded arms could also mean she is cold, shy, embarrassed by a food stain, or maybe even hiding an engagement ring. Nonverbal communication is ambiguous because one behavior can represent many different messages, which can be sent intentionally and unintentionally.

Although nonverbal communication can be ambiguous, we can play an active role in clarifying and understanding the meaning of many behaviors by asking appropriate questions. One way to create clearer understanding and thus more effective communication is to ask questions when in doubt, rather than infer or guess the meaning of any nonverbal behavior. How will you ever know if you don't ask?

TYPES OF NONVERBAL COMMUNICATION

Nonverbal communication can be pervasive, varied, and meaningful to others. In order for you to become more familiar with this silent dimension of communication, let's examine its four primary categories—body movement, paralanguage, personal presentation, and proxemics. These four categories will enable you to become more aware and sensitive to the many ways you can increase the creativity with which you communicate.

Body Movement

The study of body movement is known as **kinesics** and it deals with all the ways people use their bodies to communicate or enhance their verbal communication. Body movement includes posture, gestures, facial expressions, and eye contact.

Your **posture**—the way you position and move your body—can communicate a great deal about you. For example, leaning toward or leaning away from someone in conversation can convey your degree of interest, attentiveness, or involvement. Turning your back or standing to leave can convey a lack of interest or signal the end to the conversation.

Gestures are any movement of the hands, fingers, or arms. Open arms can signify honesty and openness. A finger can communicate accusation when pointing to another person or it can invite interaction when motioning "come here." Hands held behind the back while speaking can communicate anxiety or reluctance, whereas expressive hand gestures can convey confidence, enthusiasm, and conviction. Yet some gestures are not universal. Their interpretations are often culturally based and their meanings differ from culture to culture. For example, the "okay" gesture made with the thumb and the forefinger means "everything is all right" to an American. But in France it means "You're worth zero," in Japan it means "money," and in Turkey it's a vulgar invitation for sex. A gesture can get you a smile or a slap depending on who is interpreting it.

Facial expressions are the arrangement of facial muscles to communicate messages. They include the mouth, cheeks, eyes, eyelids, eyebrows, forehead, nose, and chin. The face is probably the most observed part of the body when we communicate with others, and this is not without reason. Our face usually communicates our internal, emotional experience. Although some individuals, such as actors and models, are trained to control their facial expressions, most of us unconsciously express our emotions with our face.

> *What you are stands over you the while, and thunders so that I cannot hear what you say to the contrary.*
>
> —RALPH WALDO EMERSON

Researchers have suggested that there are at least 640 different facial expressions when you take into account the different eyebrow/forehead, eyes/eyelid, and lower face expressions possible. The rapid speed with which facial expressions can change has been estimated at one-fifth of a second. These, plus the combinations of facial expressions displayed by different parts of the face, can contribute to interpretation difficulties.

Eye contact can also communicate several different types of messages. Direct eye contact in our culture can communicate involvement, intimidation, and intimacy. A diverted or downcast gaze communicates a different message. Our eyes can also communicate dominance and submission. We can "stare someone down" with a prolonged gaze that is not returned by the other person, or we can avoid or break eye contact when talking with a superior, such as a boss or supervisor.

As with gestures, however, eye behavior is often culturally learned. In the United Sates and many other Western nations, direct eye contact is a sign of involvement, honesty, authenticity, and liking. In Japan and other Eastern countries, direct eye contact is a sign of disrespect, rudeness, and even aggression.

Once again, we need to be aware of and sensitive to many of the cultural differences in nonverbal communication.

Paralanguage

The voice is a significant medium of nonverbal communication. **Paralanguage** is how we speak. Aside from the actual words or content of our messages, paralanguage includes pitch, volume, rate, and quality. As actor Sir Lawrence Olivier once said, "One's voice is an instrument that can play a sentence in a hundred different ways." These qualities of paralanguage enable actors, and you, to create a variety of music when they speak.

Pitch refers to the highness or lowness of our voice. The pitch of our voice is primarily determined by the physical length and thickness of our vocal chords, but it can rise if we are frightened, anxious, or excited, and it can lower if we are attempting to sound more powerful or authoritative.

> *The human voice is the most beautiful musical instrument.*
>
> —JUDY COLLINS

The relative softness or loudness of our voice is called **volume**. We often speak in a characteristic volume; some individuals talk loudly, whereas others talk in almost a whisper. We can also adjust our volume to meet the requirements of the communication setting we are in. In a noisy, crowded room we raise our volume and speak above the other voices, whereas during a movie or quiet dinner we lower our voice.

Rate is how fast or slow we speak. People tend to have their own personal rate of speech. Some speak fast, others slow. We tend to increase our rate of speech when we're excited, frightened, or nervous, and we tend to decrease our rate of speech when we're uncertain, thoughtful, and sad.

Finally, **quality** refers to the overall sound of our voice. Each human voice has a distinctive tone. One voice is loud and deep. Another voice is soft and high pitched. The quality of one's voice may be characterized as soothing, harsh, strident, or calm. We each have a distinctive quality to the way we sound. Can you recall your mother's voice? You father's voice? Your best friend's voice? Often, when answering the telephone, we immediately recognize the caller by his or her voice quality.

Try to speak with **vocal variety,** varying your pitch, volume, and rate. Don't be monotone. That puts people to sleep. Create voice characteristics that are varied, expressive, and appropriate to the message and context of the setting.

Personal Presentation

The third category of nonverbal communication is your personal presentation. This includes clothing, grooming, and touching behavior.

Our **clothing** is one of the most obvious and public displays of who we are and what we want to communicate to others. Billions of dollars are spent annually on clothing, yet the primary consideration in most of our purchases is not warmth, function, or durability, but rather popularity, attractiveness, and status.

> *What I wear affects*
> *how I perform.*
>
> —LIBERACE

Our clothing doesn't have to be outrageous, but it can reflect or communicate our moods and emotional states. On days we are feeling casual or want to communicate a less formal public image to the world, we can dress in old jeans, sneakers, and a tie-dyed T-shirt. On more formal days, we can choose a business suit, a dress, or even a tuxedo, with jewelry to match. We can create a variety of public images simply by the clothing we wear.

Our **grooming** can also reflect and communicate messages to the world. The length and style of our hair, bathing routines, makeup, cologne and perfume, finger and toenail painting (even for men these days), and many other grooming habits communicate a great deal about who we are and how we want to be perceived.

Touching is the most intimate form of nonverbal communication behavior. Touching behavior, or **haptics,** as it is called by social scientists, includes all behavior that involves the skin. Primarily, touching behavior deals with our hands and how we use them to communicate.

Touching behavior has been discovered to be essential to our development as human beings. Ashley Montagu in his book *Touching: The Human Significance of the Skin* cites vast numbers of animal and human studies supporting the theory that adequate touching during infancy and childhood is essential to healthy behavior development.

In addition to aiding our development, touching is a necessary and important means of nonverbal communication. Without it, relationships can wither. With it, deep and significant messages can be exchanged. You must be sensitive to the personal and cultural preferences of the individual you want to touch. It is always best to ask. Don't assume that your desire to touch or hug is shared by others. Remember how Rose asked her classmates and me if it would be okay to hug before she actually wrapped her arms around anyone? Be sensitive and courteous—ask.

Proxemics

Each of us is surrounded by an invisible "bubble" that we consider our personal space. This personal space is our buffer zone and is as private as our body itself. Our personal bubble varies in size according to culture, the context of the situation, and whom we are interacting with. It contracts when we're with close friends and family and expands when we're with strangers in unfamiliar environments. The purpose of this bubble is to protect us from threat, provide us with a psychological sense of self, separate us from others, and enable us to communicate intimately.

Proxemics, the study of our use of space, and was first introduced by anthropologist Edward Hall in his book *The Hidden Dimension.* By observing conversations between people, Hall discovered that our personal space could be broken down into four zones or distances:

✦ **Intimate distance** (0 to 18 inches) is reserved for intimate activities include making love, holding intimate or confidential conversations, hugging, kissing, and snuggling. This is often referred to as our "personal bubble." Only our most intimate relationships are permitted into this area. If an uninvited person invades our personal bubble, whether it's a stranger sitting next to us on an empty bench or a person getting too close for comfort during a conversation, we usually move away slightly to maintain our intimate distance.

✦ **Personal distance** (18 inches to 4 feet) is used for most conversations with family, friends, and most acquaintances.

✦ **Social distance** (4 to 12 feet) is the distance we feel most comfortable with transacting business, sitting during committee meetings, and interacting with the hotel clerk, the supermarket cashier, or the police officer giving us a ticket.

✦ **Public distance** (12 to 25 feet) is used for public ceremonies, speeches, large group meetings, and class lectures. If the distance between people is greater than 25 feet, communication is often limited to shouting and exaggerated nonverbal gestures.

The distance of your personal space changes depending on the setting, the people involved, and how you are feeling at the moment. Cultural factors also play an important role in determining proxemic distancing and personal comfort. For example, a person from Iran or Italy would feel comfortable speaking and interacting at a closer distance than someone from Japan or England.

Your awareness and sensitivity to the personal space and proxemic comfort of those you interact with will greatly increase your communication effectiveness with them. By your creative use of proxemics, you can communicate powerful messages without speaking a single word. The behaviors available for you to create more expressive, supportive, and caring messages are limited only by your own creativity.

CREATING EXPANDED NONVERBAL COMMUNICATION: THE T.O.U.C.H. TECHNIQUE

Now that you're all excited about trying some new nonverbal behaviors, consider the T.O.U.C.H. Technique to help you focus your creative efforts while using nonverbal communication to invite, enlarge, and increase your relationships with other people.

Touch others

The most intimate, expressive, and encouraging nonverbal behavior is touch. Your touch can deepen, strengthen, and heal relationships. Always be aware of and sensitive to cultural and individual differences and preferences when you consider using touch to communicate with others. Ask people if it is all right to touch or hug them. Be respectful of their response. If they give you permission, your touch can express caring, concern, encouragement, and reassurance in ways that words cannot. Reach out during your lifetime and be one who touches others. A gentle hand on a shoulder, a pat on the back, and a hug of greeting or reassurance can create more intimate and expressive communication in your life.

Open to others

Every interaction gives you the opportunity to be open or closed to others, to invite them in or keep them out. Do you want to be known as a person who is open to others? A person who embrace others? An individual who invites others in? You can. With your body, posture, eye contact, arms, and voice you can create an openness, a welcoming, and a caring attitude toward others.

Be creative when you create your welcome mat! Let your own unique qualities and personality shine through as you express your hospitality. Henry Ward Beecher said, "Every artist dips his brush in his own soul, and paints his own nature into his pictures." Do the same with the way you open up to others.

Uplift others

Without saying a word, you can be uplifting to others. You can create an uplifting experience for others by looking for little things to do for people, such as paying the toll for the car behind you, giving gift certificates anonymously to a needy family, or buying a box of doughnuts for the office next door to yours. Can you imagine receiving one of these nonverbal acts of kindness? What an uplifting experience! It would change your entire day. You can create this uplifting experience by looking for little things you can do for others—nothing big, nothing expensive, just little things to uplift those around you. So, give another driver your parking spot, pick up some trash at your favorite park, or plant a tree in your neighborhood. Be a blessing. Be uplifting with your actions.

Connect with others

One of the problems that plagues our culture is loneliness. Often, we don't feel connected to family, friends, acquaintances, and the world in general. The primary purpose of communication is connection with others. We need the company of others. We need to feel part of something bigger than ourselves. We need to belong, to be known, and to know others. Without human connections, life is meaningless. Our purpose is to come together, to share, and to love.

Look for ways you can nonverbally connect with others. It doesn't have to be anything big or special. It can simply be mowing your grandmother's lawn, sending flowers to your loved one at work, or including a treat in your child's lunchbox. You can create hundreds of ways of saying you care and maintaining connections with those you love. Seneca once said that "Good material often stands idle for want of an artist." Look around you. The world is full of a lot of good material. Don't let it go to waste. Be an artist of communication and connect with someone!

Help others

You can create a great deal of assistance, reassurance, and hope by helping others. But do not give advice, wisdom, or even kind words. Talk is cheap. Lend a helping hand and be a blessing to others. Look for ways to help others, to meet the needs of others. Holding the door for the person behind you, helping the elderly across a busy street, and giving money to a homeless person are just a few ideas.

Your decision to help others will create in you a more loving heart. It doesn't require words or speeches to help those in need. It asks that we forget about ourselves for a moment or two and lend a helping hand to those in need. You will not only create more loving communication to those around you, you may discover who you really are. Create goodness wherever you go.

Every moment of your life presents you with the opportunity to support and connect with others with your body and your behaviors. If you seize these opportunities, like Rose, you too will be a blessing to others.

EXPLORING CREATIVE TASKS

1. Make a list of ten nonverbal communication behaviors you appreciate a family member, friend, or loved one doing, such as giving rides to school, smiling, making eye contact, mending clothing, cooking a meal, hugging, or giving a back rub. Share this list with the person and thank him or her for communicating support and connection. What was his or her response? How did it feel to you?

2. Make a list of ten supportive nonverbal behaviors you do to others regularly. Next to each behavior, list the name(s) of the person(s) you do this behavior to. Are there some behaviors you do to many people? Are there behaviors you do to only a few? Why? Would you like to do these behaviors to other people you know? Why or why not?

3. For one week, increase your touching behavior with family and friends. Be sensitive to others. Don't force yourself on anyone, but take some risks. What happened during that week of increased touching? What was the response of those you touched more? How did it feel to you? Will you continue to touch more? Why or why not?

4. Select a family member or friend with whom you would like to improve your relationship. Meet with this person for twenty minutes and ask him or her what specific nonverbal communication behaviors he or she likes having you do and doesn't like having you do. Then ask for suggestions for behaviors to do in the future. Be open to his or her comments and suggestions. Don't evaluate anything he or she says. Just be open and listen. What did you think about this meeting? How did it feel? What suggested behaviors could you try in the future?

EXPANDING YOUR CREATIVE THINKING

1. How would you describe the nonverbal behavior of your family of origin—the family in which you were raised? Was your family physically affectionate or reserved and detached? How did your family's nonverbal behavior influence your present nonverbal behavior and preferences? Are you satisfied with the way you nonverbally communicate affection and support with your family and friends now? If not, what would you change or modify? How? When do you want to begin?

2. Look at three of your favorite photographs of you and your family or friends. In each picture, identify all the nonverbal communication behavior that makes these treasured photos. What are the settings? What are you doing? What do you look like? What do the other people look like? What things do you notice about the facial expressions, postures, gestures, clothing, and hair? What feelings do you have about the pictures?

3. What would your life be like if you became blind? What nonverbal behaviors would you no longer be able to observe in others? What nonverbal behaviors would you become more aware of and sensitive to? How would your life change? How would you communicate support and connection? How would being blind make you feel?

4. Where do you go when you're feeling low? What room, building, location, or place do you go to in order to be soothed? What is it about that place that soothes or rejuvenates you? How does it make you feel? Do your loved ones know about this place of yours? Why or why not? Do you think this place will still be important to you twenty years from now? Why or why not?

FIVE

Creating Spacious Communication with Another Culture

> *Human beings draw close to one another by their common nature, but habits and customs keep them apart.*
>
> —CONFUCIUS

"Randy, can I treat you to an Ethiopian lunch?" It was a simple invitation. One sentence. Spoken softly, yet delivered with cheerfulness and a strong sense of self.

Shenar was a part-time geography instructor at our college. He used the office next to mine. During the first week of the semester I heard loud music coming from his office. Annoyed, I got up and knocked on his door.

Shenar greeted me warmly as we introduced ourselves. After a moment or two of pleasantries, I asked him to turn down his music. He apologized and turned down the music.

The next day, however, Shenar's music was blasting again. I knocked on his door again and asked him to turn down the music.

"I'm sorry, Randy," he replied. "In my country, we begin our day with music."

"Well, here it's considered impolite to disturb others," I protested.

"Okay," Shenar said smiling. "I'll not play the music." I turned to leave.

"Randy, let me treat you to an Ethiopian lunch," he offered. "You'll love the food of my country."

Well, how could I refuse his friendly invitation? During that semester, Shenar and I shared three Ethiopian lunches. The food was strange at first, but I quickly developed a love for the cuisine. I enjoyed listening to Shenar's stories. We shared a great deal about our cultures and more importantly, about ourselves. Over Ethiopian food, we became friends.

Shenar could have responded to my complaints with rudeness, coldness, or detachment. Instead, Shenar chose to respond with spaciousness and an invitation to friendship. He chose to create a warm, vast environment where friendship could blossom between two individuals of different cultures. I'm thankful he did.

CREATING SPACIOUS COMMUNICATION

Our world is becoming increasingly more diverse. Changes in transportation, communication, global economics, political dynamics, and immigration have created a world in which individuals of different cultural backgrounds are interacting with one another with greater frequency than ever before. Within seconds, we can talk to people halfway around the world. Within hours, we can fly to countries that once took weeks or months to reach. Within a decade or two, it is generally accepted that the United States will experience dramatic cultural changes that will forever alter our nation.

Great artists belong to no country. They belong to all.

—ALFRED DE MUSSET

How will you respond to the changes that will confront us in the years to come? What will be your response to people who look and behave in ways that are "different" from your ways? In recent years, this question has come up more frequently, as people of different cultural backgrounds make this country their country too.

As author Paul McElroy warns, "We must learn to live with those whose manners annoy us, whose practices offend us, and whose ideas disturb us. We must somehow learn to get along with these people or else be forever at odds with them, with ourselves, and the world." Often, our initial response is to judge, criticize, and distance ourselves from those who differ from us. But as we move farther and farther away from others, we soon discover ourselves increasingly more alone in the world. McElroy concludes by saying, "Our tendency is to build a wall that will shut those who differ from us, but each time we erect a barrier to shut someone out, we also shut ourselves in." So that we won't find ourselves in a prison of our own making, we can develop a spaciousness, an openness to those who are different than us. It might even create a friendship.

COMPONENTS OF CULTURE

People in Japan often bathe communally, while people in the United States bathe privately. People in India worship cows, while people in Canada eat cows. Some people pray to one god, while others pray to hundreds of gods. Some people spend thirty years of their lives paying off a home, while others build a tent in a few days that will last ten years. What makes for these differences in behavior? The answer to this question is culture.

The definitions of culture range from "culture is everything" to "culture is art." Although there is no single definition of culture that is accepted by all scholars, I define **culture** as the learned set of perceptions about thinking, feeling, and behavior that affect the behaviors of a large number of people. In this definition, thinking includes all knowledge, experiences, beliefs, values, notions of time, concepts of the universe, and any other shared cognitions of the specific group of people. Feelings are the shared emotional responses to various situations, circumstances, and people. Behavior includes all nonverbal communication, rituals, material objects, and possessions. This definition emphasizes that these three areas of culture involve perceptions of right and wrong, good and bad that are learned from infancy and reinforced throughout life.

The primary function of culture is to make sense of our world. Without the rules of culture, our daily lives would be chaos. Culture structures and shapes our thinking, feeling, and behavior in such way as to make our lives predictable, manageable, and enjoyable. Can you imagine even one day without the rules of culture to guide your thinking and behavior and those of others? All the rules of communication, interaction, and etiquette would no longer hold true. Everything from greeting an acquaintance to sexual behavior with an intimate would be unpredictable. Without the rules of culture, we would be lost.

To better understand culture, let's examine the basic ingredients of any culture. Communication researchers A. J. Almaney and A. J. Alwan have suggested three primary ingredients to any culture—artifacts, concepts, and behaviors. An **artifact** is any physical object made or modified by humans that has utility or meaning, such as a book, money, chain saw, stop sign, diploma, jet airliner, and computer microchip. A **concept** is any notion, idea, or construct, such as religious beliefs, values, ideas of right and wrong, and ethics. Finally, a **behavior** is any physical action that refers to the actual practice of any of the concepts of the culture, such as communicating with others, driving a car, dating, child rearing, dancing, and standing in line at the grocery store. These three basic ingredients of culture are not necessarily distinct categories. Consider a wedding ring. The ring itself is an artifact, the value placed on it is a concept, and the sliding of the ring on the finger during a wedding ceremony is a behavior.

CHARACTERISTICS OF CULTURE

Some characteristics apply to all cultures. By understanding these characteristics, we can be better equipped to communicate more effectively with those who are different from us.

Culture Is Learned

Culture is not innate. We are not born with a set of rules governing our thinking and guiding our behavior. From the moment we are born we learn about our culture—the cultural concepts, behaviors, and artifacts that are passed from one generation to the next within the culture. Without this continuity, there would be no culture.

Every culture views beauty in different ways. You expand your world every time you can see beauty through the eyes of others.

—BARBARA DOSKER

Enculturation, the activity of learning one's culture, is the single, most important activity of our childhood and early adulthood. From infancy we are taught important cultural lessons of thought and behavior. Our cultural training occurs through our interactions with others, observation, and imitation. The older members of the culture teach us to eat, drink, bathe, play, speak, listen, pray, problem solve, share, and countless other behaviors that allow us to interact and live effectively within the culture. It is through this learning that we also become familiar with the concepts and artifacts of the culture.

Learning one's culture occurs both consciously and unconsciously. We are consciously taught the process of driving a car, eating dinner, saluting the flag, learning to read, and being punctual for appointments. But much of the learning process occurs at the unconscious level through observation and imitation. By observing and imitating how parents interact with each other, how men and women behave and communicate, and how individuals space themselves when standing in line, children learn the culture unconsciously. Both conscious and unconscious enculturation processes shape each individual into an effective participant within the culture.

Culture Is Transmissible

The concepts, behaviors, and artifacts of a culture can be transmitted from person to person, group to group, and generation to generation. We are able to pass on the contents of our culture to others. We can use the spoken word to tell others about our nation's history and achievements. We can use the written word to communicate to others about landing a man on the moon in 1969. We can use audio and videocassette recordings to let others actually hear and see important historical events and figures. We can let our artifacts communicate success, loyalty, and status to others.

Not only can the culture's collective history be passed on to individuals, groups, and future generations, but your own cultural experience can be stored and shared with others. Your scrapbooks, videotapes, and personal heirlooms contain important information about who you are and can be passed on to your children and grandchildren. Be an artist of communication so future generations of family members will enjoy your photo albums, a song you recorded, and a poem you wrote.

Culture Is Ethnocentric

All cultures teach their members the "right" or "preferred" way to behave and respond to the world. These "preferred" ways are often labeled "natural" and "appropriate." In the United States, we grow up behaving, thinking, and believing that direct eye contact demonstrates confidence, honesty, and interest. We are taught that we should "look others in the eye" if we are telling the truth or if we want to communicate confidence. It's the right or appropriate way to communicate. But it's not necessarily the "natural," "appropriate," or "right" way to communicate for most Asians, who view direct eye contact as disrespectful, aggressive, and even hostile.

Ethnocentrism is the belief that one's own culture is central and superior to all other cultures. It is the learned belief in cultural superiority. Members of every culture believe that their concepts, behaviors, and artifacts are the "correct" and "natural" ones, and all other cultures are inferior. For example, in the United States, we hold certain beliefs about body odor. Most Americans bathe or shower at least once a day. In addition to bathing, we replace our natural body odors with artificial ones when we apply shampoos, perfumes, shaving lotions and deodorants, and eat breath mints.

Individuals in cultures where water is not so plentiful do not share this belief in daily bathing, let alone the application of so many artificial odors. From our ethnocentric perspective, we react negatively to those from different cultures who bathe only once a week. We often respond with disgust at their "unnatural" personal hygiene. Equally valid would be their ethnocentric response to our practice of daily bathing and preference for artificial odor as being "unnatural," wasteful, and even a little neurotic.

Until we are aware of and sensitive to our own ethnocentrism, our attempts to communicate with people from other cultures will be ineffective.

Culture Prioritizes What Is Important

One of the most important functions of a culture is that it prioritizes what is important and good. From this ranking of what is considered important and good, the culture will determine and shape the desires, efforts, and achievements of those individuals living within the culture. For instance, if a culture values material possessions, most of the individuals within the culture will desire and seek material possessions. If a culture values honoring the elderly, then the individuals within the culture will seek to honor the elderly. In many ways, what a culture prioritizes or values defines that culture. A culture that values politeness is a polite culture. A culture that values material possessions is a materialistic culture. We are what we value.

Culture Is Dynamic

Cultures seldom remain constant. As ideas and products evolve within a culture, the culture itself changes. For example, the invention of the microchip has changed the American culture by giving us personal computers, cellular phones, pagers, answering machines, the Internet, computer-operated automobile engines, and a hundred other devices that have radically changed our concepts and behaviors. It has changed the way we conduct business, talk with our loved ones, and even the way we eat our meals.

A culture changes primarily because of invention and diffusion. **Invention** is defined as the discovery of new concepts, practices, or tools. Assembly line production, voting rights for women, education for all residents, the civil rights movement, and two-income families are concepts and practices that have changed our culture. The microchip is an example of a tool that has changed our American culture. In addition to the microchip, inventions such as the radio, automobile, telephone, airplane, television, movies, convenience stores, and video games have brought about tremendous changes to the United States and the world.

Diffusion is the borrowing or assimilation of concepts from other cultures. We especially adopt the practices from another culture when two cultures are geographically close to each other or their interaction increases such as due to commerce or national security. For example, American businesses adopted many of the Japanese practices of decision making, employee input on quality control, and assembly line robotics to enhance productivity in American factories and plants.

VERBAL AND NONVERBAL CULTURAL VARIABLES

When communicating with individuals from different cultures, keep in mind that there are verbal and nonverbal communication differences between cultures. Let's briefly review some verbal and nonverbal cultural variables that distinguish one culture from another.

Verbal Communication Variables

Recall that verbal communication is all communication that is spoken and written. Every culture on earth has a spoken language and almost every culture possesses a written language. It is impossible to separate a culture from its language because language is used to communicate and transmit the content of the culture to people.

The most obvious difference in the verbal communication between two cultures is their language. We cannot communicate effectively if we don't share the basic vocabulary of another culture. Our culture teaches us that the word "cow" represents a large farm animal that provides milk and meat for us to consume. People from India have a different symbol and word for the same animal. At the surface level, if we don't know the word for "cow" in Hindi, we cannot communicate the concept of "cow" to an Indian. That seems obvious. But it goes even deeper.

Remember the difference between denotative and connotative meanings for a word? Denotative meaning is the dictionary meaning for a word or symbol. In this instance, the dictionary meaning for the word "cow" cannot be communicated because we do not know the Hindi equivalent. Even if we did, we would have a secondary difficulty—the connotative meaning.

The connotative meaning captures the emotion or feeling that is attached to a word. For a Hindu, "cow" has sacred, reverent emotions attached to it because cows are given religious significance in India. Even if an Indian knew English, the word "cow" would convey a very different message. Can you imagine how the statement "I love to eat hamburgers" would be received by your Indian acquaintance?

How people from various cultures use language is another verbal communication difference you need to be sensitive to in order to be an effective communicator. The use of language varies from culture to culture. In American culture, we value verbal communication. We want to fully explain our ideas. We desire to share our feelings. We value the individual who speaks eloquently. In Japan, people hold the opposite view of communication. Verbal communication is kept to a minimum. It is not encouraged in many social and business settings. In fact, excessive talking to the Japanese is a sign of impoliteness and self-obsession. So you need to keep in mind that even the uses of verbal language may be very different for the individual with whom you are communicating.

> *We create reality with our language.*
> —SHUNRYU SUZUKI

Related to verbal communication differences are the different ways of thinking that distinguish one culture from another. Most Westerners believe that action is desirable and passivity is undesirable and a sign of personal weakness. Westerners think that they need to take action to solve problems, achieve their aims, and reach their goals. Asians hold a different worldview. Patience and stillness are the paths to problem solving. Rather than immediately setting out to get things done, they wait. The solution to problems and answers to questions will make themselves apparent when it is time. These different perspectives of problem solving are just a few examples of the many ways in which cultures think differently. To communicate effectively with individuals from another culture, you need to be sensitive to their patterns of thinking and worldview.

Nonverbal Communication Variables

Not only do the language and emotions associated with many words differ from culture to culture, so do the behaviors of the people themselves. The nonverbal communication differences between cultures are so great that I will not attempt to discuss even a small portion of the hundreds of behaviors that are recognized and used by even one culture. My purpose is to increase your awareness of four nonverbal categories of behaviors of touching, use of space, time, and clothing.

Touching. In Spain, touching is perceived and practiced as a positive nonverbal behavior, whereas in Japan, touching is perceived as inappropriate, even among intimates in public. Americans fall somewhere between the Spanish and Asian cultures in touching behavior. When you communicate with a person from another culture, you need to be aware that the touching behaviors you perceive as natural and appropriate may not be perceived as such in other cultures.

Use of space. The use of distance or space is another way that culture helps determine nonverbal communication. In the United States, we generally feel comfortable talking to acquaintances from a distance of one and a half to four feet, whereas Arabs feel perfectly comfortable interacting more closely. Asians, on the other hand, would feel uncomfortable at either distance, preferring greater space.

Privacy or territorial distances can also differ. Many Eastern Europeans feel comfortable standing right next to a complete stranger while waiting for a bus or in a store, whereas Americans would view this as a violation of personal space. When interacting with people from a different culture, be aware that their use of space may differ from yours.

Time. The concept of time and its relative importance to people vary from culture to culture. Americans view time as a linear process that moves from the past into the future. Given this linear view, we value time in schedules and calendars because once time is lost, it can never be regained. The Swiss are even more time bound, with an almost religious emphasis on punctuality and adherence to schedules. The Vietnamese, on the other hand, view time not as a linear process, but as a circular one. Perhaps this perspective is derived from the Buddhist belief in reincarnation and the notion that you are given many lives to realize your Buddha nature. In that sense, time is never really lost, but ever returning. The Vietnamese are not as time bound as Westerners, and being late to an appointment by fifteen or twenty minutes does not carry the same meaning for a Vietnamese as it does for a German or a Swiss.

Clothing. Aside from skin color, clothing presents one of the most obvious and striking differences between people of different cultures. The clothing a person wears sends important messages about who they are and how they perceive themselves. In some cultures, uniforms are popular. In Mexico and many Central and South American countries, the military, police, government officials, and even schoolchildren enjoy wearing uniforms, whereas in Israel uniforms are very unpopular. Even the Israeli military are often seen wearing casual attire such as T-shirts and shorts.

It's important to remember that no matter what people are wearing, their clothing is just one aspect of who they are. People from any culture are more than their clothing and jewelry. To communicate effectively with individuals from different cultures, you need to suspend judgment on their appearance long enough to get to know them beneath the surface.

CREATING COMMUNICATION WITH ANOTHER CULTURE: THE I.N.V.I.T.E. TECHNIQUE

There are two primary ways we can improve our communication with an individual from another culture. A **culture-specific** approach to improving our communication involves learning about a specific culture and applying that knowledge when communicating with an individual from that culture. For instance, if you were to travel to Spain, you might enroll in a beginning Spanish course, read books and articles about Spain and Spanish culture, and perhaps even interview individuals who are familiar with Spain and its customs. This approach focuses on one culture and applies the knowledge gleaned for a specific purpose.

On the other hand, a **culture-general** approach examines and explores those aspects of communication that seem to apply to all cultures. Instead of focusing on the differences between cultures, the culture-general approach seeks to highlight universal communication aspects and skills that we can use when we interact with individuals from any culture.

I believe that people of all cultures have more in common than they do differences. The I.N.V.I.T.E. Technique provides a summary of communication attitudes and skills to help you create more spacious and inviting communication with people of all cultures.

Increase your frame of reference

Each of us carries a frame of reference or model of the world that divides all people into "us" and "them." "Us" may include people within your culture, your friends and loved ones, your immediate family, or maybe only yourself. Everyone outside this circle or frame is "them"—people you consider outsiders. To communicate effectively with individuals from other cultures, you need to increase your cultural frame of reference to include more people. You need to enlarge your circle of "us" to include more of "them." You need to accept the fact that all people are different, even within your own specific culture. You need to consider that these "differences" are aspects that can be appreciated and even enjoyed.

No evaluation

Oftentimes an individual's skin color, clothing, accent, nonverbal behavior, or topic of discussion can cause us to evaluate him or her as strange, unnatural, or different. We judge and condemn a person for not looking or behaving as we do. If you do this, you have already closed off any real possibility of making contact with this individual. Our negative evaluation of another person can be communicated verbally or nonverbally. Verbal expressions include negative comments, criticism, or humorous remarks that could cause the other person to feel defensive, threatened, or put down. Negative evaluation is more commonly communicated nonverbally with, for example, a frown, raised eyebrows, rolling eyes, an audible sigh, turning aside, or walking away.

Especially valuable when communicating with an individual of another culture is to suspend judgment and make no evaluation, either verbally or nonverbally. This is perhaps the most difficult requirement because our ethnocentrism encourages us to view the behaviors and habits of those from other cultures as inferior. By not evaluating verbally or nonverbally, we make room for connection and dialogue with another individual to occur. This nonevaluative stance enables meaningful communication to take place.

> You can experience your everyday life as art by bringing to it the qualities of the artist—inspiration, creativity, absorption, and delight. Go beyond yourself.
>
> —LAWRENCE BOLDT

When people from another culture are talking to you, listen without interrupting. Nonevaluative listening can be difficult, especially if their fluency or pronunciation is weak, their nonverbal behaviors are distracting, or the topics they are sharing are unfamiliar to you. By remaining silent, you create the spaciousness required for connection. By your open, nonjudgmental listening, you will begin dialogue with them.

To create an atmosphere where genuine meeting can begin, you must convey an attitude of wanting to learn and not wanting to judge or teach, wanting to explore and not wanting to direct or guide. Like looking at a painting for the first time, you must stand back and take it in, being open to what it has to say to you.

Venture out from your comfort zone

Each one of us has a comfort zone that separates those activities, ideas, and feelings that are comfortable from those that are uncomfortable. We tend to do things, think things, and feel things that we are comfortable with and avoid the rest. Personal growth comes when we venture outside our comfort zone by taking risks and experiencing new things.

Here are just a few ways you can take risks and venture out beyond your cultural comfort zone: enroll in a foreign language class, attend an ethnic carnival or fair, visit a museum featuring art from another culture, learn a skill or hobby from another culture, go to a foreign film festival, read a book about another culture, subscribe to *National Geographic*, interview someone from another culture, share a meal with a foreign visitor, visit an ethnic section of town, date someone from another culture, host a foreign exchange student for a year, travel to a foreign country, or live in a foreign country for a year. I'm certain you can think of many more ways to broaden your cultural experiences.

Inquire of others

Author Frank Kingdon states that "Questions are the creative acts of intelligence." The questions you formulate and ask can be pieces of art created by your mind. One question, carefully chosen, can change the course of a discussion and even alter the direction life takes.

You can improve your communication with individuals from another culture by asking them questions. By inquiring, you create a situation in which the other person is encouraged to talk. In a sense, whenever you ask a question, you place the person in a teaching role and yourself in a student role. The person provides information and you receive the information. This is especially helpful because that person may already feel inadequate with her English proficiency and knowledge of American culture. By asking questions about her culture, you put her in a one-up position. She knows the answers to the questions and you do not. The questions don't have to be philosophical or deep. You can simply ask how to say something in her language.

The process of asking questions—inquiring about culture, perceptions, thoughts, and feelings—creates communication wherein the focus of attention is on the other person, not you. You honor people by your questions. By showing your interest in their culture, you also have increased your cultural frame of reference to include a little more of their culture.

Talk about things in common

After asking all these wonderful questions, you need to listen carefully to what people have to say. During the conversation, seek similarities. Look for common ground that can serve as the foundation for further inquiries and dialogue. This is not the time to debate, argue, or find fault in what people share. The purpose is to create an atmosphere where the other person feels safe to speak, encouraged to disclose, and happy to be chatting with you. This is the time to talk about things you have in common.

What could you possibly have in common with an individual from a different culture? Plenty. Each of us lives on this planet for a relatively short period. We come into the world from the womb of our mother. We will experience infancy, childhood, adolescence, and early adulthood. We will eat food. We will attend school. We will fall in love. We will experience heartbreak. We will most likely marry or bond with a significant other. Most of us will become a parent and belong to a family. We will be employed or work at a job for much of our lives. We will celebrate birthdays, anniversaries, reunions, and retirements. We will experience the deaths of parents and other loved ones. We will become older and our bodies will begin to fail. We will experience ill health, disease, and loneliness. Then we die. Each one of us will participate in most of these experiences, no matter what culture we belong to. That's the human journey. Regardless of skin color, language, and culture, we will all experience these events. Through these similar experiences, we can connect with individuals from another culture.

When you are interacting with others, seek those things you have in common. Look for the common experiences that point to your connections as human beings, not as individuals from different cultures. You have more in common with those who are different from you than you think. Open to the things you have in common. Create a place where you and a person from a different culture can meet and share the human experience.

Encourage social interaction

Once the two of you are busily chatting about all the things you have in common and the hour is growing late, do not end the conversation here. Consider getting together again at a later date. Offer to treat him or her to coffee, tea, or a hot fudge sundae sometime soon. Arrange a little get-together for thirty minutes or an hour at most. It doesn't even have to be much—just a cup of coffee, a walk during a break at work, or dessert at a fast-food restaurant. Something brief will provide the best opportunity to continue your delightful conversation.

Every friendship begins with one conversation. Remember, your greatest creations will be the friendships and love relationships you establish and maintain during your lifetime. So, extend the invitation for further discussion and maybe you will create a friendship that will last you a lifetime.

Can I treat you to an Ethiopian lunch?

EXPLORING CREATIVE TASKS

1. Select one classmate from a different culture and meet with him or her for a twenty-minute informational interview (see chapter 12 for suggestions for successful interviewing). Ask the student to share his or her observations and feelings about Americans. How are Americans different from people in his or her

native country? How are we similar? How did this interview go? What did you like best? What did you like least? Why?

2. List ten specific traditions, beliefs, or artifacts from your cultural or ethnic background that are significant to you. Share this list with a friend or classmate. What was it like sharing your culture or ethnicity with another individual? What did you like about sharing? What did you like least? Why?

3. Spend an entire day in an ethnic part of a city. Visit shops, eat in restaurants, visit churches or temples, talk with the people. What was the experience like for you? What did you like best? Why? What did you like least? Why? What did you learn about yourself?

4. Take an individual from another culture to lunch (your treat). Remember to ask questions, be open, and listen without judging. What did you like best about the lunch? Why? What did you like least? Why? What did you learn about the other person? What did you learn about yourself?

EXPANDING YOUR CREATIVE THINKING

1. How would your life change if you lived alone in a foreign country (one that you have not lived in or visited)? Select a specific country. Why did you select that country? If you moved there, what modifications or changes would you have to make in terms of language, living situation, transportation, employment, eating, recreation, friends, and so on?

2. What do you like about your country of origin? Why? Of the things you liked best, what might you do to enhance, support, or strengthen those things?

3. What do you dislike about your country of origin? Why? Of the things you liked least, what might you do to improve things? What have you tried thus far?

4. What would your life be like if you were blind from this day forward? How would that influence the way you interacted with people of different cultures? How would you change?

SIX

Creating Receptive Communication as a Listener

> *Do you listen to confirm what you already know, or do you listen to explore and learn new things?*
>
> —JIDDU KRISHNAMURTI

The woman with the silver hair listens to the eleven-year-old as he talks reluctantly about his parents' divorce. They both sit in comfortable sofa chairs, facing each other in the quiet of her office. He pauses for a long time, glancing at the woman for some gesture or nod for him to continue his story, but she doesn't move. She doesn't speak. With kind eyes meeting his, she sits motionless with hands folded, listening deeply, listening patiently, as if time were standing still.

No one ever listened to him like this before. It feels unfamiliar, strange, not being rushed. Not being judged or criticized. Not being interrupted or having your sentences finished for you. She doesn't even ask many questions. Mostly, she listens to what he has to say. And to what he doesn't say.

He will grow to trust the silver-haired woman, to even like her. She will create a safe harbor for him to open, to explore, and to heal. She will change how he sees his parents, himself, and his life, mostly by her listening.

THE IMPORTANCE OF LISTENING

In our culture, talking is valued much more than listening. But listening is important. We cannot be successful without developing this skill. Studies show that we spend 45 percent of our communication time in daily life listening, and only 30 percent speaking, 16 percent reading, and 9 percent writing. To make matters worse, studies also suggest that we remember only 25 percent of what we hear after two days. Listening is important and yet we don't do it very well.

Sure, we know to keep silent for a few moments when someone speaks, but during our silence we're already forming our response or rebuttal to what is being shared. We interrupt without ceasing. We judge without thinking. We often redirect the conversation to our point of view without trying to understand what is being shared. When we listen like this, we create a communication atmosphere that encourages a tug-of-war contest, rather than deeper disclosure, mutual sharing, and understanding. How can we create receptive communication as a listener?

> *The real art of listening involves an awareness and sensitivity to the feelings of the speaker, because it is at the feeling level that genuine connection, relationship, and healing occurs.*
>
> —HENRY GANZLER

THE PROCESS OF LISTENING

The process of listening isn't as simple as you may first think. It is not just keeping quiet long enough for the next pause so you can speak. **Listening** is the process of receiving, attending, understanding, responding, and remembering. The first step in the listening process is **receiving** or hearing sounds from your environment. Hearing is limited to the physiological process of receiving and processing the sounds. The second step is **attending,** which is paying attention to some of the sounds you receive and disregarding or filtering out the others. For instance, you hear all the voices around you at a party, but you attend to the voice of the person you're talking with. **Understanding,** the third step, involves comprehending the message. **Responding,** the fourth step, includes asking questions or giving feedback to the speaker. The final step in the listening process is **remembering** what was said. Listening is a process that requires your active participation.

LISTENING STYLES TO AVOID

There are many different ways you can listen to another person and there is no one style of listening that creates or encourages effective, positive communication in every circumstance. However, you should avoid four listening styles.

Refusing to Listen

The most obvious behavior that prevents effective listening is to refuse to listen to the other person. Here are some examples of refusing to listen:

> Simply walking away when someone begins speaking.
> "I don't want to talk about this anymore."
> "No, I don't want to hear what you have to say."

Pseudolistening

With **pseudolistening,** or pretending to listen, the listener may demonstrate many of the nonverbal behaviors of true listening—open posture, eye contact, nodding, and appropriate facial expressions—but there is no attempt to receive, attend, or understand the content of what the speaker is saying. Here are some comments suggesting pseudolistening:

> "Yes, dear."
> "Okay, I got the message."
> "Whatever."

Listening Selectively

There are times when the listener attends and responds only to those subjects he is interested in and skips the rest. We've all endured the individual who listens to us just long enough to bring up a topic he's interested in and then continues to dominate the conversation. Here are some examples of statements suggesting selective listening.

> "Well, now you're talking about something I'm interested in."
> "Yeah, I'm glad you brought that up because I had that happen
>   to me . . ."
> "That reminds me of a time when I . . ."

Listening to Evaluate

Listening to evaluate focuses on judging the correctness, rightness, or worth of the speaker's statements. Rather than hearing and trying to understand the speaker's opinions, feelings, and frame of reference, the listener is concerned about judging the message from her own point of view. It doesn't matter whether the listener's evaluation is negative or positive, the goal is to judge what the speaker is saying. Whether the listener's response is "That's a wonderful point!" or "That's the most ridiculous opinion I've ever heard!" the deeper message is "I am the judge of your comments." Listening for the purposes of judging does not encourage or provide a basis of understanding. Here are some common responses that suggest listening for judgment:

"No one should say that."

"Yes. That's a good point."

"How can you say that?"

We often create the opportunity for others to open up or close down by the way we listen and respond to them. The pictures you paint with your evaluations are far different from the ones you can paint with your openness and receptivity.

There are occasions when using one of these four styles of listening may be appropriate. But when your primary purpose for listening is to create a receptive listening atmosphere, you should avoid these four styles.

BARRIERS TO LISTENING

The reasons why most of us listen in ways that are ineffective are not that we are bad, malicious, or mean. Listening is a difficult process. There are many barriers to listening that we experience and must contend with on a daily basis.

The first barrier is the **abundance** of messages that bombard us every day. Messages crying out to be heard, to be listened to—the sounds of the radio, television, endless conversations, business meetings, e-mail messages, phone conversations, and the list goes on and on. There are just too many things to listen to in our lives.

External noise, or interference from outside sources, is the second barrier to listening. Some examples of external noise are traffic, barking dogs, machinery, and the music from the neighbor's stereo. These external noises make listening difficult.

The third barrier to listening is **rapid thought.** We can understand a person's speech up to 500 words per minute, while the average person speaks about 125 words per minute. With all this spare time on our hands, our thoughts can drift, and we can think about our response to what is being said or just daydream about food. Rapid thought can be a barrier to listening.

Preoccupation with self is the fourth barrier to listening. We think in terms of how communication affects us, what it means to us, whether it agrees or disagrees with what we think, feel, and believe. It is through this filter that we listen to what others say.

The final barrier to effective listening is that listening requires **effort.** Effective listening demands that we pay attention, process what is being said, and interact appropriately.

Receptive listening ultimately requires that we put aside our ego, pay attention to what is being shared, ask questions to clarify the messages, and respond in ways that demonstrate understanding. More than anything else, receptive listening requires our acceptance of others.

ACCEPTANCE—THE BASIS OF LISTENING

Acceptance is receiving "what is." The basis of all listening is acceptance—to be open to receive whatever the speaker is sharing with us. No receptive listening can occur without being open to the other person. Some of the barriers to effective listening discussed earlier—listening selectively and listening to evaluate—prevent us from being receptive to what is being shared.

To be truly accepting, you must be willing to put aside *your* thoughts, ideas, beliefs, and values for a few moments and receive what is being shared. The information you hear may be new, unfamiliar, and even strange. Yet, you will need to put aside your evaluation for a moment or two and listen with an open mind. This is the most difficult requirement of listening. It is also the most important, because without it, you will hear only the echoes of your own mind—your constant judgment and evaluation of what is being shared.

To listen with acceptance requires that you abandon your preoccupation with yourself. Maybe that's the reason we are such poor listeners. We cannot get outside ourselves to experience another person. Now, before you throw your hands up in defeat, thinking that receiving "what is" sounds impossible, consider this example.

Anytime you watch a beautiful sunset, you are, in a sense, receiving "what is." You accept or enjoy the sunset just the way it presents itself to you. There is no judging, fixing, changing, controlling, adjusting, teaching, redirecting, rejecting, blaming, insulting, criticizing, helping, or manipulating the sunset. You don't yell out for more red and less purple. You don't blame it for the cooling temperature of the air. You don't try to stop the sun from setting. There's just an "Ah, how beautiful." You simply receive "what is."

The same can be true for human beings. When we listen, we need to accept more things about others that we may not agree with, find desirable, or even like. If we don't, and continue to evaluate, criticize, and attempt to control other people's thoughts and behaviors, we will only alienate and distance ourselves from them. We must learn to listen to different ideas, thoughts, and feelings when we listen to others, or forever be at odds with them, ourselves, and the world.

Nonverbal Signs of Acceptance

Can you imagine what it would be like to initiate a conversation with an individual when all he did was frown and look away every time you tried to speak? Can you imagine what it would be like to talk and have him respond with labored sighs of disgust and disapproval? Wouldn't that be an enjoyable experience?

The way you communicate nonverbally sets the tone of acceptance or rejection long before you speak. The manner in which you make yourself available to people by your posture and gestures, eye contact, facial expressions, and nodding demonstrates your acceptance of them.

Posture and gestures. How you stand or sit can communicate acceptance or rejection. Facing away from another person or speaking over your shoulder can communicate rejection, whereas facing the person directly can communicate acceptance. A slouched, withdrawn posture can communicate negative messages, whereas an erect posture or one in which you lean toward the person can communicate positive messages. The way you gesture with your arms and hands can also show acceptance or rejection.

> *The artist, above all else, should maintain an open heart and mind to the beauty he has yet to notice.*
> —B. M. BURRELL

Eye contact. Eye contact communicates acceptance in American culture. It can be a sign of acknowledgment, approval, and agreement, especially when accompanied with a smile. Refusing to look at someone can be interpreted as a sign of rejection.

When you are practicing receptive listening, your eye contact should be direct. As someone speaks to you, maintain eye contact to demonstrate your interest and involvement. Don't look away or close your eyes and fall sleep. Look at the speaker for three or four seconds at a time. Don't stare for long periods of time, however. Staring can make others feel uncomfortable, so maintain direct eye contact for short periods.

Facial expressions. Your face can communicate a great deal about how you are feeling and what you are thinking. A frown, raised eyebrows, and rolling eyes are just a few facial expressions that can convey your thoughts and feelings. So, if you are trying to communicate acceptance, remember to reflect the appropriate facial expressions as someone else speaks. Supportive facial expressions create a sense of acceptance when listening to others.

Nodding. This isn't nodding-off-to-sleep nodding. Occasional nodding is an encouraging nonverbal message that says you are paying attention and acknowledging the words of the speaker. Don't overdo this behavior, but nod your head as a way of saying, "I hear you" and "What you're saying is important."

Verbal Signs of Acceptance

In addition to the nonverbal signs of acceptance, there are a number of verbal ways to communicate acceptance while listening. These verbal signs of acceptance are not interrupting, nonevaluative listening, words of acceptance, and invitations to share.

Not interrupting. Two people cannot speak at the same time and expect communication to occur. Whenever a person speaks, someone else needs to listen for communication to occur. So your willingness to listen is a very important message. Don't interrupt the speaker as he or she talks. Instead of interrupting or adding your own comments every twelve to fifteen seconds, let the speaker talk for thirty to sixty seconds without interrupting. In some instances, it may be beneficial and helpful to remain silent for a minute or two without interrupting.

Nonevaluative listening. Nonevaluative listening is your decision to verbally and nonverbally withhold evaluation or judgment as the speaker talks. Many people cannot refrain from evaluating what is being shared. Like a judge, they listen with gavel in hand, ready to pronounce judgment with their words and body expressions even before the speaker has finished the sentence.

Recall that according to linguistics professor and author Deborah Tannen, American men are more inclined to evaluate what a speaker is saying than American women are. Tannen adds that men are more likely to interrupt, judge, give advice, and offer solutions than are women. So, men need to be especially aware and sensitive to their listening responses: Don't interrupt, give your opinion, or offer your advice; just keep silent and listen.

Remember to use supportive nonverbal responses to create receptive communication. Smile, nod your head, and lean toward the speaker as she talks. The speaker is then freed to explore her thoughts and feelings in the presence of another human being without the usual verbal interruptions or nonverbal judgments that characterize most conversation in this culture.

Words of acceptance. Words or phrases such as "Oh," "Um," "Really?" "Okay," "I see," "Is that so?" "That's interesting," and "Say more" are words of acceptance. They are not evaluations of right or wrong, good or bad, or agreement or disagreement. They are intended to communicate your attentiveness and acceptance of what is being shared. It is your way to cheer the speaker on and say, "Keep going, you're doing a great job of sharing!"

Invitations to share. You can invite others to share by issuing invitations such as "How's it going?" This invitation is relatively neutral and gives the person the choice to talk or to decline. Either way the person responds to your invitation, honor his decision. If he decides to talk, listen nonevaluatively. If he declines, accept that also. What is important is that you are inviting the person to share and creating the opportunity for him to talk. Other invitations to share are:

> "Tell me about it."
> "Would you like to talk about your situation?"
> "I'm interested in your point of view."

These are just a few ways you can encourage someone to open up. Many times people don't share because they feel no one wants to listen. Your invitations to share can create an atmosphere in which disclosing is made possible.

ACTIVE LISTENING

To create an atmosphere that encourages sharing, you can use active listening to demonstrate your understanding of what the speaker has said. **Active listening** is the process by which you paraphrase or restate in your own words what the speaker has said to clarify or confirm the accuracy of the message.

Listening is often mistakenly viewed as a passive activity—the speaker talks and the listener listens. The speaker is active and verbal, and the listener is passive and silent. When the speaker finishes talking, the assumption is that the message has been accurately received by the listener,

> *To affect the quality*
> *of the day is*
> *the highest of arts.*
>
> —HENRY DAVID THOREAU

with no observable effort or participation on the listener's part. What could be simpler? The speaker talks and the listener listens. But it's not so simple.

The assumption that the listener truly understands what the speaker has said is one of the most dangerous assumptions in communication. Chapter 1 discussed how the listener's decoding process can be a very complex and how the listener's perception can be influenced by a multitude of variables.

The listener can use active listening to ensure that he or she understood what the speaker said. Using active listening, the listener is an equal participant in the communication process. True communication requires the active participation of the listener as well as the speaker.

The Four Steps of Active Listening

There are two types of active listening. Active listening for **content** (accuracy) and active listening for **feelings** (empathy). The four basic steps to the active listening process are the same for either content or feelings. If you follow these four simple steps, you will master one of the fundamental skills in creating receptive communication as a listener.

Step 1.   Speaker makes a statement.
Step 2.   Listener paraphrases speaker's statement ("Are you saying . . . ?").
Step 3.   Speaker accepts paraphrase ("Yes, that's what I meant")
          or rejects paraphrase ("No, that's not what I meant").
Step 4.   If rejected, the speaker clarifies the original statement (the
          process repeats).
          If accepted, the listener is free to express his or her thought
          or feeling.

Don't overuse active listening. You don't want to sound like a parrot, repeating every sentence the speaker says. This can irritate the speaker and discourage communication as much interrupting or judging. Use active listening as you would spices in cooking. Just use it enough to clarify those statements you're unsure of.

Active Listening for Content

The first type of active listening is listening for content or the accuracy of what is being shared. Here are some examples of active listening for content:

Jill:	"I'd like you to pay more attention to me."
Tim:	*"Are you saying* you want us to talk more?"
Jill:	"That's exactly what I mean!"
Leo:	"I hope our supervisor doesn't check on us today."
Al:	*"You mean* you're afraid we're not doing our work correctly?"
Leo:	"Yeah, I'm still not certain about our specific duties."

Did you notice how in both examples the listeners actively reflected what they thought they heard by asking "Are you saying . . . ?" and "You mean . . . ?" Remember not to parrot word for word what the speaker has said. Just try to restate in your own words what the speaker has said.

The next dialogue shows an example with an incorrect first paraphrase. The listener and the speaker negotiate for shared meaning by using steps 3 and 4 of the active listening process.

Sue:	"I think you should be nicer to my friends."
Hassan:	*"Are you saying* I don't include them in our conversations?"
Sue:	"No. You do, but I'd like you to show more interest in them."
Hassan:	*"You mean* you'd like me to ask them about their lives?"
Sue:	"I'd love that! It would make them feel like you were interested in them."
Hassan:	"That would be fine. I am interested in what's going on with them."

Did you see how the listener and the speaker had to repeat the process one more time to accurately communicate the message? This simple technique of actively reflecting the content of the message back to the speaker is effective in assuring the accurate reception of the thought or idea sent by the speaker.

Three variations of the active listening technique for content are the You Technique, active listening questions, and active listening statements.

You Technique. The most basic form of active listening is with a question beginning with the word "you." Here is an example of the You Technique:

> Jared: "I think I need to look again at the cost of graduate school."
>
> Tyler: "*You* think the tuition and books might be too expensive?"
>
> Jared: "That's right. Anyway, I don't know if I want to do the studying."

Active listening questions. The second type of active listening involves beginning your interpretation with statements such as "Do you mean . . . ?" "Are you saying . . . ?" "Do I understand you to say . . . ?" and "Are you feeling . . . ?" Here is an example of an active listening question:

> Ned: "Being married is more work that I thought."
>
> Jan: "*Are you saying* it demands a lot of your time?"
>
> Ned: "No, my wife just wants to talk and I'm not a talker."

Active listening statements. The third way you can reflect the content of the speaker's message is by using statements that introduce your interpretation: "I hear you saying . . ." "What you're saying . . ." "What you're feeling is . . ." "I understand you to mean . . ." "It sounds like you . . ." and "I'm feeling that you . . ." Here are a few examples of active listening statements:

> "I hear you saying that you want to sell your house."
>
> "It sounds like you wish you were younger."
>
> "I'm understanding that you want to see your folks this weekend."

All three active listening techniques for content will help you more clearly understand the thoughts and ideas presented by others. They will enable you to make certain that the pictures you construct in your mind's eye are the same as those the speaker is attempting to communicate.

Active Listening for Feelings

There are occasions when communicating at the feeling level is required. This is especially true if you are trying to help someone through a problem or difficulty. Rather than clarify and validate the content of the speaker's message, you shift to the speaker's feelings. To go beyond the content of what people are saying and to be sensitive to their feelings is a powerful way to encourage a deeper connection and relationship.

The three ways you can listen for feelings are by observing the speaker's nonverbal communication, reflecting the speaker's nonverbal behavior, and responding to the speaker's verbal communication.

Observing the speaker's nonverbal communication. The first way you can listen to the speaker's feelings is not with your ears, but with your eyes. An individual's posture, physical position, facial expressions, eye contact, gestures, tone of voice, rate of speech, breathing pattern, and touching behavior are just a few of the numerous nonverbal cues that communicate messages to you.

Feelings and emotions are communicated primarily at the nonverbal level, so during your next conversation, pay attention to the speaker's facial expressions, posture, gestures, tone of voice, breathing, eye contact, and anything else you can observe. Be creative and listen for feelings, with your eyes!

Reflecting the speaker's nonverbal behavior. A second way you can listen to the feelings of others is to make them consciously aware of their nonverbal messages. We are often so unaware of our feelings in this culture that many times we are blind to the emotions our bodies are communicating to others. Frequently an individual is unaware of a downcast eye, raised voice, increased breathing rate, or reddening face. Many times these nonverbal behaviors go unnoticed by both speaker and listener.

If, however, you are observing any significant nonverbal behavior in the other person, you may want to share it. Share your perception without attaching any value judgment to it. This could invite the individual to talk about his feelings. Here are some examples of listening to feelings:

> "I see that you're looking at the clock."
> "I hear you sigh when I . . . ."
> "I notice that you're smiling when I talk about . . . ."

Responding to the speaker's verbal communication. There are two ways the speaker will verbally invite you to communicate at the feeling level. First, the speaker will share a feeling statement with you such as "I'm feeling happy" or "This situation makes me feel discouraged." Be sensitive to such feeling statements and respond to them with a paraphrase to encourage the speaker to explore or comment further. Here are some examples:

> "I'm feeling happy."
> "So, you're feeling pretty pleased?"

> "This situation makes me feel discouraged."
> "Sounds like you're feeling defeated?"

The purpose of paraphrasing or reflecting the speaker's feeling statement is to prove that you have received the message and to encourage the speaker to remain at the feeling level to explore or expand on the statement.

Second, the speaker will ask you how you are feeling about a particular issue, person, or situation. You can then respond with an appropriate feeling response, instead of remaining at the content level. Here are some examples:

"Are you angry with your father's decision?"
"Yes, I am upset with Dad."

"Am I making you feel comfortable?"
"Yes, I'm not feeling nervous or frightened."

In addition to these two ways to respond to the speaker's invitation to talk about feelings, you can issue an invitation yourself. You can follow up a speaker's content statement with a feeling-level question. This is one of the basic tools of therapists and counselors, especially when the client is unaware or unwilling to explore his feelings. Here are some examples of feeling-level questions:

"I just passed my math test." (content level)
"How are you feeling about that?" (feeling-level invitation)

"I don't have time for anything." (content level)
"Are you feeling frustrated?" (feeling-level invitation)

By responding to the speaker's feeling statement (their invitation for you to share feelings) and by issuing a feeling-level invitation to a content message, you can participate in the discussion of feelings. Instead of changing the subject and diverting the conversation back to the content level, you accept the invitation to shift to the feeling level of communication.

FOUR TYPES OF QUESTIONS

Creating receptive communication as a listener depends on knowing the right kinds of questions to ask. Your questions can direct, encourage, and even inspire the speaker to clarify, focus, and explore their thoughts and feelings. There are four types of questions.

Closed Questions

Closed questions can be answered in a word or two. They don't really encourage the speaker to develop, expand, or explore the topic. Instead, they focus, limit, and highlight. Here are some examples of closed questions and possible answers:

Are you right or wrong? right/wrong
Do you go to the store yesterday? yes/no/maybe
Do you mean you want to stay in the relationship? yes/no/maybe

The purpose of closed questions is not to develop and explore, but rather to focus and specify.

Open Questions

Open questions encourage the speaker to develop, expand, and explore a topic in greater depth. Open questions usually begin with the words "Why," "What," and "How," or contain the words "Explain" and "Describe" within them. Here are some examples:

> Why do you think you're right?
> Why did you go to the store yesterday?
> What made you decide to stay in the relationship?

The purpose of open questions is to evoke more information from the speaker than closed questions.

Probing Questions

Probing questions are open and closed questions that are directly related to the preceding statement in a conversation. The purpose of probing questions is to further encourage the speaker to explain, expand, and develop a thought, idea, or feeling. Here is a brief dialogue to help you get the feel of open and closed probing questions:

Ted:	I'm feeling disappointed about my life.
Cara:	What part of your life? (open probe)
Ted:	I guess my job.
Cara:	How is your job not meeting your expectations? (open probe)
Ted:	I haven't advanced like I thought I would. I thought I'd be a manager by now.
Cara:	So promotions haven't come as you expected? (closed probe)
Ted:	Yeah. I'm always passed by when there's a management opening.
Cara:	What do you want to do about this? (open probe)

Did you notice how Cara didn't evaluate or give advice? Instead, she asked open and closed probing questions to help Ted express his problem more specifically and then led the discussion to possible solutions.

Loaded Questions

Although they are structured like questions, loaded questions blame, accuse, and judge. They also indirectly force your own opinion and advice on the listener. Here are some examples of loaded questions:

Are you always disgusted with everything I do?
How long will this relationship last?
Do you still criticize your sister?

Avoid asking loaded questions. If you want to discuss issues that are bothering you with another person, you need to be more direct and gentle about raising such topics. You often create the communication climate and context by the questions you choose to ask. So be thoughtful and sensitive when selecting your questions when talking with others.

CREATING RECEPTIVE COMMUNICATION: THE E.A.R.S. TECHNIQUE

Being an active listener requires that you participate in the process of communication—that you put aside your ego, receive the message being sent, and paraphrase and negotiate, if necessary, to prove understanding. By creating more receptive communication, you will increase the accuracy, understanding, and empathy of your listening.

You can create more receptive listening by keeping silent long enough to hear what someone has to say and using active listening to check your understanding of the content and feelings of their messages. Lending a receptive ear to another human being is a joy you can provide others. Use the four suggestions in the E.A.R.S. Technique when you set out to create receptive communication as a listener.

> *What a great joy it is to be able to create something. Creativity is one of the great privileges of being human.*
>
> —THOMAS KINKADE

Elevate the person

The first step in listening to another person is acceptance—to receive "what is." You must be willing to put aside your opinions, preferences, and prejudices and really be open to the thoughts and feelings of another human being. But it's more than that. Receptive listening demands that we shift the spotlight from ourselves to the other, to elevate the speaker above us, to make room for the speaker's thoughts, opinions, and feelings, even above our own. Receptive listening demands that we put the person we are listening to first and ourselves second. This is not an easy task, but it is the only way we can prepare to receive the speaker's message.

Attend to the person

Once we have elevated the person above our own needs, desires, and judgments, we are prepared to attend to the person. Attending involves our presence, our nonverbal behavior, and our verbal signs of acceptance. We must be present physically to communicate that there is nowhere else in the world we would rather be. We must attend to what the speaker is sharing with attentive nonverbal behavior, such as an open, relaxed posture, silence, direct eye contact, affirmative nodding, warm facial expressions, and appropriate touching of support.

We must be attentive verbally as well to voice interest, concern, and understanding, to tell the speaker to continue sharing, to tell the speaker we are interested in what he is saying, and to encourage him. Most important, the speaker must feel that we are there to listen, not to change, fix, judge, direct, teach, or rescue. We must listen as the silver-haired woman did.

Henry David Thoreau once remarked, "The greatest compliment that was ever paid to me was when one asked me what I thought and attended to my answer." By attending to the speaker, you are creating an atmosphere that not only encourages the speaker to disclose and share, you are also giving him or her one of the greatest compliments you can give—your undivided attention.

Reflect the person

Once the person is sharing, you need to reflect or paraphrase what the speaker is saying to clarify, negotiate, and demonstrate understanding. Your active listening will not only ensure that the speaker's messages are being communicated accurately; it will also show the speaker that you understand what is being shared.

Many times, a person can experience relief, satisfaction, and even healing by just being heard and validated. This is what active listening can accomplish. Your nonjudgmental mirroring or reflecting can have a surprisingly positive and healing effect on the speaker. A simple "Are you saying . . . ?" or "Do you mean . . . ?" without evaluation or advice can change an entire conversation. By reflecting the speaker's content and feelings, you have created a communication setting wherein the speaker is free to disclose at even greater depths, encouraged by the trust and openness you have established. What a masterpiece!

Support the person

The final guideline in creating reflective communication as a listener is to support the speaker wherever and however possible. This does not mean that you rescue, take control, or solve her problem. It means that a word of encouragement, a gesture of support, or an invitation to coffee can provide a real gift to the individual you have been listening to.

The purpose is not to solve the speaker's problem, reduce her fears, or make her happy. It is to go one step further than simply demonstrating your understanding; it shows that you care, that you want to support her, and be on her side. Supporting a person doesn't have to be a major endeavor. It can take the form of dropping a note in the mail, making a phone call to check in, or even delivering a bouquet of flowers. Mother Teresa said, "You can create heaven on earth by every act of kindness." Create that heaven on earth for others by doing things to show your support.

You were given two ears and one mouth so that you might listen more than you talk. Your ears can create a place in every relationship, regardless of setting, where others feel welcomed, safe, and understood. By using your receptive listening, you too can create a safe harbor for others to enjoy, just like the silver-haired woman.

EXPLORING CREATIVE TASKS

1. For the next few days, try listening without interrupting for thirty to sixty seconds during your conversations with friends and family. What was the response from those you listened to? What was that like for you? What did you feel while you kept silent for thirty to sixty seconds? What changes were there compared with conversations in which you speak every ten to fifteen seconds?

2. After trying Creative Task 1, use active listening when conversing with family or friends. Use the four-step process outlined in this chapter. Keep in mind that the purpose of active listening is to check content accuracy and prove understanding. Don't overdo active listening. Try paraphrasing the speaker's statements every fifth statement. What was the speaker's response? What was that like for you? What changes were there compared with your usual conversational style?

3. Try listening for the speaker's feelings the next time you are in a conversation. Watch the speaker's nonverbal behavior, listen between the lines of conversation, and paraphrase the feelings you think he or she is conveying to you, either in word or behavior. What was the speaker's response? How did it feel to paraphrase the feelings you thought the speaker was communicating or experiencing?

4. List five ways you show can more acceptance of a friend next week. Try one or two of them. How did your friend receive your demonstrations of acceptance? What happened? How did you feel doing this task?

EXPANDING YOUR CREATIVE THINKING

1. How would your listening change if you knew that the person you were listening to had only one day to live, but you couldn't tell the person of his or her impending death? Would you be more accepting? Would anything he or she said irritate or upset you? How would you feel about this individual? Why?

2. Think of an individual from your personal life whom you have difficulty listening to without interrupting, judging, or giving advice. What is it about this person that makes listening difficult for you? In what ways are you and he or she similar? What would have to change for you to listening effectively to this person?

3. Who listens to you the most effectively? What is it about this person's listening that makes you say this? Have you ever told this individual that you appreciate his or her listening? If not, why? Do you reciprocate his or her listening? Why or why not?

4. What would your life be like if you were deaf? How would you communicate with others? What changes would you have to make in your personal life to maintain the quality of relationships you now experience with loved ones?

SEVEN

Creating Healthy Communication in Relationships

> *We create the form and content*
> *of our relationships.*
>
> —VIRGINIA SATIR

A successful businesswoman was introduced by her associate to a sixty-eight-year-old acquaintance at a luncheon. The associate bragged to the older woman about the businesswoman's many accomplishments—her fame, power, properties, and vast wealth.

The successful businesswoman smiled as her associated rattled off her many achievements. Finally, the businesswoman excused herself from the table to attend another function. After she left, her associate quickly turned to the older woman and asked, "Don't you think she's the most successful person you've ever met?

"Well, I don't know," said the old woman.

"What do you mean, you don't know?" demanded the associate.

The old woman smiled and replied, "I haven't met her children yet."

We devote much our time, energy, and resources trying to create a successful life. To get an education, work hard at our job, and maybe even start a business of our own. We strive to save our money, to invest, and even dream of becoming rich. We can spend our lives trying to make this happen.

But success should not be measured by money, power, or fame. Like the old woman observed, we should measure the quality and impact of our lives on the relationships with those we love. Do we create and sustain healthy, loving relationships that make life worth living?

THREE KINDS OF RELATIONSHIPS

You will be involved in many relationships during your lifetime. Although each of them will vary in intensity, duration, and depth, they will fall into three basic categories—acquaintances, friends, and intimates.

Acquaintances

Acquaintances are those people with whom we have limited interactions on a regular or semiregular basis and whose names and faces we know. An acquaintance may be the supermarket cashier, a neighbor, or a work colleague. Our interactions with acquaintances are limited in number and duration. For example, your interactions with a coworker may be pleasant and enjoyable, but you don't make arrangements to meet outside the workplace and your depth of self-disclosure is limited.

Friends

People with whom we are more personally involved are called **friends**. Oftentimes, our relationships with acquaintances can evolve into friendship as the interactions increase in both quantity and quality. Maybe a coworker invites you to lunch after a meeting and you discover you have mutual interests and enjoy talking with each other. Over time, you both realize you like being together and voluntarily seek out each other's company. As friends, people disclose more information about themselves over time, develop trust, and in general, like each other.

Intimates

Intimates are those people with whom we share our deepest thoughts and feelings during our lifetime. Intimates differ from friends and acquaintances mostly in our degree of intimacy with them. People who qualify for this kind of relationship are spouses, lovers, and close friends. Many of these relationships are lifelong. From them we often learn our most valuable lessons. Our experiences with these people teach us our most important lessons—to forgive, to endure, to show us our limits, and to love. These lifelong relationships show us how to accept other human beings—their shortcomings and weaknesses, as well as their insights and strengths.

THE CIRCULAR STAGES OF RELATIONSHIPS

The relationships you experience are not static. They go through changes or stages of development. There are numerous models of relationship development. The simplest model I know is the circular model of "sparkle/conflict/resolution." Just about every relationship model includes some variation of these three stages.

Sparkle Stage

The **sparkle stage** is when the relationship begins and everything is going well. This includes the euphoria of first romance, the optimism of a new friendship, or the arrival of a first child. Everything sparkles with newness, freshness, and possibility. Time seems to fly. Each meeting is anticipated with longing and excitement, and nothing seems to go wrong. There is little or no conflict during this initial stage.

Conflict Stage

The second stage is the inevitable **conflict stage. Conflict** is any disagreement or dispute between two individuals. Usually, when the relationship develops and disclosure increases, conflict also increases when differences of opinion, taste, and preference arise. The conflict stage is not a bad thing, but rather an invitation to a deeper, more authentic relationship. Conflict in the relation-

*Art is the process
of redefining
our relationships
one to another.*

—RUBY DEE

ship indicates people are beginning to assert their individuality, their truer selves. How they deal with their conflict will determine the quality of their relationship.

Resolution Stage

The third stage is **resolution,** which represents the outcome or solution to the conflict the individuals have come to. If conflict is cooperatively addressed, there is a good chance the individuals will discover common ground and resolve their conflicts, and their relationship will continue to grow. Many times, however, the resolution involves an impasse, separation, and even the termination of the relationship. Not all conflicts can be resolved. But those conflicts that are successfully managed and negotiated by the individuals are the source of greater relationship strength and satisfaction. All successful relationships require the accommodation and negotiation of conflict to remain healthy.

The Circular Nature of Relationships

The most important feature of this model is its circular nature. Unlike a linear model, which moves from points A to B to C in a straight line and then ends, the circular model returns to its beginning, time and time again. After one conflict has been resolved, another conflict may surface. As family therapist Jay Haley warns, "Relationship is one damn thing after another."

We can return to the sparkle stage of a relationship, experience new conflicts, resolve them, and once again return to the sparkle stage. The challenge is in creating new forms of sparkle, while cooperatively solving the conflicts that arise in relationships.

Family therapist Virginia Satir believed that "There is an art to exploring new and creative ways of relating to the same person year after year." These "new and creative ways" don't necessarily have to be expensive, extravagant, or ingenious. Simple, ordinary little pleasures, such as a surprise gift, a poem you wrote, or a moonlit walk on the beach, can often rekindle the sparkle in any relationship. You're full of creative ideas! Let the artist of communication within come forward!

PRINCIPLES OF HEALTHY RELATIONSHIPS

There is no one approach or prescription that guarantees a successful, satisfying relationship with another human being. It doesn't matter whether your relationship is with a spouse, a parent, a child, or a friend—each journey is unique. No map charting every curve, hill, and valley of any relationship is available. Every relationship is unlike any other, and yet there are some general principles of healthy relationships.

Relationships Are Not Perfect

Most good relationships are far from perfect. There will always be those irritations, shortcomings, failures, and disappointments. I believe that 80 percent of a healthy relationship is working at any given time and only 20 percent of the relationship is not. The trouble is we often focus our attention on the 20 percent that is not working and fail to notice all the wonderful aspects of a relationship. We sabotage the relationship by choosing to focus on the negative. A healthier choice is to focus more of our attention on the 80 percent of the relationship that is working well. You can create a healthier, more satisfying relationship by identifying, complimenting, and rewarding those areas of the relationship that are working.

Relationships Do Not Give You Everything

There isn't a single relationship that will satisfy all your needs, desires, and longings. No relationship will provide you with everything you need. The mistake we often make is to believe that one individual or relationship will complete us, make us whole. But that's a myth. Each one of us is far more complicated and our needs are much more varied than we may believe. We thrive and grow more fully with the interaction, support, and love from a variety of people during our lives, not just from our family or best friend.

Relationships Will Die If Not Nurtured

Each of your relationships is a living entity. Like a plant or tree, each relationship has to be watered, pruned, and nurtured with loving care, or it will die. The grandmother who peers out her window in hopes of seeing your car in the driveway, the friend waiting for a response to her letter, and the child waiting for your promised trip to the movies are all like parched, brittle trees waiting for you to water them. Relationships cannot survive on their own. They require your participation and will die if not nurtured.

Artist Georgia O'Keeffe once said, "Nobody sees a flower, really. It is so small, we haven't time, and to see, takes time—like to have a friend takes time." Your friendships take time to attend to, to nurture, and to enjoy. Don't overlook the beauty of your relationships. See them. Appreciate them. Nurture them. Take the time.

Relationships Are Both Pleasurable and Painful

You will experience both pleasure and pain in your relationships with others. When we open our hearts to another person, we discover both pleasure and pain. There is no journey into intimacy without the pain that accompanies it. Pleasure and pain are two sides of the same coin.

Psychiatrist and author Elisabeth Kübler-Ross says that "Grief is the price we pay for loving." Although her comments describe the pain we experience with the death of a loved one, her observation can also apply to the pain we feel when a loved one disappoints, frustrates, or neglects us. Relationships are both pleasurable and painful. Ultimately, you don't get one without the other. So if all you're seeking is fun and laughter, relationships may not be what you're looking for, because they require the full range of feelings and emotions.

Relationships Require Flexibility

All relationships change. No healthy relationship remains the same forever, nor would you want it to stay the same. All relationships change because people change. We get older, more experienced. We learn new things about ourselves and about life in general. Our comfort zones expand to encompass new territory as we grow older and things that used to frighten or intimidate us no longer pose the same threat.

There is one attribute you can develop that will create more enjoyable and successful relationships. That attribute is flexibility—your willingness and ability to be flexible, bend, and adjust to the changes the relationship will require. Flexibility is essential in providing your relationship with the room to grow and the spaciousness to develop as it should.

BEST RELATIONSHIP INTERVIEW

One of the best ways to explore these relationship principles is to examine a healthy, loving relationship firsthand. Select a couple you regard as having a healthy, loving relationship. Arrange for a twenty-minute interview to ask them the questions listed below. You can add your own open and probing questions if you'd like.

1. How did you meet?
2. What were your initial feelings/thoughts about one another?
3. How would you describe your dating/courting experience?
4. How did you know you wanted to marry?

5. How would you describe your marriage?
6. What are the three major strengths of your relationship?
7. What are your communication strengths?
8. What are your communication weaknesses?
9. How do you resolve conflict within your relationship?
10. What are the weaknesses or areas needing improvement?
11. How do you keep the sparkle or romance in the relationship?
12. How have children changed your relationship?
13. How do you see your relationship ten years from now?
14. What are the keys to a good relationship?
15. What specific advice do you have to give me about relationships?

Seeking the advice and counsel from people who are in healthy, loving relationships is one of the best ways to learn about relationships. Don't be reluctant to seek out and ask questions of those individuals who truly demonstrate love, respect, and trust in their relationships. You will never know until you ask.

CREATING HEALTHY RELATIONSHIPS:
THE B.O.N.D. TECHNIQUE

Four conditions are required to establish healthy relationships. These conditions are necessary for the maintenance and growth of any relationship you are hoping to establish. The four conditions are B.O.N.D.—bridging, openness, nurturance, and discovery.

Bridging

The first requirement of a healthy relationship is your willingness to reach out and connect to another person—to build a bridge to another individual. **Bridging** means that you are willing to move from "me" to "we." It requires that you move from the self-centered nature of childhood to the "other-centeredness" of mature adulthood. It means that you invest energy and time into considering another human being—to walk over to his side of the river and see and experience the world from his perspective. It may even require that you put another person before yourself. To yield or submit, at times, to the wants, desires, or wishes of another.

This doesn't mean that you are less powerful, subservient to, or less important than the other individual. Instead, it suggests a yielding or providing space for the ideas, beliefs, feelings, and desires of your friend or loved one. It is the realization that the other person in a relationship is not you. She is her own person, with ideas, beliefs, feelings, and desires that might not always coincide with or be identical to yours. To respect what she wants and desires, even if you have to occasionally sacrifice what you want. In losing yourself, you just might find yourself.

Openness

The second requirement is **openness**—knowing and understanding the deeper thoughts, feelings, and behaviors of another person. In our friendships and intimate relationships, it is the voluntary sharing of our deepest thoughts and feelings that bonds us to others. Intimate self-disclosure from a friend or intimate makes us feel special, unique, and set apart from the rest of the world. We are given information about the other that few, if any, are privileged to know.

Nurturance

The third requirement of a healthy relationship is **nurturance**. Like a home, a healthy relationship should be a place where you can go and let your guard down, relax your defenses, and breathe in perfect assurance that you are in a safe environment. More than that, however, a healthy relationship should provide you with the opportunity to give and receive support, comfort, encouragement, and care, to cherish and be cherished.

Your relationships should have an enlarging impact on you and the other person. Do you feel better or worse? Do you grow or remain stagnant? Are you encouraged or discouraged? Are you nurtured or drained of energy? Are you enlarged or diminished? These are simple but essential questions that need to be asked of any relationship. Your relationships should nurture, encourage, and even inspire.

Discovery

One of the most important requirements for a healthy relationship is your willingness to discover new things about yourself and the other person. Your willingness to explore, experiment, and expand on the current relationship enables the two of you to chart out new territories and extend the boundaries of who you are and what you're about.

People are sometimes threatened, frightened, and angered by a friend or loved one's desire to set out on a path of discovery—whether it is to vacation in a different place, enroll in a class, or change vocations. A fundamental requirement for a healthy relationship is our remaining open to discovery. We need to keep an open mind, a flexible attitude, and a willingness to try new things as we live our lives. The sure way to stifle a relationship is to insist that it remain the same, for all time. But people, and thus relationships, do change. Nothing remains the same forever. To establish and maintain a healthy relationship, we must be open to discovery, to change.

These four conditions—bridging, openness, nurturance, and discovery—are the basis for creating a healthy relationship. Your ability and willingness to create a relationship when these four conditions are met will determine your success in establishing and maintaining healthy friendships.

CREATING HEALTHY SELF-DISCLOSURE

The most essential component of communication for intimate and healthy relationships is self-disclosure—volunteering information about yourself that would otherwise be unobtainable. Chapter 3 discussed the characteristics of self-disclosure, the Johari Window, and suggestions for its use in communication. These same suggestions apply to creating healthy communication in your interpersonal relationships.

Disclose to Significant People

Before you disclose information to someone, ask yourself if this person is significant or important enough for you to invest your time and energy. Disclosing personal information usually deepens and increases a person's understanding of you. Is that your intent? Is this a person with whom you want to deepen a relationship? It is wise to avoid disclosing personal information about yourself to anybody you happen to be speaking with because it might send the wrong message or invite inappropriate or premature disclosure on the other's part. Sharing personal information needs to be done carefully and with conscious intent.

Begin with Safe, Low-Risk Disclosures

To disclose too much, too soon, can be detrimental to a conversation as well as to a developing relationship. Relationships need to develop gradually over time, disclosing safe, low-risk topics initially, and then moving to more intimate topics after trust has been developed. Begin with safe topics such as your interests, favorite foods, and happy childhood memories; then as your relationship develops, introduce more personal and intimate topics. As friends or intimates bond over time, the rate and depth of disclosure can increase.

Is the Risk of Disclosing Reasonable?

Be careful not to disclose personal information to those who might betray or ridicule your confidences. If the person is untrustworthy or overly critical of others, you are wise to keep personal information and reactions to yourself. On the other hand, if the other person has proved to be trustworthy and supportive of you in the past, self-disclosure can bring greater depth and intimacy to the relationship. There is nothing more gratifying than sharing who you are with someone who is significant to you.

Match the Level and Amount of the Other's Disclosure

This is the most important guideline I can suggest because it focuses attention on the equality of the relationship. Disclosure between two individuals in a healthy relationship should be matched in quantity and quality. In other words, both parties should share personal information at approximately the same level and in the same amount.

In an unhealthy relationship, one person may do all the disclosing, while the other person does very little. You don't need to become a "parent" to someone who discloses all the time to you, nor do you want to become a "child" who dominates the discussion. What characterizes a healthy relationship is a balance of sharing and listening, both in quantity and depth.

Maintaining a Healthy Relationship

There are several important communication skills you can use to maintain healthy sharing and boundary maintenance within a relationship. Any successful relationship requires that each individual have needs met and boundaries stated and observed. Here are a few questions and statements that can help you maintain a healthy relationship.

How Are We Doing?

One helpful question you can ask is "How are we doing?" If this open-ended question is asked sincerely, it can serve as the invitation to some very informative and confirming discussions.

> *The more I think about it, the more I realize that nothing is more creative than to love others.*
>
> —VINCENT VAN GOGH

Any relationship can go along for months, even years, without both people ever discussing the relationship itself. We can get hung up on the details of just getting through the day, but we rarely pause to take a deep breath, really look at the person we're in relationship with, and ask, "How are we doing in this relationship?"

Invite someone you are in relationship with to share his or her perceptions about the relationship. You may learn something helpful or be pleasantly surprised.

How Can I Love You More?

Another question you can ask someone is "How can I love you more?" Other variations of this question are "What can I do to help you more?" "What can I do to be a better friend (spouse, parent, son, etc.)?" "How might I improve being your friend?" and "In what ways can I be more supportive of you?" No matter which question you ask, the purpose is to encourage specific feedback or self-disclosure about ways you can improve or satisfy your friend's needs.

When you listen to the answers to this question, don't judge, criticize, or defend yourself. The purpose is to learn what you can do to be more useful, more caring, and more loving. You may not be able to do everything he or she wants or desires, but at least you've opened up the topic for discussion. How are you to know if you don't ask—"How can I love you more?"

No (That's Not Okay, That's Unacceptable)

The word "no" has been called the most effective boundary statement there is. To understand what a **boundary** is, think of a circle. Within the circle are beliefs, opinions, behaviors, and activities that are comfortable or acceptable to you. Outside the circle are beliefs, opinions, behaviors, and activities that are not comfortable or acceptable to you.

To establish and maintain a healthy relationship, you must be able to communicate readily and easily what is acceptable and unacceptable to you. You must be able to say no or that's not okay when the occasion arises. If someone wants you to do something you feel is wrong, unethical, improper, or deceitful, you should be able to say no. Even if you're uncomfortable or unwilling to participate in an activity or behavior, you should be able to say no.

Saying no has more to do with your stomach than your brain. It often takes courage to tell someone that you're unwilling to do something or that something is not okay with you. But to be silent and comply with the request will often make you resentful, angry, and bitter. One of the most important skills you will develop in a healthy relationship is your ability and willingness to say no, and to encourage others to do the same.

May I State a Need?

The ability to state needs is another skill that is required in healthy relationships. You should be able to make your needs known to the other person. One of the easiest ways to introduce the topic of needs is to ask, "May I state a need?" By asking this question, you invite, not force, the person into a dialogue about your need. Most people agree to the question. If the person is willing to listen to your need, phrase your need as specifically and succinctly as possible.

> "I need to use the car this afternoon for one hour."
> "I need you to ask for my permission to borrow the computer."
> "I need you to compliment me when I finish my homework."

Your needs may not always be met, but at least you brought your request to the person's attention. You will often experience satisfaction by making your needs known—to speak up for yourself instead of remaining silent. You can create what you want by asking for it.

If You Continue to . . . , I Will . . .

If your need is not being met or you feel that your boundaries are being violated, you can address these issues by **stating boundary consequences.** This two-part statement contains (1) the boundary violation ("If you continue to . . .") and (2) the consequence or action you are willing to take ("I will . . .").

"If you continue to criticize me, I will leave the room."

"If you continue to refuse paying rent, I will evict you."

"If you continue to come home after midnight, I will lock the door."

Stating boundary consequences is helpful because you specify the behavior that is unacceptable to you and communicate what you are prepared to do if the person does not comply with your request. If your request is not honored, then you are free to act on the consequence you set forth.

These five communication skills can help maintain healthy relationships. They will not necessarily guarantee that you will always get what you ask for, but they will create the circumstances in which they can be heard and addressed.

RESOLVING RELATIONSHIP CONFLICTS

As people in relationships begin to share more deeply and honestly about their thoughts, opinions, and feelings, the potential for conflict also increases. During the course of any healthy relationship in which there exists open and honest communication, you will experience conflict. No two individuals see the world in exactly the same way. No two people hold identical tastes, opinions, beliefs, and desires, so conflict is natural. Whether or not you address the conflict in a healthy manner is the important question.

Two common responses to interpersonal conflict are fight or flight. Fighting can take the form of verbal argument and/or physical conflict. Taking flight from conflict can occur by leaving the relationship, physically fleeing the conflict setting, or placating and giving in to the demands of the other person.

The **Five Step Problem-Solving Process** is a positive, constructive response to interpersonal conflict that combines skills you learned in earlier chapters. These five steps provide a win-win approach to resolving conflicts—one that emphasizes listening, negotiation, and compromise. This technique works for serious conflicts as well as minor disagreements.

Step 1. Retreat to a Quiet Place

The first step in problem solving is to do nothing. Don't talk, discuss, or attempt to debate the conflict initially. Agree to retreat to a quiet place where the two of you won't be disturbed. Also agree on a time limit for the session. Usually ten to twenty minutes is a reasonable amount of time to take for one session. Identify only one specific issue to discuss. Don't try to talk about every difference and difficulty in the relationship. Select only one. Don't feel obligated to settle your conflict in one session either. Be gentle on yourselves.

Step 2. Listen to Each Other

The second step is the most difficult to accomplish. It requires you to listen to your partner for one to three minutes *without* verbal interruption. Let your partner go first because you're the one who issued the invitation.

Your partner may hold a pencil as a reminder that she has the "microphone" for the first phase. You are not to interrupt while your partner is talking. During this time, your partner is to:

1. Describe her perceptions of the issue. ("I see the issue as . . .")
2. Share her feelings about the issue. ("I feel . . .")
3. State her need(s) regarding the issue. ("I need . . .")
4. Reveal her fear(s) about the issue. ("I'm afraid that . . .")

As she talks, you are not to interrupt in any way. You cannot talk. You cannot blame, judge, criticize, bring up past mistakes, or discuss another issue. All you do is sit silently and listen. By remaining silent, you will prevent making the worst mistake in conflict communication—interrupting the speaker. Listening without interrupting will create a shift in the communication climate. It will provide a space for your partner to be heard, perhaps for the first time.

When she feels she has completed her statements, she will say, "Okay, let's go to step 3." You can't talk until she gives you the okay.

Step 3. Paraphrase Each Other

In the third step you paraphrase your partner's statements from step 2. By asking questions, you prove your understanding of her perceptions and feelings. During this stage you ask the following questions:

1. "Are you saying the issue is . . . ?" (Let her respond.)
2. "Are you feeling . . . ?" (Let her respond.)
3. "Do you need . . . ?" (Let her respond.)
4. "Are you afraid that . . . ?" (Let her respond.)

The purpose of step 3 is *not* to give your side of the story; rather it is to show you are attempting to understand your partner. You are trying to prove to your partner that you have heard her perceptions and feelings of the issue at hand. Many times, this alone is enough to change the dynamics of the situation.

When the other person feels you understand her (you've reflected her comments on all four statements), she will give you the pencil ("microphone") and you can return to step 2 for your turn. You now will have a chance to share your perceptions of the problem, your feelings, your needs, and your fears, without your partner interrupting.

After you have completed your statements, you will say, "Okay, let's go to step 3," and your partner will ask *you* questions about *your* statements. Make sure your partner has accurately paraphrased or reflected all four of your statements before going on to step 4.

Step 4. Create a Compromise

Now that you and your partner have completed steps 2 and 3, you will be in a position to better understand each other's feelings and concerns about the conflict. The next step is for the two of you to begin the compromise.

Before you compromise, you must each suggest two or three different solutions to the problem you would be willing to try. There is to be no evaluation or criticism. Just like step 2, simply listen to each other's suggestions. After you both share, you should have at least four to six possible solutions to consider.

Discuss the solutions suggested. Try to see their strengths and weaknesses and ask for clarification. As you discuss the solutions, you may both decide on one that is worth trying. If not, select your favorite solution from your partner's list. This will let her know you are willing to acknowledge that at least one of her solutions is worth considering. Your partner then selects the solution she liked best from your list.

> *When it comes to giving love, the opportunities are endless and we are all gifted.*
> —LEO BUSCAGLIA

Try to reach a compromise between the two solutions. Maybe you would both be willing to try one of the solutions for a period of time. Keep in mind that this is a tentative compromise that can be altered, modified, or dropped if it doesn't work.

Chances are you will not get your number-one choice of solutions, and neither will your partner. But, you will compromise on a solution you can both "live with for a while." Remember, a win-win, not a win-lose compromise, is the goal of this process. Also agree on an implementation schedule and a time period to try the solution. When you have agreed on a solution or compromise, go on to the final step.

If you cannot reach a compromise in step 4 and you're running out of time or steam, go to the final step and then take a break for an hour or a day. Be gentle on yourselves. Many conflicts have taken months and years to develop. So, table the discussion for now, and go on to step 5.

Step 5. Compliment Each Other

End the session with a compliment or two. Spend a few minutes discussing the strengths of the relationship. Remember the 80/20 rule—80 percent of any relationship is working and only 20 percent of the relationship is not working or in need of improvement. Look for and focus on the 80 percent of the relationship you can commend or compliment.

GUIDELINES FOR RESOLVING CONFLICT

Whenever you attempt to resolve a conflict with a loved one, follow these four guidelines: keep the relationship in mind, limit the conflict to one issue at a time, think of the conflict as an invitation to growth, and be soft and slow.

Keep the Relationship in Mind

While you are in a conflict, keep the relationship foremost in mind. There are very few conflicts worth ending a relationship for, and you need to remind yourself of this fact as you try to solve your differences. Ask yourself, "Would I rather be right or be in a healthy relationship that could last a lifetime?" This question helps keep the issue in the proper perspective. Be flexible and spacious. A good relationship is worth all the effort in the world.

Limit the Conflict to One Issue at a Time

One of the most common mistakes in attempting to solve a conflict is to bring into the discussion other areas or issues of disagreement in the relationship. In the heat of an argument, it's tempting to bring up other problems we feel the other person is responsible for or mistakes from the past. Don't get sidetracked with other issues. Just address one issue at a time.

Think of the Conflict as an Invitation to Growth

No human being is born with the ability to resolve interpersonal conflicts with skill and finesse. Listening, compromising, negotiating, cooperating, and forgiving are learned skills. They require time, effort, and, in many instances, discomfort and pain.

In relationships, it is the conflicts we experience that force us to take a closer look at our partner, ourselves, and the relationship itself. Conflict is not something to avoid. Conflict is an invitation to create and use new skills—listening, empathizing, negotiating, compromising, and forgiving.

Be Soft and Slow

During conflict, the last thing we probably want is to be soft and slow. Everything tells us to speed up, tighten up, gear up. Often our breathing becomes fast and shallow, our face becomes flushed, and our speech becomes rapid and loud. These nonverbal behaviors can trigger similar responses in our partner. Before long, the discussion can turn into a heated screaming match and the prospect for a mutually satisfying solution disappears. Remind yourself to speak in a slow, gentle tone of voice. This will help keep the discussion on track and the atmosphere more supportive and relaxed.

FORGIVENESS

We will all hurt others and be hurt by them. In any relationship, we will suffer disappointment, frustration, and pain. The hurt you experience will most likely be minor—an unfair criticism, a broken promise, or a bit of gossip. A few may be more serious in nature. But you will experience hurt in any relationship. We have little control over that. However, we can control what we do with our hurt. We can let go of the hurt and guilt, decide to forgive others, and ask for forgiveness.

Forgiveness is the act of granting free pardon for an offense. In essence, it is the act of letting go of the desire to get even, to make someone pay for the hurt he may have caused you. It is the act of letting someone off the hook for hurting you. To grant free pardon means you voluntarily pardon or excuse the individual who hurt you, at no cost to him. There is nothing the person has to do, no price he has to pay, for you to excuse him for his offense.

> *Forgiveness cures people. Both the ones who give it and those who receive it.*
>
> —KARL MENNIGER

Forgiveness is one of the most difficult communication acts to engage in. It also can be one of the most liberating. No relationship can survive long without forgiveness. In creating healthy relationships, you will have to learn to ask for forgiveness and to forgive others. There are two specific instances of forgiving others. In the first instance, you forgive those who ask for forgiveness. In the second instance, you forgive those who do not.

Forgiving Those Who Ask for Forgiveness

If someone who has wronged you asks for your forgiveness, seriously consider forgiving her. Instances of repeated or chronic physical or emotional abuse does not warrant the same consideration as less dangerous offenses, but you need to consider the violation, the person's sincerity, and the probability of recurrence.

Forgiveness is not a feeling, but a decision. You may not feel like forgiving the individual, but you can decide to begin your personal journey of forgiveness by accepting her request to forgive. You need to forgive if you are to be free from your anger and resentment. Forgive those who ask for forgiveness, if it's possible.

Forgiving Those Who Are Not Apologetic

At times, someone who hurts you will not be apologetic and refuse to ask for forgiveness. In this instance, you can choose to forgive him anyway. Initially, you may not want to forgive him. But remember, forgiveness is not a feeling. It is your decision to be free of hurt and anger. You will probably never feel like forgiving him. However, you can make the conscious decision to let go of your pain. Forgiving those who have hurt you, even if they are not repentant, is the only way to go beyond or transcend the anger you feel.

One helpful way to forgive someone who has not asked to be forgiven is to do an imaginary role-play. Sit in a chair with an empty chair before you. Imagine that the person is sitting in the empty chair and is asking for your forgiveness. Imagine the person's body, face, and voice as her "request" is being made. Then *verbally* accept her offer to forgive her. I realize that you're talking to an empty chair, but talk as if she were seated there. Close your eyes and relive the role-playing scene in your mind once or twice. See what happens. You may notice that it is a little easier to think about that person after having imagined her asking for your forgiveness.

Asking for Forgiveness

If you have wronged someone and want to ask for his forgiveness, try the AAA Forgiveness Method.

Admit you were wrong

Apologize for the offense

Ask their forgiveness

Let's assume that you criticized a friend unfairly. There was a brief argument over the incident, but you defended your actions. The incident was never mentioned again. Yet in the days that followed you began to feel guilty. You decide to ask your friend for forgiveness. This is how the AAA Forgiveness Method works:

You:	"Stan, do you remember our little argument last Saturday night?"
Stan:	"I've been trying to forget."
You:	"Well, *I was wrong* to criticize you." (admitting you were wrong)
Stan:	"You bet you were. That was a terrible thing to do. Would I ever do something like that to you?"
You:	"No. Probably not. But *I apologize* for criticizing you. *I'm sorry.*" (apologizing for the offense)
Stan:	"Apology accepted, I guess."
You:	"*Would you forgive me* for criticizing you?" (asking for forgiveness)
Stan:	"Well, yes. Of course I'll forgive you."

Not all attempts at asking for forgiveness will go this smoothly, but I wanted you to see how the AAA Forgiveness Method can work.

By deciding to ask for forgiveness, you have changed position regarding your offense. Instead of denying, justifying, rationalizing, blaming, or projecting your offense, you have chosen to take responsibility for it. By taking responsibility and asking forgiveness, you have altered the balance of your relationship with that person.

You can choose to create, develop, and maintain the kinds of relationships with others that are satisfying, meaningful, and significant. If you do, you will experience satisfaction and success in your life that will exceed wealth, fame, and power.

EXPLORING CREATIVE TASKS

1. Select an individual with whom you would like to improve a relationship. Meet with him or her and ask, "How are we doing in our relationship?" Ask specifically about the degree of bridging, openness, nurturance, and discovery he or she experiences (B.O.N.D.). How did the meeting go? How did you feel about the discussion? What did you learn? How can your behavior change in the future?

2. Select an individual to whom you would like to state a boundary consequence. Write the boundary consequence on a piece of paper before meeting with this person ("If you continue to . . . , I will . . ."). Meet with him or her and share your boundary consequence statement. How did the meeting go? What was his or her response? What will you do?

3. Use the five-step problem-solving process with a family member or loved one. Review the five steps with the person before beginning the process. Remember to address only one specific issue and give yourselves a couple of sessions to discuss the problem. How did the process go? What was his or her response to the process? How did you feel about the process? What did you learn? What was the outcome?

4. Select a person you have wronged and want to apologize to. Use the AAA Forgiveness Method and ask that person for forgiveness. What was his or her response? How did it feel asking for forgiveness? What was the outcome of the encounter? What did you learn about yourself?

EXPANDING YOUR CREATIVE THINKING

1. What do you think your relationships would be like if you consistently asked questions such as "How are we doing?" "How can I love you more?" and "Will you forgive me?" How would your relationships be different? How would you be different? What would you like about the new "you"?

2. What things do you need in terms of bridging, openness, nurturance, and discovery that you may not be getting or experiencing now in your current relationships? What would it take to have you share your needs with the individuals involved? What do you think will eventually happen if you don't share these needs?

3. What things have you done to others or to yourself that need forgiveness? What prevents you for asking for forgiveness either from others or yourself? What would happen if you did ask for forgiveness? What do you think will happen if you don't ask for forgiveness?

4. Will you forgive me if I don't write this question? My wife and kids just invited me to Don's Chinese Cafe and I'm starved. I've been at this computer for the past five hours and I want to be with my family. Thanks. I owe you one!

EIGHT

Creating Cooperative Communication in Groups

> *Light is the task*
> *when many share the load.*
>
> —HOMER

It had been more than two hours since this group of seven people first sat down to talk. Their faces expressed fatigue, boredom, and frustration, as I silently coded each remark made during this employee relations meeting as either a personal declarative statement or a guiding statement or question.

After tabulating the entire discussion, I discovered that more than 85 percent of all contributions made were declarative statements expressing individuals' opinions, suggestions, feelings, rebuttals, and criticisms. The vast majority of contributions were statements of personal opinion! Less than 15 percent of all contributions were coded as paraphrasing, clarifying, requesting for information, summarizing, guiding, analyzing, information and reasoning, or negotiating statements. I had never realized how self-centered group discussion could be.

Most people want to tell what they think, feel, and want, while paying very little attention to the opinions of others and the direction of the discussion itself. We've never learned that we can actually create a cooperative, productive group process by our contributions. No wonder most problem-solving meetings are long, exhausting, and unproductive. The participants often lack the skills to create cooperative communication in a group.

WORKING IN SMALL GROUPS

Working in groups is a part of your life. Whether you're the vice president of marketing, a member of a PTA group, or the head of the high school reunion planning committee, you will be working with others in small groups to solve problems.

Working in a group may seem easy at first. All you do is sit around a table, talk, and get things accomplished. What could be easier? Yet instead of experiencing unselfish cooperation, responsible preparation, and open communication in our problem-solving efforts, we are often shocked by the lack of cooperation, inadequate preparation, and poor communication skills of group members. If we are honest, we also have to admit our own inabilities and lack of understanding of this complicated process called group problem solving.

But don't get discouraged and avoid opportunities to work with others. You can learn the basic skills necessary to participate in a problem-solving group in productive, positive, and helpful ways.

ELEMENTS OF A PROBLEM-SOLVING GROUP

A **problem-solving group** is three or more people who share a common task, interact in a face-to-face setting, and influence one another. Let's consider each of these four elements of this definition.

Three or More People

A small group consists of three or more people. Two people do not make a group because their interaction is that of a couple, or **dyad**. In a dyad, no third individual witnesses the discussion between the other two, or influences the interaction by serving as an audience to it. So for our purposes, a group consists three or more people.

Sharing a Common Task

A task or goal is the primary purpose for the existence of a problem-solving group. The group shares a problem it feels is worth solving. Whether it's brainstorming ways to generate money, selecting a candidate for a hiring committee, or planning a retirement dinner for a coworker, the group has an identified task or goal to accomplish.

Interacting in a Face-to-Face Setting

The third element of a problem-solving group is that the group interacts in a face-to-face setting. This means that group members be able to see one another. Usually, the meeting will occur in the same room, with all members physically present. But with video technology, group members can see and hear one another through teleconferencing. Although teleconferencing satisfies the "face-to-face" criteria of our definition, it loses much of the nonverbal communication that occurs when people meet in person.

Influencing One Another

No one exists and operates in a vacuum, isolated from others. Each group member is influenced and affected by the other group members. Each member's statements and behavior affects every other member in some way, be it small or great. A thoughtful compliment, a subtle criticism, a raised eyebrow, or a complaining moan can communicate a powerful message.

You can learn from other group members' feedback and grow from their suggestions; be persuaded by their arguments and challenged by their proposals; be hurt by their remarks and healed by their praises. Each member influences and is influenced by other group members, whether or not she acknowledges this fact.

CHARACTERISTICS OF GROUPS

To more effectively work in groups, we need to explore some common group characteristics: the group as a system, the power of one, group formation, the task and social dimension of groups, norms and conformity, and the four phases of group development.

The Group as a System

A **system** is a set of objects that interrelate with one another to form a whole. If one object in the system changes, the other objects change in response. Any group of people working together to solve a problem meets this definition of a system. The emphasis in a systems perspective is not on the individual members, but rather on the group as a whole.

We can view group interaction in terms of a group of individuals getting together to solve a problem where each member is distinct and unconnected to the others. We can also view group interaction as a living organism. Each group member is a part of this living organism. You're the heart, I'm the lungs, and so on. When something happens to one part, all the other parts experience the effects.

Four principles of systems theory (introduced in chapter 1) specifically relate to your understanding of group process: interdependence, synergy, adaptation, and equifinity.

Interdependence. Each group member depends on all the other members in one way or another. An obvious example is the absence of four of the five members at a meeting. Even though you alone are present at the meeting site, their absence makes it impossible for you to participate in the meeting. Each member's behavior or lack of behavior prevents the entire group from progressing. In many ways, you are connected to and dependent on the actions of the other group members.

Synergy. The focus of attention in group work is on **wholeness,** or the entire group, rather than on any one individual. Once the individual members become interrelated and form a working group, they acquire a collective life and synergy—the whole becomes greater than the sum of its parts. The group can take on characteristics—productivity, creativity, and responsiveness—that might not be characteristic of any individual member. The group product is usually superior to the best individual product.

Adaptation. A system seeks to adapt or change to fit the demands of a changing environment. The ability for a group to remain flexible enough to adapt or change its procedures, rules, communication patterns, even its way of thinking and feeling, is indicative of its ability to survive. The problem-solving group must remain flexible and willing to adapt in order to cope with the changing environment of people, issues, and circumstances.

Equifinality. The group's ability to accomplish its goal in many ways and from many starting points is called **equifinality.** The group must accept the fact that there are many ways to accomplish a goal or task, not just one way. The concept of equifinality opens up the possibility for creative approaches to solving problems, which includes seeing the "problem" from a variety of viewpoints. This encourages groups to create their own unique solution to problems they face.

The Power of One

According to systems theory, a change in one object in the system changes all the other objects in the system. Every behavior affects the group—regardless of whether the behavior is negative and counterproductive, or positive and productive. In other words, your behavior, be it negative or positive, influences the group's interaction and final product.

As an artist of communication, you can use your skills to create a group process that is more effective, productive, and enjoyable. You have the power to influence and determine the direction and the outcome of the group, and that's the beauty of a systems perspective.

Group Formation

Individuals join groups for a variety of reasons. Every member receives something personally from his or her affiliation with the group. Many of these reasons are conscious; some are unconscious. Four of the more common reasons that people join groups are interpersonal attraction, group goals, group activities, and group identity.

Interpersonal attraction. We join certain groups because we are drawn or attracted to the group members themselves. Not attraction in the sense of romance and love, but rather in the sense of similarity and affinity. We often join groups because of our similarity in beliefs, ethnicity, economic status, and age. A synagogue, the NAACP, a country club, and a retirement center lunch group are examples of interpersonal attraction.

Group goals. People often join groups because of the objectives the group seeks to achieve. Groups such as a volunteer wilderness rescue team, a Little League fund-raising group, and a politician's election campaign provide opportunities for individuals to join groups to help advance a cause or accomplish a specific goal.

Group activities. People join groups because they are attracted to the activities. A social dancing club, a fraternity or sorority, a weight-lifting group, and a bird-watching club provide opportunities for people to gather with others who enjoy similar activities.

Group identity. As discussed in chapter 2, our self-identity is determined to a great extent by those people with whom we associate. Birds of a feather often flock together. Once again, many of the groups we identified earlier, such as religious groups, social organizations, and even the Hell's Angels, can provide an individual with a strong sense of identity and purpose.

You may have noticed that some groups satisfy more than one reason. For example, a church can provide interpersonal attraction, common goals, activities, and identity. This is true for most groups people join—there is rarely only one reason for group affiliation.

Task and Social Dimensions of Groups

Once an individual joins a group, he or she becomes involved in the group's process. It is important to realize that this process or interaction occurs in two different dimensions—the task dimension and the social dimension. Each dimension covers a different aspect and purpose of the group's interactions.

The **task dimension** is the work of the group. All efforts directed at solving the problem are considered the domain of the task dimension. Researching the problem, analyzing the problem, brainstorming solutions, discussing the strengths and weaknesses of the solutions, reaching consensus on the best solution, and implementing the solution are all elements of the task dimension of the group.

The **social dimension** is the interpersonal relationships among group members, between one member and another, and with the group as a whole. While the group is busy working in the task dimension, it is also involved in the social dimension. The social dimension is not separate from the task dimension, but rather it is intertwined within the task dimension. A change in the social dimension produces a change in the task dimension and vice versa. For example, a severe personality clash between two members can affect the productivity of the group. A group that is overburdened with task responsibilities can quickly experience interpersonal tension and conflict.

Norms and Conformity

The behavior of all group members will be determined and regulated to a great extent by the norms operating at the explicit and implicit levels. **Norms** are the rules that regulate the behavior of the group. They make smooth, predictable interaction possible. The concept of norms or rules is the basic building block of group interaction. Without norms of behavior, the group could be thrust into confusion, alienation, and even hostility.

Implicit norms are rules that are understood by group members, either consciously or unconsciously, but are not announced verbally or in writing. Norms such as not speaking when others are speaking, being polite, sitting facing one another, and not using obscenities are examples of implicit rules or norms.

Explicit norms are those rules that are orally stated or written down as a code of conduct or expected group behavior. Many groups, such as military organizations, sports clubs, and religious sects, establish formal rules of behavior that members are expected to follow. On receiving membership to a group, the new member may receive a list of expected behaviors.

Conformity is the adherence to group norms. Why do group members conform to norms? First, conformity to norms makes our lives orderly, predictable, and organized. Rather than always having to consider when to talk, whom to face, and which hand to shake, we allow norms to prescribe these behaviors. Second, adherence to norms makes group interactions more productive. Rather than spending time debating which behaviors are acceptable and unacceptable, group efforts can be directed to the task dimension. Third, conformity to norms provides each member with a sense of belonging and acceptance. Whether it's a secret group handshake, a moose lodge hat, or a certain style of dress, norms can make us feel like one of the group.

The Four Phases of Group Process

Each problem-solving group has a life all its own. No two groups are exactly the same. However, communications professor Aubrey Fisher has identified a four-phase sequence of group development that applies to most problem-solving groups. This four-phase model consists of periods of orientation, conflict, emergence, and reinforcement.

Phase 1. Orientation. Most members of new groups spend their first meeting or two getting to know one another. Group members often have a high level of anxiety and uncertainty because they have little or no previous history with one another. The orientation phase is devoted to letting the group members "break the ice" and get acquainted. Humorous remarks, polite behavior, social chitchat, and avoidance of conflict characterize this phase of group development. **Primary tension**—the uneasiness group members feel because they are unfamiliar with one another—usually occurs during the orientation phase. The social dimension of the group is emphasized during this time because the establishment of a warm, supportive, and trusting environment is crucial to the group's task dimension in later phases. If the mood of the group is defensive, suspicious, and uncooperative, the group will experience greater task dimension difficulty later on.

During the orientation phase, members begin to initiate discussion about the nature and scope of the task before them. They will often state their opinions and feelings in tentative, vague language, because they may not yet be comfortable fully disclosing their positions.

Phase 2. Conflict. Once group members are comfortable enough to share opinions and feelings at a deeper level, they begin the second phase of group process, the conflict phase. During this phase, group members discuss the nature and background of the problem, propose solutions, debate the relative merits of the solutions, and select the best solution or solutions. During the conflict phase, group members begin to clarify opinions and feelings about the issues. They devote more energy to sharing differences of opinion, arguing positions, and debating the issues. The feelings of uneasiness experienced during this phase is called **secondary tension**— the tension caused by disagreement or criticism over one's ideas, evidence, or proposed solutions.

> *Art has something to do with the achievement of stillness in the midst of chaos.*
>
> —SAUL BELLOW

When conflict arises within a group, our immediate reaction oftentimes is to defend ourselves, blame someone, discipline someone, or correct something. This need to immediately fix the problem is natural in our culture. But sometimes the best course of action is no action.

When conflict arises, be still and don't do anything for a brief period, even if chaos is swirling around you. Take a breath, relax, and just observe what's going on. Others might be rushing around, but you can choose to be still and observe. Once you've caught your breath and relaxed for a few moments, you can the join the discussion. Don't blame, judge, or criticize. Be open, listen, and see what unfolds. In this way, you can help create a safer, more supportive atmosphere in which the group members can work.

If a group develops a safe, supportive social dimension during the orientation phase, it is more likely to successfully weather the secondary tension experienced during the conflict phase. Groups that have not devoted sufficient time to the orientation phase can buckle under the pressures of conflict.

Phase 3. Emergence. During the third phase, group members move from debate and conflict to a possible solution that is acceptable to all members. It's a time when the group negotiates, compromises, and begins to discover common ground. Whereas the conflict phase emphasizes differences of opinion, the emergence phase focuses on similarities. During this time, decisions slowly emerge, so all group members are comfortable with the process of forming a solution. Statements of agreement, acceptance, and approval are increasingly heard within the group. Finally, the group makes a decision or adopts a solution.

Phase 4. Reinforcement. The final phase occurs when group members congratulate themselves on a job well done. During this time, the group also constructs an implementation plan and timetable for the agreed-on solution. The social dimension is reinforced in this phase with the expression of positive feelings about the group and its accomplishments. Members often feel a strong sense of group identity and belonging. Disagreement, conflicts, and arguments were successfully negotiated and the group is stronger because of it.

No matter how good the group feels about its success, be aware of groupthink. **Groupthink** describes the situation when a group departs from rational, reality-based decision making to irrational, nonreality-based decision making because the group is too cohesive. Having accomplished task success and felt tight member cohesiveness, groups can occasionally experience groupthink and believe that they can "do no wrong." In such cases, the group can become closed minded, pressure group members into conformity, and forbid any outside input or critical evaluation, thus affecting future decision making. The group becomes a closed system.

There are four steps you can take to create a more open communication system within the group if you believe it is beginning to experience groupthink:

1. Stress critical evaluation of the group process. You can share your observations about weaknesses in the group's operation.
2. Discuss the group's decision-making process with a trusted colleague or coworker outside the group and report these "outside perceptions" to the group members.
3. Play the **devil's advocate** and challenge prevailing opinions and attitudes, even if you personally agree with them.
4. Invite a qualified individual from the outside to observe the group's decision-making process.

If you feel your group has reached an acceptable solution to the problem it has been assigned and you don't think the group is experiencing groupthink, then celebrate your group's task achievement and reinforce the good feelings of the group.

Groups, however, rarely move from step to step as Fisher has proposed. A group may go through these phases for each issue it addresses. One group may devote most of its time to orientation and socializing, whereas another group will bypass orientation altogether and focus solely on the task at hand. Groups can also move from emergence back to the conflict phase and begin the process again as new issues and obstacles arise. Groups can get sidetracked, abandon their discussion track, or even disband. The journey a problem-solving group takes is much more complex and the stages it experiences are not as clear cut as one might hope. But Fisher's model provides a framework from which to view and understand the basic phases of group work.

DECISION-MAKING TECHNIQUES

The primary role of the problem-solving group is to make decisions in order to solve problems. During the conflict and emergence phases of decision making, groups can use a variety of methods to reach their decisions. The five most common methods are decision by the leader, majority vote, compromise, arbitration, and consensus.

Decision by the Leader

The leader decides for the group either after hearing discussion from group members or without their input. The advantages of this method of decision making are that it minimizes wasted time, reinforces the traditional hierarchical business structure, and can be efficient. The disadvantages are a lack of commitment to the solution by the group, superficial or minimal group discussion and analysis, and the development of an adversarial relationship between the leader and group members.

Decision by Majority Rule

Decision by majority rule or voting is the most commonly used method of group decision, when 51 percent or two-thirds vote determines the outcome of an issue. We've all experienced the end to conflict resolution when someone in the group yells, "Well, let's vote on it! I'm tired of arguing about this topic!" The vote is taken and the matter is settled. Or is it really?

The disadvantages of majority rule are that there are always winners and losers and that majority rule provides no protection for the minority. Additionally, the losers often suffer because they feel their position was discarded by the majority.

Majority rule has advantages too. Decisions can be made quickly. Time can be saved. Majority rule can be used effectively in procedural matters within the operation of the group, such as voting on meeting times, placement of items on the agenda, and other administrative tasks.

Decision by Compromise

Decision by compromise is a bartering technique—"If you give us this, we'll give you that." Members of one point of view will give up some aspect of their solution in exchange for support from the other members. Compromise combines aspects of the leading alternatives or most popular solutions being discussed. Compromise is not all that bad. Isn't life a compromise? But compromise often results in low commitment to the solution, because final solution may be weakened or diluted. Compromise is good when the position of members representing one point of view is incompatible with those representing another point of view. It will permit the discussion to continue, whereas no compromise would have killed discussion long ago.

The disadvantage of compromise is that it is often used too early in discussion and prevents productive exploration of alternatives. It also produces decisions or solutions that are watered down, "averaging out" differences between various points of view.

Decision by Arbitration

There are times when decision making needs to come from outside the group. For instance, a dispute between labor and management often requires decisions to be made by an **arbitrator,** an impartial third party whose decision both sides have agreed to be binding. In other words, both groups will accept the arbitrator's decision.

The disadvantage is similar to that of majority rule. The loser in the decision must accept the ruling of the arbitrator. The advantage is that the arbitrator will break an impasse or stalemate. Arbitration gets the ball rolling again, whereas an impasse between the two sides could polarize them even more, increase tension and hostility, and prevent compromise from ever occurring.

Decision by Consensus

One of the most effective small group decision-making methods is consensus. Consensus occurs when all members of the group find the decision acceptable. The decision may *not* be each member's first choice, but each member regards it as *workable* and *acceptable.* Consensus is not an "averaged-out," hybrid decision between two different points of view. It is a new, different point of view. You can test for consensus during group discussion by asking, "Can we live with this solution for a period of time?" In other words, does the group feel the decision is workable and acceptable?

> *People tend to resist that which is forced upon them. People tend to support that which they have helped create.*
>
> —VINCE PFAFF

The advantage of decision by consensus is that it increases member satisfaction with the decision, because *all* group members must buy into the decision of the group. *Any* member can prevent or block the acceptance of a decision. So the ultimate decision is the product of thorough discussion. It promotes a stronger social dimension in the group by increasing cohesion. It also increases the information base, because discussion cannot be terminated by vote or compromise. Finally, it increases the quality of the decisions.

One of the primary disadvantages of decision making by consensus is that it requires a tremendous amount of time. Whereas the other four methods of decision making—by leader, majority rule, compromise, and arbitration—can terminate discussion with the imposition of the decision, consensus demands the members talk until they discover a decision that is workable and acceptable to all members.

Guidelines for reaching consensus. Here are five guidelines for reaching consensus within a group:

1. **Be open to the ideas and opinions of others.** Present your views and positions. Then *listen* to the views and positions of other group members.
2. **Seek win-win solutions.** Try not to view the discussion as an activity that someone has to win and someone has to lose. Look for the next acceptable option for all members.
3. **Encourage difference of opinion.** Difference of opinion is natural. Critically listen to and evaluate the arguments and evidence of others. Yield only to the views and opinions that make sense to you. Difference of opinion makes for higher-quality decisions.
4. **Avoid conflict-reducing techniques.** Don't vote, flip coins, compromise, or average. These techniques require someone to win and someone to lose.
5. **Include the participation of all members.** Make certain all group members are included in the decision-making process. Ask low-verbal members for their opinions, reactions, and feelings.

THE STANDARD PROBLEM-SOLVING AGENDA

The majority of current problem-solving agendas are based on John Dewey's reflective thinking model, whether they include all the steps he provided or some modification of them. An **agenda** is an agreed-on set of steps the group will follow to solve a problem. Although Dewey's book *How People Think* was originally intended to identify the steps most people use to solve personal problems, his steps have been followed as a way to organize problem-solving agendas for small groups.

The problem-solving agenda presented here is a modified version of Dewey's model, with the addition of an orientation, or check-in, step at the beginning.

Step 1. Check In

The first step the group must take is to provide members with the opportunity to establish a supportive and trusting social dimension. Without a healthy social dimension, the group will not be able to reach its maximum effectiveness. The check-in for the group encourages members to introduce themselves to one another by sharing any pertinent professional and personal information they feel may be helpful in letting the other members know who they are.

After the group has established a supportive, friendly social dimension, the check-in step of each meeting becomes less involved. Usually, members will each take thirty to sixty seconds to share how things are going in their lives since the group last met. Much useful information can be provided during the group's check-in and I've found these five minutes to be important to maintaining the group's social dimension.

Step 2. Analyze the Problem

Fruitful problem analysis requires that group members research the problem before coming to the meeting and are ready to discuss the following questions:

1. What is the problem?
2. What is the question of policy? ("What should be done about_____?")
3. What is the nature of the problem?
4. Whom does the problem affect?
5. How serious is the problem?
6. What are causes of the problem?
7. What solutions have been attempted before?
8. What will happen if the problem is not solved?
9. What are the constraints for a workable solution?
10. What are three possible solutions? (Each member brings three to the discussion.)

These ten questions for problem analysis are not the only ones that can be considered when investigating a problem. Feel free to modify, delete, and add to this list as you and your group see fit.

Step 3. Brainstorm Possible Solutions

Creativity is seeing something that doesn't exist already.

—MICHELE SHEA

The purpose of **brainstorming** is to generate a large number of ideas for potential solutions without evaluation. The most serious threat to selecting a workable and acceptable solution to any problem is the group's inability to generate more than two or three possible solutions. Your group should never stop brainstorming until it has generated at least twenty to thirty possible solutions.

During the brainstorming process, group members sit in a circle and contribute possible solutions. They also write down every suggestion made during the session (even their own suggestions), numbering each suggestion as the group moves from item to item. The primary rule is no evaluation of any idea during this stage of the problem-solving process. There is no rationale, explanation, or justification for each suggestion, only the suggestion. Assign a number to it, then go to the next suggestion until the group reaches at least twenty to thirty suggestions!

Generate as many ideas as possible. Don't hold back. As Pablo Picasso once commanded, "The important thing is to create. Nothing else matters." Follow his advice for this step of the problem-solving process.

Here are some guidelines for a successful brainstorming session:

1. Evaluation of any idea is not permitted.
2. Questions, storytelling, explanations, and tangential talking are not permitted.
3. Quantity of ideas, not quality, is desired.
4. The wilder the ideas the better.
5. Combine ideas from ones you have already listed.

Step 4. Evaluate the Better Solutions

Before you actually evaluate the better solutions, you need to spend some time eliminating the ridiculous, illegal, and absurd suggestions created during the brainstorming session. This is where the numbers come in handy. Instead of reading the entire proposal or idea you want to discard, you simply announce the number. If members agree or disagree, they'll tell you. Using the number will save you time, energy, and effort.

Once the group has deleted one-half to two-thirds of the ideas, then the real task of step 4 begins—discussion of the strengths and weaknesses of the better solutions on the list. Here are some guidelines for a more effective discussion:

1. Discuss one solution at a time.
2. Consider both its strengths and weaknesses.
3. Move to another solution quickly. Don't get stuck.
4. Avoid lumping solutions into one large conglomeration.
5. Don't be afraid to challenge a solution.

Evaluation of the better solutions will take time. Keep these five guidelines in mind when considering the better solutions. Speak your mind. Now is the time to share your reservations. But above all, listen for understanding while other members are sharing their reservations and preferences. You may hear or see something they don't.

Step 5. Reach Consensus on the Best Solution

During the discussion of the better solutions, two or possibly three solutions will keep surfacing. When you notice this occurring, let group members know they may be arriving at some agreement or common ground. Begin looking for areas of agreement within the group as members narrow the selection to two or three. Try to discover any common ground contained in the remaining solutions. Bring these to the attention of the group.

You may need a second minibrainstorming session at this time to generate a few related solutions to the two or three remaining in hopes of discovering one solution that is workable and acceptable to all the group members. Remember, for consensus to occur, each group member must find the solution workable and acceptable.

Test for consensus by asking group members if they can live with the solution. They might object, stating it's not their first choice or they're not overly pleased with it. Just smile and repeat the question that tests for consensus: "But can you live with this solution for a period of time?"

After the group has reached consensus on a solution, take a break and celebrate. The group deserves it!

Step 6. Implement the Solution

After the group reaches consensus, you need to implement the solution. Implementation involves three steps—planning a timetable, assigning implementation tasks, and evaluating the implementation process. If the group is not required to implement the solution, disregard this final step.

You can dream, create, design, and build the most wonderful idea in the world, but it requires people to make the dream a reality.

—WALT DISNEY

Plan a timetable. The group needs to divide the implementation of the solution into its component objectives and assign dates for the completion of those objectives. Be as specific as possible when you describe the component objectives.

Assign tasks. Assign individual members to complete the various tasks. Make certain each member knows the task and the date by which the task must be accomplished. Everyone should have the phone numbers of all group members because communication is critical to the success of the project at this stage.

Evaluate implementation. Evaluation of the group's effectiveness in implementing the solution to the problem can be accomplished during a face-to-face meeting or over the telephone. Changes in procedure or approach may be necessary for future groups. Additional resources can be secured. Members may need to be encouraged, reminded, or congratulated. If the implementation was a success and all the members are satisfied with their performance and the performance of the group, then the group should consider it a job well done.

Reanalyze the problem (if necessary). If the solution fails to meet the group's expectations or standards, members may need to return to the beginning of the standard agenda and reanalyze the problem in step 2. Evaluation of the implementation may have provided valuable information or a new perspective that was not initially available to the group. Many times, it's only after a solution has been implemented that incomplete, inaccurate, or faulty analysis of the problem becomes apparent. In any case, the group can return to step 2 and begin the entire process again.

Reanalysis of the problem involves additional work and effort and it can discourage group members, especially when they thought the problem was solved. But don't get too discouraged. Author John Updike observed that "Any activity becomes creative when the doer cares about doing it right or better." Be an artist of communication and invest the time and effort to do things right, or even better.

The Circular Nature of Problem Solving

The standard agenda provides groups with the most complete and time-tested problem-solving method, but that does not mean groups necessarily follow a linear, step-by-step process when they solve problems in the real world. More often, the process is circular and dynamic, not following clear-cut divisions. Your group may begin with an analysis of the problem, skip to a discussion of a solution, and then return to problem analysis. Or, as I mentioned earlier, the group may actually implement a solution, only to discover that it needs to return to the beginning of the agenda and begin again with additional information and insight. Don't get upset when these things occur. That's simply the circular nature of problem solving.

RESEARCHING FOR A DISCUSSION

The majority of problem-solving groups are made up of interested and concerned people like you and me. We want to get a candidate elected. We want to put a stop sign at the end of our street. We want to raise funds for a favorite charity. We want to make our neighborhood safer.

Regardless of the group goal, research can help the group achieve the best solution for the problem. Researching your subject and increasing your knowledge of the topic can help you make worthier decisions and implement better solutions. Television interviewer Charlie Rose believes that, "Knowing a lot is a springboard to creativity." So know a lot by researching.

The more information and evidence a group has at its disposal, the greater the probability its efforts will produce a solution that is workable and acceptable to all group members. Your own personal knowledge and experience, library resources, and interviewing are three primary sources of information when you research a discussion topic. (Chapter 10 discusses these three research areas.)

What to Research

The questions from step 2 of your standard agenda—analyzing the problem—will help you focus your researching efforts. Feel free to add, modify, and delete from this list as you see fit.

> *Often the most creative people are also the most prepared.*
>
> —LEE IACOCCA

1. **What is the problem?** The group should agree on what is the problem. Avoid vague, general descriptions of the problem. Be as specific as possible. For example, Instead of "crime," focus more specifically on the type of crime, such as "department store shoplifting by preteens in Santa Clara County."

2. **What is the question of policy?** The group should agree on the question of policy before you begin researching the topic. By constructing a question of policy, you are ensuring that the group proposes an action plan. Remember to begin the question of policy this way: "What should be done about …?" For example, "What should be done about department store shoplifting by preteens in Santa Clara County?"

3. **What is the nature of the problem?** Find information describing the specific nature of the problem you are investigating. What exactly is the problem? What are the parameters of the problem? Are there any limitations or special conditions presented by this problem? How long has the problem existed? What is the history of the problem?

4. **Whom does the problem affect?** Try to get as much information as possible about those affected by the problem. Does the problem affect primarily humans? Men, women, or children? Young or old? Does the problem affect a specific subgroup?

5. **How serious is the problem?** Not all group members will perceive the problem as serious to the same degree, but you need to establish some measurement of its magnitude, scope, and significance. Try to obtain statistical information describing the severity of the problem. Interview experts.

6. **What are the causes of the problem?** This can be both a question of fact and a question of value. It is a question of fact if you discover evidence that proves the cause or causes of the problem. It is also a question of value if experts hold differing beliefs about the cause or causes of the problem.

7. **What solutions have been attempted before?** Be on the lookout for solutions that have been attempted already to reduce or eliminate the

problem. Be as specific as possible when you describe solutions that have been previously attempted, because your group may want to consider them.

8. **What will happen if the problem is not solved?** What do experts or the literature say will happen if the problem is not solved? Once again, this is primarily a question of value because experts will have differing views.

9. **What are the constraints for a workable solution?** Suggest at least three specific constraints for a workable solution to the problem. For instance, three criteria for a solution to the problem of reducing neighborhood theft may be that the solution must (1) costs less than $500 to implement, (2) be implemented within sixty days, and (3) involve participation by all residents. These constraints will help determine the merit of the solutions considered by the group.

10. **What are three possible solutions?** After you have completed researching the problem (questions 3 through 9), brainstorm three solutions to the problem. You may want to brainstorm more, but try to keep it manageable. You will be sharing your three ideas during the group's brainstorming session.

Constructing an Information Sheet

Record your research data on an **information sheet,** which contains the ten questions from your problem analysis and the evidence you gathered for each of the questions. You should cite the author, source, and date for each piece of information you include, in the event a group member questions your data. For interviews, cite the expert's name, qualifications, and date of the interview. Here is an example of one question and the corresponding evidence and documentation for an information sheet:

---

6. **What are the causes of the problem?**
    A. "Increased drug use is the primary cause of increased home robberies."
        Police Chief Mark Henson, San Rafael Police. Interview, 8/26/02.

    B. "The increase in home robberies is due to the increase in drug use."
        Article by Sheila Graves, *San Rafael Times,* 8/18/02.

When you research, don't limit yourself to only magazines, newspapers, books, or expert opinions. Utilize as many sources of information as you can discover. Increased knowledge is a springboard to creativity.

CREATING EFFECTIVE GROUPS: THE G.R.O.U.P. TECHNIQUE

Keep in mind the following G.R.O.U.P. Technique as you prepare to work in a problem-solving group. It will focus your thinking and efforts in a constructive fashion as you work with others.

Growth is the goal

Your participation in a problem-solving group is directed, at one level, to solving a problem. At a much more significant level, your goal is to grow and learn lessons along the way. As you participate in your problem-solving group, you are learning to listen to the ideas of others, share your opinions and feelings, develop your creativity, compromise, reconsider, cooperate, fulfill your responsibilities, meet challenges, deal with conflict, forgive, laugh, feel frustration, experience success, and countless other valuable lessons. These lessons will make you a more skilled, caring, mature, responsible, patient, and loving individual. These lessons will enable you to become a better person.

Research the topic

Whether I'm working with a faculty group, a community action group, a religious group, or a special interest group, I'm always surprised at the lack of preparation and research of most group members. My experience is that most group members are insufficiently prepared for meetings, whether it's reviewing the minutes from the last meeting, preparing a report, or reading material they were assigned. Researching a topic is the last thing most group members consider. The majority of them come to the meeting and rely on personal opinion to support them during a discussion. By researching a topic, you can provide the group with relevant facts, statistics, and expert advice. Visiting a local library, making a few phone calls, and surfing the Internet requires relatively little time and effort, can take the group to a higher level of discussion, and can provide it with the information it needs to make informed decisions. This investment of time and effort can make a positive difference. Create a wealth of information for your group to consider, discuss, and use.

Organize the discussion

Whenever you are the chairperson or leader of a problem-solving group, organize the discussion following the problem-solving agenda outlined in this chapter. Group members may not be familiar with the six-step process, so review the steps with them before you begin the discussion. Make copies of the agenda (include the guidelines for each step) and distribute them to members at the meeting before your problem-solving session. If you are not the elected or assigned leader of the group, you can still share the problem-solving agenda with the individual in charge and recommend its use.

If followed, this problem-solving agenda will enable your group to more effectively and productively address the problem it seeks to solve. Create a group process that will increase the chances for group success.

Unify the group

The theory behind a problem-solving group is that "Two heads are better than one." If one head were always better than many, there would be no need for such groups. A group can analyze, brainstorm, reach consensus, and implement solutions far better than one individual, as long as the group members cooperate and work together.

This is where you come in—one of your most important goals as a group member is to unify the group during its orientation phase and to maintain this unity when conflict emerges during discussions. Without group unity, it is more difficult to reach sound decisions and propose effective solutions.

During the orientation phase, welcome group members and take the initiative to "break the ice" by expressing warmth and friendliness. Be a positive, uplifting person as the group meets for the first few times. Do your part to unify the group.

When the group experiences conflict, rather than always taking a side and adding fuel to the fire, play the role of negotiator or peacekeeper. Help bring compromise and unity to the group by saying:

> "What is the problem?"
> "Can we agree that . . . ?"
> "What do we feel/think?"
> "What things can we agree upon?"
> "Is anyone opposed to . . . ?"
> "What would make you happy/satisfied?"
> "You both have good points we need to discuss."
> "Can we disagree without disliking?"
> "We need to focus on issues, not personalities."
> "Can we all live with this solution/compromise?"

It usually takes one group member to initiate compromise, cooperation, and unity within a group. One individual can create a situation where unity can spring from conflict, where cooperation can rise from discord. When others are losing their tempers, you can choose to remain calm, balanced, and focused on bringing unity back to the group. Unity begins with one person. Let that person be you.

Participate wholeheartedly

I believe enthusiasm is contagious. A coach's enthusiasm can spark life into a downtrodden team. An inspirational teacher can light up the eyes and hearts of a roomful of children. The excitement of a speaker can bring a large audience to its feet. One individual can create enthusiasm in others.

How you participate in any endeavor or activity can have a tremendous impact on others. By choosing to participate with enthusiasm, delight, and even joy, you can spark enthusiasm, delight, and joy. One person's wholehearted participation in a group can encourage and inspire others to do the same.

George Patton said, "Always do more than is required of you." Don't just show up to a group meeting and go through the motions. Do it wholeheartedly. Arrive early, bring snacks for everyone, smile, share your ideas and opinions, compliment others, encourage others, volunteer for tasks, stay after to help clean up the meeting room. Make your presence known. Make your presence felt. Make a positive contribution by participating wholeheartedly! Create some enthusiasm. It just may be contagious.

EXPLORING CREATIVE TASKS

1. Videotape your participation in a problem-solving group, either at work or in school. Review the tape and classify each of your comments as either stating personal opinion or some other communication behavior such as asking a question, marking a transition, summarizing, stating time limits, clarifying, analyzing, negotiating, and compromising. What were your contributions? How did you feel about your participation? What can you improve? What did you like? What did you learn about yourself?

2. List of five explicit and five implicit norms of a group you are currently involved with. For example, you can list norms involving punctuality, participation, interruption, disagreement, humor, decision making, and conflict resolution. What do you think of your list? Share your list with group members and see if they agree with you. What did they think?

3. Use the standard problem-solving agenda with a group that you are involved with. You may have to instruct group members on how the agenda works. Propose a solution to a problem facing the group. What was the process like? What were your feelings about using the standard problem-solving agenda? How did other members respond? What did you learn about your group and yourself?

4. Select a personal problem and try to find a solution to it using the standard problem-solving agenda. How did you feel about addressing a personal problem in such a structured manner? What were your results? What did you think about the process? Would you ever use the agenda for personal problems again? Why or why not?

EXPANDING YOUR CREATIVE THINKING

1. What motivates you to join groups—interpersonal attraction, group goals, group activities, or group identity? Has your motivation changed as you get older and your life situations change? What is most important to you now in choosing group membership? What do you think will be important to you ten years from now?

2. How do you make decisions in your personal life? Do you seek the advice of others? Do you consult experts, books, or the Internet? Or do you let others make your decisions for you? How do you feel about the way you make decisions in your personal life? Are there any changes you would like to make in the way you decide on important issues that involve you? How could you improve your decision making?

3. Assume you could select any five individuals (either living or dead) to serve on a problem-solving committee that would help you find a solution to the personal problem you identified in Creative Task 4. Who would those five people be? What do you think the task dimension would be like in the group? What do you think the social dimension would be like? What do you think the solution to the problem would be? How would you feel about working with this group of individuals?

4. What creative things would you implement to improve the social dimension of a current group you belong to (at work, the class you're enrolled in, an interest group, or your family)? How practical are your ideas? What do you think would be the response of your group?

NINE

Creating Guiding Communication as a Leader

> *A good leader creates opportunities for others to succeed.*
>
> —MAXWELL JOHNSTON

Five minutes before the meeting was scheduled to begin, Joe Samuels's agenda and notes were neatly stacked on the large round table in front of his chair. He arrived early to the first of three planning meetings for the full-time faculty interview for our college.

Joe rose and greeted each of us in the seven-member hiring committee with a warm handshake and friendly smile as we entered the room. For the next hour, Joe led our discussion with his questions, clarifications, and occasional summaries. He guided our disagreements to areas of common ground and consensus. But most of the time, he sat quietly, watched, and listened to what the committee members had to say. In just one hour, we completed the goals we set out to accomplish. Standing at the doorway, Joe shook our hands a second time, thanking us for our time and contributions as we left the room.

While I was walking back to my office, I reflected on another successful meeting led by Joe and how I appreciated his skill and caring attitude. What Joe can accomplish in a one-hour meeting is sheer beauty in my eyes. He really does produce a work of art with his leadership skills.

DEFINITION OF LEADERSHIP

A **leader** is an individual who is perceived by the group members as having a legitimate position of power or influence in the group. The leader can be assigned or designated to that position. Or the leader can emerge from within the group's interactive process or even by group election.

> *Everyone leads.*
> *Leadership is action,*
> *not position.*
>
> —DONALD McGANNON

Leadership, however, is different. **Leadership** is the process of influencing the task and social dimensions of a group to help it reach its goal. Leadership is more of a function or behavior rather than a position, rank, or office. Leadership isn't limited to the individual who is elected or assigned the role of leader. Leadership can be shared by all group members. Every group member has the potential and opportunity to participate in the leadership functions of the group.

THE FUNCTION OF GROUP LEADERSHIP

The primary task of any problem-solving group is to keep the group focused on solving the problem confronting it. A collection of geniuses wandering off in separate directions, not coordinating and sharing their individual talents, is a waste indeed. The function of leadership is to encourage, facilitate, and focus the communication within the group.

Guiding behaviors keep the discussion on track and coordinate the participation and contributions of the individual members in the most productive manner possible. There are two two categories of guiding behaviors: task guiding behaviors, which are intended to keep the discussion on task and productive, and social guiding behaviors, which are designed to establish and maintain healthy interpersonal relationships between group members.

If every member of the group is skilled in using these guiding behaviors, the overall performance of the group will be enhanced. In fact, every group member should be skilled at guiding discussion, not just the designated leader. Knowledge and skills training vested in only one (the leader) or two individuals within a group can often lead to an imbalance of power and can thus affect decision making.

TASK GUIDING BEHAVIORS

Task guiding behaviors are statements or questions that initiate and maintain a productive task dimension during the group's discussions. The seven task guiding behaviors are requesting information, providing information, clarifying information, guiding discussion, summarizing, analyzing evidence and reasoning, and negotiating.

Requesting Information

Requesting information from group members serves to broaden the information base of the group, initiate interaction, and encourage low-verbal members' participation. It is one of the easiest ways to create communication within a group. Here are some examples of requesting information:

> "What do we think about . . . ?"
> "Does anyone have any information dealing with . . . ?"
> "Does anyone have any evidence concerning . . . ?"
> "What information hasn't been shared yet?"

Providing Information

Giving information, evidence, or personal opinion is a vital behavior each group member is expected to perform. Without the sharing of information, there can be no discussion. By contributing what you know and what you have learned, you are adding more information to the group's collective memory and thus creating a more informed group. Here are some ways you can begin your contributions:

> "In my research I discovered . . ."
> "I read that . . ."
> "During my interview I learned that . . ."
> "A recent poll concluded that . . ."
> "According to . . ."
> "It's my opinion that . . ."

Clarifying Information

When information is shared in a group discussion, some confusion may arise about the content or meaning of the contribution. This is when you need to clarify any unclear or ambiguous information. By using active listening and other clarification statements, you foster clearer understanding within the group. Here are some ways you can create greater clarity:

> "Do you mean . . . ?"
> "Are you saying . . . ?"
> "Do I understand your research to suggest that . . . ?"
> "So, what this tells us is . . . ?"

Guiding Discussion

Guiding behaviors keep the discussion on the agenda, regulate participation, and announce time limits. Without guiding behaviors, the purpose of the group would be lost. When Joe chairs a meeting, his helpful guiding behaviors let us know where we are and where we need to go. Notice how each of these behaviors is helpful in guiding the group:

Initiating the agenda:	"Let's define the problem . . ."
	"Can we move onto brainstorming solutions?"
	"I think we can move to the next step of . . ."
Maintaining the agenda:	"We need to return to the topic of . . ."
	"I think we need to return to the agenda . . ."
	"Can we get back to . . . ?"
	"How does this relate to our agenda item? We're offtrack."
Encouraging low verbal:	"What is your opinion, Mary?"
Regulating high verbal:	"So, what you're telling us is . . . ?"
	"Can you summarize your point?"
Providing information:	"Our meeting should last one hour."
	"There are five minutes remaining."
	"Our time is up. Shall we table this until next time?"

Summarizing

In any discussion, many ideas are presented, a host of evidence given, and a list of solutions proposed. Periodically, these ideas, evidence pieces, and proposals need to be rounded up and herded into a cluster for clearer viewing. A **summary** is a listing of items, without detailed development of any one item, so they can be understood and processed in a manageable way. It can serve to simplify and focus a discussion. As artist Henri Frederic Amial said, "The great artist is the simplifier." Here are some phrases that can help you to simplify and summarize discussions:

"The brainstorming list of solutions are . . ."
"So far, we've heard three explanations. They are . . ."
"I'm hearing two schools of thought on this. First . . . and second . . . "

Analyzing Evidence and Reasoning

Careful and thoughtful analysis of evidence and reasoning is crucial in the problem-solving process. You need to be able and willing to test the evidence presented and analyze the reasoning of the proposals set forth. The following questions can help you test evidence and analyze reasoning:

> "What makes this researcher qualified?"
> "Do you have additional evidence for this position?"
> "When was the article published?"
> "How does this relate to our topic?"
> "Are these two situations similar enough to warrant comparison?"
> "Could there be other positions?"

The hallmark of critical thinking is the analysis of evidence and reasoning. Your responsibility to test the thinking and information of your group cannot be overstated. Without diligence in analyzing evidence and testing the reasoning of arguments, the group process will be compromised by weak evidence or reasoning.

Negotiating

Negotiating is the skill of bringing differing parties to mutual agreement, a skill you will find particularly valuable as the group gets closer to consensus. We all possess the capacity to suspend personal judgment and appreciate the strengths of different points of view. These negotiating skills are also helpful in settling minor conflicts and differences throughout the course of discussion. By using them, you can create a place where opposing sides can meet and discuss. Here are some ways you can help in the negotiating process:

> "Can we all agree that . . . ?"
> "Is anyone opposed to . . . ?"
> "Can we combine the strengths of these two proposals?"
> "Can we all live with this solution for a period of time?"

One of the most important contributions to the success of a group is your ability and willingness to negotiate and serve as a consensus builder. Be positive and constantly alert to any common ground—areas of agreement, common ideas, and similar beliefs—where your group can meet as one. Negotiate ways to build agreement within your group.

SOCIAL GUIDING BEHAVIORS

Social guiding behaviors encourage and maintain a healthy social dimension during group discussion. Each of these behaviors is designed to ensure a friendly, supportive, and trusting atmosphere within the group. The social guiding behaviors are encouraging, expressing feelings, harmonizing, and energizing.

Encouraging

Many times group members need encouragement to continue speaking, participating, or even remaining in the group. Encouragement fosters a caring and supportive group atmosphere.

You can encourage others by acknowledging their presence, agreeing with their statements, complimenting their behaviors, or reframing negatives into positives. Here are some things you can say to encourage:

> "I see your point, Britta!"
> "I agree with you, Ted. Your comment makes sense to me."
> "Another way of looking at this is . . . " (positive interpretation).

Expressing Feelings

Although your problem-solving group is not a therapy group, the expression and acknowledgment of feelings are essential to a healthy social dimension of any group. Whether it's to congratulate the group's successes or explore the group's interpersonal conflicts, the expression of feelings is crucial to the health and maintenance of the group. Here are some ways to encourage the expression of emotions:

> "I love being in this group."
> "How are we feeling right now?"
> "Are you guys feeling as frustrated as I am? Maybe we need a break."

Harmonizing

Tension or conflict between two or more members may occasionally rise to a level that negatively affects the group's task dimension, whether it's a disagreement over a substantive issue, hurt feelings caused by an insensitive remark, or a minor feud between two individuals. Some attempt must be made to bring harmony or a sense of cooperation and unity back to the group. Here are some things you can say to reestablish harmony:

> "Maybe the two of you can discuss this matter after the meeting."
> "Let's not let our feelings get the best of us."
> "Can you two disagree without disliking each other?"
> "We need to focus on the issues, not personalities."

Energizing

You will discover that working with other people in a small group can be psychologically, emotionally, and physically draining. Extended periods of time spent discussing, debating, and deliberating is taxing and can quickly deplete our energy levels and exhaust our enthusiasm. Create group enthusiasm by showing enthusiasm yourself. Also communicate enthusiasm by what you say. When you sense the vitality of the group is slipping, you can try to energize the group by saying:

> "We've done well this far and we only have a little ways to go!"
> "I think we're doing a great job!"
> "I know we can accomplish what we've set out to do!"

LEADERSHIP STYLES

We each have our own style of writing, dancing, singing, and playing. Likewise, we have our own style of leadership. Some of us control, some of us direct and guide, and some of us do nothing. However, rather than limit yourself to only one style of leadership, you can develop and use a variety of leadership styles to do what is appropriate and most effective for the situation and the group members.

The three basic leadership styles are autocratic, democratic, and laissez-faire. The **autocratic leader** dominates and controls the group with little or no member input. The **democratic leader** emphasizes the participation of group members in discussion and decision making. Emphasis is placed on the group and the leader leads by example, not by force. The democratic leader recognizes the value of group input and participation, and seeks the majority opinion or consensus. The **laissez-faire leader** allows the group to lead itself. This "hands-off" style of leadership lets the group "do its own thing."

> *Leadership appears to be the art of getting others to want to do something you are convinced should be done.*
>
> —VANCE PACKARD

All three styles of leadership have advantages and disadvantages. The most productive styles can be the autocratic and democratic approaches. The autocratic style generally produces more efficiently run groups, which complete tasks in less time. The democratic style produces the greatest member satisfaction, but requires more time to complete tasks. The laissez-faire style is effective when group members are independent or creative and require a great deal of freedom and latitude.

But remember that no one approach is consistently more effective than the others. Each style appears to work best under certain conditions, so always try to match the style with group members and the situation and conditions they find themselves in. You must constantly be asking yourself, "What degree of leadership direction would be most beneficial now?" Maybe the group needs tighter control because group members are socializing, fighting, or getting offtrack. Perhaps the group needs less control and guidance because it works effectively and coopera-tively. Sometimes the group needs no degree of leadership control because the members work independently or in subgroups.

Your answer to the question "What degree of leadership direction would be most beneficial now?" may not always be correct, but it will keep you open to dif-fering degrees of control and guidance, rather than limit you to only one style of leadership.

LEADING AN EFFECTIVE MEETING

Leading an effective meeting is one of the most important functional skills of any leader. Many specific skills and behaviors go into running a meeting that is pro-ductive, organized, and even enjoyable. Here are twenty suggestions for leading an effective meeting. Don't try to follow all twenty suggestions for each meeting. The implementation of even one suggestion will create a much more effective and productive meeting.

Clarify the Leader's Job Description

Clarify the duties and responsibilities of the position before you volunteer, are appointed, or elected as the leader of a group. Consult your boss, supervisor, or group to review what is expected of you as a leader. Get the job description in writing if possible. What are the expected timelines for projects? When does the position end? Under what circumstances can you be replaced? What special things should you know about the duties, group members, or project?

Consider If You Want the Job

Weigh the pros and cons of being the leader. After considering the duties, respon-sibilities, and timelines expected of you, be honest with yourself. Is this some-thing you really want to do? Is this something you really need to do? Honestly consider your motives. Ask yourself if this is a position in which you would want to serve others—the group members and the organization.

You don't have to agree to any leadership position if you don't want to. How-ever, your decision to decline a leadership position at work could put you in dis-favor with a supervisor or boss or even cost you your position or job. But if you feel strongly enough about not accepting a leadership position, then you must ultimately follow your conscience. Life is too short. Be nice to yourself and don't create a hell on earth for yourself, no matter what others want you to do. This advice is not limited to leadership offers either. On the other hand, do accept positions of leadership if you feel the group is working on a task you believe in. Don't be afraid to accept the position or nomination if you have never led a group before. Every great leader had a first leadership position. This may be yours!

Determine Whether or Not to Meet

After you become a leader in a problem-solving group, you will need to have your group meet. Most of the time, the meeting times and dates are determined for you. But if they're not, you will need to contact group members and negotiate meeting times and dates.

Once the scheduled meetings begin, you may occasionally determine that certain future meetings do not require the members' physical presence, and that business can be conducted by phone, e-mail, memo, or fax. Take every opportunity to conduct the group's business in the most expedient fashion possible. If you decide not to convene a meeting, group members will love you for it, for you've just created more open time in their calendars.

Prepare and Send the Agenda Before the Meeting

An **agenda** is the list of items that will be covered and the order in which they will be addressed. Agenda formats range from a simple listing of items to a more detailed listing of items.

Prepare and send the meeting agenda (and any other additional materials) to each group member one week *before* the meeting. This gives group members ample time to read, consider, and even research appropriate material before you meet. I usually have a rule when I chair a group: Members cannot participate in discussions if they have not read the agenda *and* other material *before* the meeting. This prevents members from shuffling paper and reading material during discussions.

The agenda shown below is a standard agenda used in most formal meetings. Refer to it when constructing your own agenda.

A G E N D A

1. Call to order.
2. Approve agenda.
3. Approve minutes from previous meeting.
4. Announcements.
5. Reports (officers and committees).
6. Old (unfinished) business. List all items for discussion or action.
7. New business. List all items for discussion or action.
8. Adjournment.

Limit and Prioritize Agenda Items

Limit the number of agenda items to four to six for both new and old business. You create a much more effective meeting if you don't overload the group with too many items. There may be occasions when you list only one item on your agenda to provide focus for your group.

If there are time constraints, prioritize the items on your agenda, starting from the most important to the least important. That way, if your group doesn't get to the last item or two, you have at least addressed the higher-priority items. There will be other meetings to discuss the less important issues.

Envision What Will Happen at the Meeting

The artist Paul Gauguin said, "I shut my eyes in order to see." In an attempt to focus and get into a positive frame of mind before your meeting, take Gauguin's advice and envision a successful and productive meeting, before it begins.

For a few moments, close your eyes and imagine the meeting room and the participants seated in their chairs. Envision the discussion proceeding smoothly, cooperatively, and productively. See people contributing in positive, friendly ways. See the group generating creative solutions. See as many details of this mental picture as possible. Relax and let your mind create positive images of what you would like to occur. See the success you will help create at the meeting.

Arrive Early to the Meeting

Arrive ten to fifteen minutes early to the meeting. Arrange chairs in a circle so everyone can see one another, check the lighting, open windows if it's stuffy, and plug in the coffee maker. No, a secretary or assistant isn't supposed to do this— remember, effective leadership means effective service. You're creating a space where effective, productive work will occur. Joe says, "I like to get a feel for the room, relax, and catch my breath before everyone arrives." So should you. Create some space between the time you arrive and the time you begin. That slice of time can make a big difference in how calm and centered you are during the meeting.

Mingle with Members as They Arrive

Mingle, join in, and make group members feel welcomed as they arrive to the meeting. Thank people for coming early. Listen to them and be really present in mind and body.

Begin the Meeting on Time

Announce to the group that you'll be starting in a few minutes, right before the scheduled meeting time. Invite them to get another cup of coffee and then move to your seat. After they see you seated, they will follow. *Begin the meeting on time!*

This is the first official act you perform each meeting. Don't be sloppy or indecisive with this responsibility. Your behavior creates the norms to which group members will conform in the future. If you start late, they will arrive late because that's the behavior you are encouraging. If you begin the meeting on time, they will arrive on time because that's the behavior you are modeling.

Make Announcements Quickly

Once everyone is seated, get any announcements that weren't included in the agenda out of the way as quickly as possible. Announcements are not open to debate or discussion. Briefly answer any questions about the announcements. This is not the time to get bogged down with tangential remarks and offtrack discussions.

State Objectives and Time Limits

After you have thanked group members for attending, state the objective or objectives of the meeting. Provide a tentative time limit for each objective or agenda item, and state the ending time for the meeting. Group members appreciate a leader who announces the time limits for agenda items and the ending time of the meeting. It gets things out in the open and provides a framework for discussion.

Don't Stop the Meeting for Latecomers

Sometimes a group member will arrive late to the meeting. Do not recap what has already been covered and don't acknowledge or listen to excuses for being late. Simply continue the discussion without paying attention to the latecomer. Chronic tardiness can be a symptom of passive-aggressive behavior (indirect anger directed at you or the group) or a challenge to your power. Don't give the chronic latecomer any attention or power.

Restate the Objectives and Time Limits Periodically

Every ten or fifteen minutes, restate the current objective and how many minutes are left in the meeting. If possible, avoid holding any meeting for more than sixty minutes. People get tired and bored after an hour. If you must go beyond sixty minutes, take a five-minute stretching or restroom break and then resume your meeting. Your group will appreciate the time to stretch and get a change of scenery.

Remain Impartial

Remember, as the leader, your primary goal is to ensure the smooth functioning of the task and social dimensions of the group. Let all group members voice their opinions on a particular issue before you voice yours. Your duty is to solicit and guide the group's discussion so it stays on track and on time. Your job is to serve the group, to guide the group to its goal.

Guide the Group

Use the specific task and social guiding behaviors presented earlier in this chapter to guide the group. Keep a note card summary of these guiding behaviors in front of you during each meeting as a reminder.

Seek Participation from Everyone

Occasionally ask for the opinions of those members who have not contributed and summarize the longer contributions of those who talk too much. Your group needs to see that you are attempting to seek participation from everyone.

Summarize Often

Summarize to focus discussion, quiet high verbals (talkative people), and keep the group on time. Look for opportune moments to summarize the group's progress, especially when discussion has generated three or four good ideas.

Compliment Members Often

Be aware of the positive contributions from members and compliment them during the meeting. Someone once said, "A person can accomplish a great deal if he doesn't worry about who gets the credit." Don't worry about who ultimately gets credit for anything the group does. Give credit (and compliments) liberally to group members. You will not only boost their self-confidence, you will create an atmosphere that encourages participation and member loyalty to you.

Keep the Meeting Moving

Try not to get bogged down on any one item or issue for too long. Table items to the next meeting if additional information is required or if the tension in the group is getting too great. Remember to summarize and state the time remaining in the meeting. During the last five minutes of the meeting, I usually give time remaining announcements a couple of times: "We have four minutes left," and "We have two minutes left."

In your attempts to keep the meeting moving, you will have to prohibit tangential talk, long-winded speakers, and inappropriate discussions. You will have to say no to others occasionally to get the job done. But as British Prime Minister Tony Blair says, "The art of leadership is saying no, not saying yes. It is very easy to say yes." You need to create boundaries within which effective discussion can occur.

End the Meeting on Time

By ending the meeting on time, you establish one of the most powerful norms of group work. That norm is "This leader ends when she says she will end, so I'd better say what I want and accomplish what I intend during the time or I'll have to wait until the next meeting." Or, stated another way, the norm you establish is "This leader keeps her promises."

Group members will love you for ending the meeting on time. Each one of them has a life outside the group. So end on time and let them get on with their lives. During the last minute or so of each meeting, summarize the objective or objectives the group has accomplished and remind members of the next meeting time and date.

CREATING HEALTHY LEADERSHIP: THE L.I.G.H.T. TECHNIQUE

The duties and responsibilities of a leadership position can be psychologically taxing, emotionally fatiguing, and physically draining. To avoid leader burnout, use the L.I.G.H.T. Technique to take good care of yourself when you are the leader of a problem-solving group. These five suggestions help you remain centered, open, and productive in your role as leader.

Learn new things

Every experience in our lives can be viewed as a lesson we were meant to learn during our lifetime. Your role as the group leader can provide a rich and wonderful learning experience for you. You will learn many new things about yourself— how you handle greater responsibility, how you deal with conflict, how you encourage and inspire others, how you react to criticism and failure, and how you respond to success and achievement. These and many other lessons will be yours when you become a leader.

Involve group members

As the group leader, don't attempt to do all the work yourself. Many individuals who aspire to leadership positions want to control the group process so much that they become overly involved and committed to the process. Before long, they are involved in every aspect of the process, from researching to implementing the solution. Without being careful, they can easily become overwhelmed by the many things to accomplish.

To avoid leader burnout and bitterness, involve other group members whenever you can. Delegate. Delegate. Delegate. Don't attempt to do everything yourself. You are dispensable. If you were to quit the group today, another leader would take your place and the tasks that face the group today will be solved tomorrow or the next day.

Give yourself a break

Self-doubt, self-criticism, and self-punishment can cripple and immobilize even the best leaders. No one is perfect. We all make mistakes. No leader is blameless or beyond error. We need to accept our faults and weaknesses, as well as our strengths.

When you become a group leader, don't be too demanding on yourself. Don't beat yourself after every minor mistake. You don't have to be perfect. You don't have to lead like someone else. You do, however, have to discover your own natural way of leading others. In the long run, you have to be yourself or you'll exhaust yourself by pretending to be someone you are not. Give yourself a break.

Hide your ego

You will need to create ways to detach from your ego if you are to be an effective leader. Once you enter the meeting room, you will have to hide or protect your ego, or forever be pulled and tugged, hurt and angered by every questioning remark and critical suggestion directed to you during the heat of discussion. Remember, you're not supposed to be their friend. Your role is to lead.

Take time for other things

Sometimes, being obsessive is one of the most common mistakes leaders make. They do nothing but eat, think, and sleep their role as leader. The leadership position consumes their days and haunts their nights. To avoid this, make sure you leave time in your daily life for other things. Talk with loved ones and friends about anything other than your problem-solving task. Take up a new sport or hobby. Spend more time with your partner or children doing things you meant to do last summer. See more matinees during the week. Take walks around the neighborhood and make some new acquaintances. Teach your dog new tricks. Create balance in your life. Take time for other things.

> Great artists are people who find the way to be themselves in their art.
>
> —DAME MARGOT FONTEYN

"Leadership," observed Adlai Stevenson, "is an art; like painting, it can't be learned by reading." So take the opportunity to lead a group sometime in the near future. You won't really learn how to lead until you actually walk into that room and take your chair as the leader. Like Joe Samuels, arrive early, be a guide, and end on time. Your group will love you.

EXPLORING CREATIVE TASKS

1. Interview an individual you consider an effective leader at work, at school, or in the community. Make a list of questions about this person's role as a leader, his or her leadership style, specific suggestions about managing people and meetings, and what he or she has learned about himself or herself as a leader. How did your interview go? What did you learn about leadership and the individual you interviewed? Would you like his or her job? What did you learn about yourself?

2. List behaviors or characteristics that describe your current leadership style. As you review your list, which leadership style—autocratic, democratic, or laissez-faire— seems to be the one you are most comfortable with? Why? Which aspects of the other approaches could you benefit from using? Why?

3. The next time you're in a discussion with a group of friends, try using one or two of the guiding task behaviors presented in this chapter. Don't make your contributions too obvious. What were your friends' responses to your contributions? How did your guiding behavior affect the discussion? How did you feel about doing something new in this group?

4. Conduct a meeting at work, at school, or in the community, using some of the twenty suggestions presented in this chapter. What suggestions were you able to follow? How did your meeting go? What might you do differently if you were to lead the same group again? Why?

EXPANDING YOUR CREATIVE THINKING

1. In terms of social guiding behaviors, such as encouraging, expressing feelings, harmonizing, and energizing, which individuals in your personal life have contributed to your well-being? What can you do to acknowledge or thank these individuals for their contributions?

2. Who is the most effective leader you have ever worked with? What was his or her leadership style? What specific behaviors made this individual effective in the task dimension? What specific behaviors made this individual effective in the social dimension? How did he or she respond to conflict within the group? Have you ever shared these perceptions and feelings with him or her? Why or why not?

3. To what community, religious, or work group could you volunteer your time and your leadership skills? How could you specifically put your leadership skills to use? What do you think it would be like to volunteer for this group for six months? What benefits would you derive from working with this group?

4. What leadership positions do you see yourself assuming in your professional career? How could your leadership skills improve your job performance? What leadership skills might improve your future relationships? If you could improve one specific leadership skill in the future, what would it be? Why?

TEN

Creating Skillful Communication in a Speech

> *Your speech, like life,*
> *has a beginning, middle, and end.*
>
> —GLENN MILLS

Sarah is a neighbor and a gifted artist whose paintings hang on the walls of a number of homes in our little town. Recently she knocked on my door to talk about a problem.

"Randy, I've been asked to give a speech at a regional art conference and I'm terrified," Sarah confessed. "What should I do?"

"What are you afraid of?" I asked.

"I just keep thinking that I'll freeze up," she complained. "I want to do well, to have them like me. I've written the whole thing out, but I can't seem to memorize it. What's the problem?"

"You're the problem, Sarah," I said. "You're thinking too much about yourself."

"What do you mean?"

"I mean you're focused on yourself—how well you'll do, how much you want them to like you. The secret to giving a good speech is to focus on your audience rather than yourself."

"How do I do that?" she asked.

"By seeing yourself as a blessing to your audience. To see yourself as a giver of gifts—giving your listeners that will be helpful, encouraging, and even inspiring. That's the secret."

Sarah's speech was a hit at the conference! She kept her speech focused, relevant, and simple. From the perspective of giving a gift rather than making a speech, her speech topic, material, and delivery took on a different goal—to be a blessing to her listeners rather than a contestant to be judged. That made all the difference.

Giving a speech can be seen as a way of creating and bringing a gift to your audience. A speech can be your gift to others—a way you can enlarge, inspire, and improve those who listen to your words.

PUBLIC SPEAKING

During your lifetime you will be called on to speak in front of others. At school, you may deliver an oral report, chair a panel discussion, or speak at an awards banquet. At work, you may give a sales presentation, present your ideas about a new product line, or serve as master of ceremonies for a retirement dinner. In your community, you may address a city council meeting, speak at a public forum, or run for public office. In your personal life, you may share a story at a family reunion, give a toast at a wedding reception, or talk at an anniversary party.

Public speaking is speaking before an audience for a specific purpose. Each of the examples just mentioned involved delivering a speech, in front of an audience, with a specific purpose in mind. The three general purposes of speaking are to inform, persuade, or entertain. The purpose of **informative speaking** is to expand or broaden your listener's knowledge and skill. A lecture, a gun safety demonstration, and a sales report are examples of informative speaking. The purpose of **persuasive speaking** is to change what your listeners think or do. A sales presentation, a campaign speech, and closing arguments in a court trial are examples of persuasive speaking. The purpose of **speaking to entertain** is to amuse, please, or charm the audience. After-dinner speeches, the welcoming speech at a convention, and stand-up comedy are examples of speaking to entertain. The first step in creating a successful speech is to determine the general purpose of your speech. Are you going to inform, persuade, or entertain?

DETERMINING YOUR SPECIFIC PURPOSE

Once you have decided on your general speaking purpose, you can proceed to the specific purpose for the speech. The **specific purpose statement** is the goal you hope to achieve for your speech. Your specific purpose statement includes your general purpose, the intended audience, and the desired result or goal of the speech. Here are some examples of specific purpose statements:

To *inform* the audience about *making a coffee table*
To *persuade* the audience to *buy mutual funds*
To *entertain* the audience with a *poem*

A specific purpose statement should clearly state your intended purpose of informing, persuading, or entertaining. It should have only one goal, such as "making a coffee table" or "buying mutual funds." Having more than one goal divides your efforts and focus as well as your audience's attention. Keep your purpose as specific as possible. Have only one goal in mind for every speech.

ANALYZING THE SPEAKING SITUATION

Once you have decided on the specific purpose for the speech, you are ready to analyze the speaking situation, which includes the speaking occasion and the audience. This information will help you focus your speech research and preparation.

The Speaking Occasion

The following questions will help you analyze the speaking occasion. What is the nature and intent of the occasion? Will it be a formal occasion or a backyard gathering? Is your speech expected to be informative, persuasive, or entertaining? What are the time limits? Will there be a question-and-answer period following your speech? How many speakers will there be? What type of dress or attire would be appropriate? What is the size of the audience? Where will the speaking event be held? Your inquiries regarding the speaking occasion will help focus and shape the speech you are about to prepare.

The Audience

Once you understand the speaking occasion, consider your audience. There are four areas of audience analysis to explore before you research and prepare your talk—the audience's interest, attitude, knowledge, and demographics.

Is this an audience or an oil painting? I should have prepared for you guys a little more.

—MILTON BERLE

Interest. The first area of analysis is the audience's interest in your topic. Will they be interested in the topic you have chosen? Or will they be bored? The answers to these questions will often determine the topic of your speech. Most of the time, however, you will be asked to speak on a topic that is of interest to the audience.

Attitude. The audience may be interested in your topic, but what is their attitude toward it? Are they in favor of it? Are they against it? Or do they hold a neutral attitude? The answer to these questions will determine how you approach the audience with your topic. If they are in favor of your topic, consider presenting new or creative information about the subject. If they hold a neutral attitude, consider raising their curiosity or stimulating their interest. If they hold a negative attitude, consider trying to neutralize or minimize their opposition to your topic. You may even consider changing the topic if their opposition is too great.

Knowledge. How much does your audience know about your topic? Speak at an appropriate level so your audience will understand. Don't talk about material they already know and avoid introducing information they are unable to understand. By considering their knowledge of the topic, you can avoid boring or confusing your audience.

Demographics. Determine the demographics of the audience members. What is the gender of the audience? Are they male, female, or both genders? What is average age of the group? Are they children, young parents, or retired folks? What is the economic status of the audience? What is the cultural background of the audience? Is it a homogeneous group of people from the same ethnic or racial background or will there be individuals from a variety of cultures?

The information you gather about your audience will help you research and shape a speech that will interest your audience. But in the end, your enthusiasm and interest in your topic will ultimately determine its success. You must be interested in your topic to deliver a speech that will interest your audience, no matter how they may feel about it beforehand.

RESEARCHING YOUR SPEECH

After you have determined your specific purpose and analyzed the speaking occasion and audience, you are ready to begin gathering information to include in your talk.

Sources of Information

There are four sources of information from which you will collect the material for your speech—your personal knowledge and experience, library resources, the Internet, and interviews.

Your personal knowledge and experience. Before you begin your formal research at the library, on the Internet, or with an interview, survey your own knowledge of and experience with the speech topic. What do you already know about the topic from classes you have taken, books and magazines you have read, television programs you have seen, and people you have talked with? What personal experiences have you had with the subject of your speech? Many times your personal experience and knowledge will provide some of the most stimulating, compelling, and memorable information on your topic.

Library resources. College, university, and community libraries are a wonderful source of information. Don't be overwhelmed by all the books, computers, magazines, reference books, and equipment that are contained in even the most basic library. If you aren't familiar with them, ask a librarian for help. No matter what size library you use, you should know how to search the library catalog, the *Reader's Guide to Periodical Literature,* newspaper indexes, the Internet, and reference books.

The **library catalog** is the main source of information about the books that are available to you. Most library catalogs are computer listed, although some libraries may still use the card catalog system. The books are listed by author, title, and subject.

The ***Reader's Guide to Periodical Literature*** is an index of articles published in popular magazines, such as *Time* and *Newsweek,* and many major newspapers, such as the *Wall Street Journal* and the *New York Times.* There are other guides to scientific and specialty areas of research and investigation, so talk to the librarian about your topic for additional information.

Newspaper indexes are the third source of information you should be familiar with when you're conducting research, because they can provide local and up-to-date information and stories for your subject.

The Internet. The **Internet,** a worldwide collection of computer networks, is one of the most powerful tools you have to access information from all over the world. With it, you literally have the collective knowledge of millions of organizations, groups, and people at your fingertips. Chances are you have already used or will use the Internet to research a paper, check the stock market, or buy a concert ticket. The Internet can also be a great source of information for researching your speeches. If you are unfamiliar with using the Internet, ask a librarian for help or consider enrolling in an Internet class. The few hours you invest learning how to use the Internet will produce countless benefits in the coming years.

When using the Internet, keep these two facts in mind. First, much of the information on the Internet lacks authority. Anyone with a computer and Internet access can post information, so some of the information you get can be outdated, misleading, or false. You will need to evaluate the information with care. Second, many valuable sources of information are not available on the Internet, such as copyrighted books, encyclopedias, index and abstract services, and scholarly journals. Therefore, you will still need to make a trip to the library when researching a speech topic.

As you access and evaluate information from the Internet, ask the following questions:

1. Is the author of the information a qualified expert in the field? What are the credentials of the author, the organization, or agency posting the information?

2. Is the information accurate? Is the information consistent with your library research?
3. Is the information current? Are the sources up-to-date? If no date is given, the information may be old.
4. Is the information objective? Are sources cited? Are the conclusions based on fact? Are personal opinions and bias clearly stated?

Whatever Internet information you consider, you owe it to your audience to present data from reliable, objective, and current sources. Subject your Internet information to the same standards you would library information. You don't want to create a misleading or false message in your speech.

Interviews. The final source of information to consider using is interviews with experts. By conducting an interview with an expert in the subject, you can gather a different perspective on your subject. It's one thing to read about the topic you are researching, but another thing to talk with an individual who has training and experience with the subject. As well as gathering interview material, you will be adding to the credibility of your speech with the inclusion of expert opinion. (Chapter 12 discusses information-gathering interviews. Read it before conducting an interview with an expert.)

Supporting Material

When you are researching your speech topic, look for material that will support the main points of your speech. The six types of supporting material to look for are definitions, examples, stories, comparisons, statistics, and expert opinion.

Definitions. The most basic form of supporting material is the definition. A **definition** is the meaning of a word. That dictionary on your desk or the one you have in your computer is a convenient source of information when you are looking for definitions of important or uncommon terms to use in your speech. Define important or key terms in your speech if they are not commonly known or understood by your audience. For example, if your speech is on the Jungian concept of the "archetype," you may need to define the term because it may not be familiar to your audience. By the way, an archetype is "an original model after which other similar things are patterned."

Examples. Examples are brief illustrations that support or back up a point you are attempting to make. They can also help add interest or clarify points of your speech. For example, the definition for an "archetype" may not be clear to your audience, so an example or two could help them better understand the term. An example of an archetype would be the model or concept of the "wise old woman." In every culture from the beginning of recorded history, the archetype or model of the "wise old woman" has shown up in stories, myths, and traditions. When researching your speech, look for examples that will illustrate, clarify, and explain important terms and ideas.

Stories. A **story** is a detailed account of an incident that illustrates a point. Stories are remembered long after statistics, quotations, and expert testimony are forgotten by your audience. A well-told story can serve as the cornerstone of a skillfully constructed speech. Use stories often in your speeches. Stories can be factual or hypothetical. Hypothetical stories are fictional accounts that may easily have happened, and factual stories are accounts of incidents that actually happened to you or someone else.

Comparisons. One of the most effective ways to present new information to an audience is to use a comparison. A **comparison** shows how one idea or object is similar to another. Comparisons usually connect something that is new or unfamiliar with something that is known or familiar to the audience. For example, you can compare an archetype with a template or a mold, so your audience can see the similarities and begin to understand the concept of the archetype.

Statistics. **Statistics** are numerical facts that can be highly effective in making a succinct point. For example, one out of two marriages end in divorce, college graduates will earn an average of 40 percent more income than people with only a high school education during their first year of employment, and only 7 percent of all household garbage is recycled. Statistics can provide a great deal of information in a very small amount of time.

When using statistics, keep these five guidelines in mind:

1. Take your evidence from reliable sources.
2. Cite the author and source of your statistic before you present the figures.
3. Limit the use of statistics to one or two per main point.
4. Round off your statistics. Instead of 247.65 million, say nearly 250 million.
5. Use visual aids to present more than two or three related statistics. (Chapter 11 discusses the use of visual aids.)

Expert opinion. An **expert opinion** is a citation or testimony from an authority. Expert opinions can often state a point or explain a concept much more effectively than you. In addition, their expertise, training, and experience lend authority and credibility to your speech. It's one thing for me to say, "I believe that archetypes are important for us to study." But this assertion has added authority and credibility when I can use expert testimony to make my point: "Swiss psychiatrist Carl Jung states that 'The understanding of archetypes is the first step we must take to understand the longings, dreams, and fantasies we experience in our lifetime.'"

Your use of expert opinion can be more effective if you consider these guidelines:

1. Cite the source of the expert opinion before you present the citation.
2. Use experts who have credibility with your specific audience.

3. Keep your quotation brief—twenty words or fewer; paraphrase if longer.
4. Restate the quotation in your own words if the language is too technical or confusing for your audience. ("What the author is saying is...")

Recording Your Information

When you are researching your speech, record any useful information. There are many different methods you can use from writing every piece of information on a single sheet of paper to making audio recordings with a microcassette recorder. The most functional and convenient method utilizes 3 x 5" or 4 x 6" index cards. For each piece of information, record the author, source, date, and information on an index card. A research card looks like this:

> "Don't take yourself too seriously on this journey. Give yourself permission to make mistakes along the way."
>
> Randy Fujishin, *The Natural Speaker*. 2008.

The advantage of the index card technique for recording research information is that you can use the cards to construct the main points of your speech when you are ready to outline your talk. By sorting the evidence cards into piles representing different categories, you can visually see your speech taking shape. They also helps you to rearrange, add, and delete information as you see fit, without your having to rewrite, erase, or draw arrows.

Plagiarism

As you research information for a speech, give proper credit to the sources of your evidence. This is essential to your role as an ethical speaker. To do anything less is a serious breach of ethical speaking. Plagiarism is the use of another person's ideas or words as your own. Be careful to guard against using the information of another person as if you wrote it yourself to avoid any appearance of plagiarism.

Failing to cite the sources of your speech material is unethical and a form of stealing. If you're caught plagiarizing by your instructor, a member of the audience, or even someone viewing your speech on DVD long after you've made your presentation, the consequences for your act of stealing can be serious. Students can be flunked from their class and even placed on academic probation. Public figures can have their reputations tarnished or ruined because they stole words and ideas without giving proper credit.

A helpful rule for avoiding plagiarism is this—any piece of information in your speech that is not common knowledge should be documented in your speech outline and cited orally in the speech. The sources of expert testimony, statistics, facts, or study findings should always be cited in your speech. Anything less is stealing.

ORGANIZING YOUR SPEECH

Once you have completed your research, you can begin to organize your speech. Every speech should be organized in a way that is easy for both the speaker and the audience to understand and remember. The old newspaper saying "First, tell them what you're going to tell them, then tell them, and finally tell them what you told them" also holds true for speeches. To create an effective speech, divide your message into an introduction, body, and conclusion. This organizational pattern gives a sense of wholeness to the speaking process.

The Body

Start by developing the body of your speech. Most of your speech will be made up of the main points or body. The body of the speech should constitute about 70 to 80 percent of your total speech time. You should have only three or four main points in your speech. More than five main points will dilute your efforts and will often confuse your listeners. You can give the body of your speech shape or structure by organizing your main points in a variety of ways.

Topical order. When you use topical order, the main point structure is up to your discretion. Your points can go from specific to general, from most important to least important, or in any order you determine to be most effective. Here is an example of topical order:

Specific purpose: To explain three aspects of homelessness.
I. Homelessness affects people from all walks of life.
II. Homelessness affects children.
III. Homelessness affects the community.

Chronological order. You can arrange the main points of your speech in chronological, or time, order. This organizational pattern lets your audience see a sequential order to your points. Here is an example of chronological order:

Specific purpose: To describe the steps to overcome homelessness.
I. The homeless individual learns employable skills.

II. The homeless individual acquires a job.

III. The homeless individual rents an apartment or home.

Spatial order. The third way you can arrange the main points of your speech is in spatial order. When you use spatial order, you arrange the main points according to physical or geographical sequence. This arrangement can help your audience visualize the subject of your speech. Here is an example of spatial order:

Specific purpose: To describe the three largest sections of the
California homeless.

I. The first section is the Los Angeles area.

II. The second section is the San Diego area.

III. The third section is the San Francisco Bay area.

Developing the main points of your speech. Once you have determined the order of your main points, begin selecting supporting material. This is where your research index cards come in very handy. Place your index cards in three or four piles, depending on the number of main points in your speech. Each pile will constitute one of your main points.

After you have three piles, look through each pile and begin selecting the cards you feel best develop each main point. Don't throw the unused cards away. Just put them to the side for the moment. It's funny how your idea of each main point can change. Before you know it, you may be rearranging, adding, and discarding your index cards many times before your speech takes its final form.

> *The real art of public speaking rests in exhausting your subject before you exhaust your audience.*
>
> —ADLAI STEVENSON

Keep these suggestions in mind when you're developing your speech:

1. Develop each main point equally. Evenly distribute your supporting material so that every point gets approximately the same development.
2. Use at least one piece of evidence to support each of your three points.
3. Include at least one well-developed story in the body of your speech.
4. Provide a variety of supporting material. In addition to evidence and stories, use comparisons, examples, definitions, and visual aids.

Transitions within the body. After you have adequately developed each main point, select transitions so you can guide your audience from one point to another. Remember the second point of the old newspaper adage, "tell them." Well, in the body of the speech, tell them, or signpost, each main point with a numbered transition. "The first point . . . ," "The second point . . . ," and "The third point . . ." are numbered transitions that tell your audience where you are in the speech.

The Introduction

Now that you have developed the body of the speech and set numbered transitions, you can move on to the introduction. Every speech should open with an introduction that contains an attention getter and a preview of main points. The entire introduction should consist of approximately 10 to 15 percent of the total speech time and should grab the audience's attention and focus it on your speech topic. Here are a few attention getters you can consider using.

Audience question. One of the easiest and most direct ways to open a speech is to ask an audience question: "Do you know a homeless person?" or "Have you ever wondered what it would be like to be homeless even for a day?"

Hypothetical situation. Begin a hypothetical situation with the words "Imagine yourself. . ." followed by the situation or condition you want to establish in the minds of your listeners: "Imagine yourself losing your job and not being able to pay your rent. Within two months you find yourself evicted from your apartment with no one to help you and nowhere to go. You've joined the ranks of the homeless."

Quotation. You can begin your speech with an appropriate quotation: "In her article on the homeless of San Francisco, reporter Holly Chin cautions, 'Many of us are just one or two paychecks away from being homeless, regardless of income level, so we need to rethink our vulnerability and our compassion.'"

Statistics. A startling statistic is an impressive way to begin your speech: "According to a recent *San Francisco Chronicle* article, one in five homeless are children under the age of twelve." A statistic also can add credibility to your speech.

Story. You can open your speech with a brief story. A well-told personal or hypothetical story can provide a powerful way to create intimacy with your audience. Stories often can state the theme or moral you want to convey in your speech, as well as establish rapport with your audience. If you use a brief story as an attention getter, be certain that it directly relates to the subject of your speech. An irrelevant story will confuse or distract your audience.

The second purpose of the introduction is to preview the main points of your speech. Remember, "tell them what you're going to tell them." A **preview of main points** is a one-sentence statement that lists the three or four points of your speech. "In my speech, I will define homelessness, discuss its causes, and suggests some solutions." Your preview of points prepares the audience for what is to follow.

The Conclusion

Once you finish organizing the body and introduction of your speech, you can organize the conclusion. Every conclusion should contain a review of your main points (remember to "tell them what you've told them") and a final thought or appeal. The conclusion should take approximately 10 to 15 percent of your total speaking time.

After you have completed your third or final main point of the speech, pause for one or two seconds. This gives your listeners a chance to catch their breath, collect their thoughts, and focus on your final words. Review the main points of the speech in one sentence. "Today, I've defined homelessness, discussed its causes, and presented some solutions." Use one sentence to summarize your three points. Then present a final thought, using one of the following devices.

Appeal. You can end your speech with an appeal to your audience. "I ask you to remember the homeless children whom I have spoken about today. I hope you will think about the statistics and stories I have shared with you describing the terrible, hopeless conditions of their young lives."

Call to action. You can conclude your speech with a call to action. "I want each of you to donate three dollars to the Save the Homeless Children Foundation. I have given you their envelope and placed a stamp on it. Now I want you to place just three dollars in that envelope and mail it today. Your generosity will feed a homeless child this very week. Thank you!"

Vision for the future. You can create a positive vision for the future in your final words to the audience. "I can see a society where there are no homeless children. I can envision a society in which every child is well fed, has a roof over his head, and a warm bed to snuggle in at night. With your help, we will all see this society come to be."

Return to the attention getter. You can end by coming full circle to the attention getter. "Like the young woman in my opening story, I hope you will donate your time and money to help homeless children receive the food, shelter, and love they so richly deserve. And like the woman in the story, I know you will experience a sense of satisfaction and accomplishment that comes when you help the homeless. Thank you!"

Whatever final-thought device you select, don't ramble or introduce new material. This is not the time to deliver a second speech. Know when to quit. Remember, your conclusion should take only 10 to 15 percent of your total speaking time.

CREATING YOUR SPEECH OUTLINE

Now that you've arranged your main points, selected the supporting material, and decided on your introduction and conclusion, you can create your speech outline. A **speech outline** is a brief full-sentence model of your speech.

I know what you're thinking: Do I have to write an outline for a speech? Yes, you do! It will save you a lot of headache and heartache. If you spend a few minutes outlining and structuring the framework of your proposed speech, you will be able to plan and test the ideas, organization, and reasoning of your talk before you face your audience. The framework of a speech holds the secret to its success by ensuring that its organization and content are sound.

Your speech outline is not a word-for-word manuscript of your speech. Instead, your outline will contain only about 20 to 30 percent of the actual number of spoken words in your speech. The introduction and the conclusion are written word for word to prevent rambling and give you the confidence when you'll need it the most, especially during the first minute of your speech. The body, however, is not written word for word. Instead, only the main points and subpoints are written and all the other material is shared in a more conversational fashion. For instance, one subpoint might read, "B. Story about the fishing trip to Lake Tahoe." It's only one sentence, but the story will take you forty-five seconds to share, in your own conversational speaking style.

Let's review some basic guidelines before you attempt to create your first speech outline:

1. Use a standard set of symbols. The main points of the speech can be divided by Roman numerals (I, II, III), subpoints with capital letters (A, B, C).
2. Use a complete-sentence structure for your introduction, conclusion, and main point transitions. Your subpoints can also be written in full sentences to give you a better idea of how your speech will sound.
3. Each of your main points should reinforce or clarify your specific purpose statement.
4. Every main point and subpoint should contain only one idea.
5. Limit your main point structure to three or four points.
6. Keep the number of words in your outline to 20 to 30 percent of your total for the speech.

To give you an idea of what a basic outline could look like, the sample on the following page is a sample informative speech outline.

BEING AN ETHICAL SPEAKER

As a speaker you have responsibility, above all else, to tell the truth, to speak honestly. You are never to lie, insult, or take advantage of your listeners. You need to be an ethical speaker. An **ethical speaker** is an individual who will choose to uphold the highest standards of integrity in truthfulness, topic selection, level of research, citation of evidence, and respectful delivery.

SAMPLE SPEECH OUTLINE

Specific purpose: To inform the audience about touching.

Introduction
When was the last time you received a hug? How about the last time you got a neck rub? Or maybe just a pat on the back? Well, touching is an important part of our human experience. Today, I'd like to tell you about touching. I want to explain what it is, how it can relieve stress, and how it can improve relationships.

Body
I. The first thing I want to share is what is touching.
   A. Touching is any form of skin-to-skin touching between individuals.
   B. Share 12 of the most common forms of touching in American culture.

II. The second thing I want to share is how touching can relieve stress.
   A. Story about massage during final exam week last spring semester.
   B. Helen Colton in her book *The Gift of Touch* says that "Human touch can relieve stress and reduce anxiety."

III. The third thing I want to share is how touching can improve relationships.
   A. Touching can express emotions at a level that words cannot.
   B. Touching deepens ties between individuals.
   C. Story about hugging my father during the last two years of his life.

Conclusion
Today I've shared what touching is, how it can relieve stress, and how it can improve relationships. It is my hope that you will make a conscious effort in the next day or two to increase the amount of touching you do with people you care about. Happy hugging!

Truthfulness. The most important guideline of an ethical speaker is truthfulness. You can present impressive information and have the most dynamic delivery style, but if you are not telling the truth, you are simply a liar. You have the ethical responsibility to tell the truth to your audience. If your audience discovers that you are exaggerating or lying, your credibility is forever tainted and held in question. Even if your lies are never discovered, you'll always know.

Topic Selection. You have an ethical responsibility to present topics that will benefit the audience, not insult or harm them. Select topics that you feel passionately about. Think of your speech as a gift you are giving, so avoid commonplace, boring, or harmful topics. Present your audience with a gift that will interest them, improve their lives, and inspire them to be better than they were before you spoke. Make a positive difference in the lives of those who listen to your words.

Level of Research. You also have the responsibility to research your topic as thoroughly as possible. Don't be satisfied by just collecting the minimal amount of content material needed to fill their speaking time. Your audience deserves the most relevant, accurate, and recent information you can provide. As an ethical speaker, give your audience the best information available.

Citation of Evidence. Give credit where credit is due. Cite the source of any information or evidence you present in your speech. When you quote someone directly, provide the name of the person and the source you are quoting. When you present statistics remember to cite the source of your information. Plagiarism is taking someone else's idea and trying to pass it off as your own (this topic was explored in greater detail earlier in this chapter).

Respectful Delivery. You have a number of ethical responsibilities to consider when you are actually addressing your audience. First, be punctual. Arrive on time. Or better yet, arrive early. Second, be the best-dressed person at the speaking event. Avoid clothing that is inappropriate to the occasion, sloppy, or provocative. Third, avoid offensive, rude, or vulgar language. Speak to the highest interest and motives of your audience. Honor your listeners with the words you select and the manner in which you speak.

In the end, you are only as good as your word. Tell the truth, respect your audience, and live a life of integrity.

SPEAKER DELIVERY

Delivery is all the nonverbal communication you express when you are giving a speech. It includes your appearance, eye contact, rate of speech, volume, pitch, vocal variety, facial expressions, posture, body movement, and hand gestures. Your delivery is the overall impression your audience develops about "who" you are, not "what" you say.

Everyone has a very distinctive yet natural way of speaking. Your voice doesn't sound exactly like anyone else's in the entire world. Your posture, movements, gestures, and facial expressions are, in many ways, unique to only you. How you talk and how you express yourself naturally is who you are. So, rather than wishing to sound, act, or be someone else, you should appreciate your uniqueness—your voice, body, and movement—and speak in a manner that is natural to you.

Delivery Methods

No matter what unique style of delivery you possess, there are four different approaches or methods for presenting the content of any speech. Each method has its own strengths and weaknesses. The four delivery methods are manuscript, memorized, impromptu, and extemporaneous.

Manuscript delivery. **Manuscript delivery** is reading the speech word for word from a manuscript. Using this method, you write out the speech word for word and read the manuscript to the audience, without straying from the text.

The advantage of the manuscript delivery method is that the content of the speech is guaranteed. For the purposes of the president's State of the Union Address, a scientific report, or a press conference announcement, the manuscript delivery method is appropriate.

Delivering a speech from a manuscript, however, has some distinct disadvantages. First, the speech oftentimes sounds read and not delivered with spontaneity and life. Second, your eye contact with the audience is limited or eliminated because the speech is being read and your attention is on the manuscript. Third, you cannot modify the content of the speech to accommodate feedback from the audience because the text has already been determined.

Memorized delivery. Using the **memorized delivery** method, you memorize the entire speech word for word, and then recite the speech without the use of the manuscript or even notes.

One advantage that the memorized delivery method provides is greater eye contact with the audience because there is no manuscript to read. Another advantage is that body movements and gestures are more spontaneous because you are no longer reading and flipping the pages of the text. Actors, tour guides, and an occasional professor will utilize this method.

There are some disadvantages to this delivery style. First, you have to write the entire speech word for word, like a term paper. Second, you have to memorize the entire speech word for word, which, of course, is not required when you write a paper. The time and effort spent memorizing even a brief speech is taxing to say the least. Third, even assuming you've memorized the speech, if you forget just one word—just one—you run the risk of panicking and forgetting everything else that follows.

Impromptu delivery. The **impromptu delivery** method is when you give a speech without any prior preparation or practice. This style is appropriate when you respond to an inquiry during a business meeting or answer a question during an interview, but most formal speaking situations require research, preparation, and practice for a successful speech.

Extemporaneous delivery. **Extemporaneous delivery** is speech that is prepared and practiced ahead of time, but whose exact wording isn't determined until you deliver the speech. This method of speaking combines the strengths of the manuscript, memorized, and impromptu methods, and eliminates most of their weaknesses.

The greatest advantage of extemporaneous speaking is that you are organized and know what needs to be covered, much like the manuscript and memorized methods, but without losing the natural delivery or forgetting one of the hundreds of words in the text. Extemporaneous speaking is the best method for creating an effective and successful speech in almost every speaking situation.

With extemporaneous speaking, you research, outline, and practice the speech ahead of time. The outline contains 20 to 30 percent of the wording of the speech, which you commit to memory. But you determine the exact wording of the remaining 70 to 80 percent of the speech when you deliver the speech. This provides you with the flexibility and creativity to respond to the audience and make minor modifications to the speech according to the feedback from the audience. In other words, you have the opportunity to make your speech fit the specific audience. However, you memorize the introduction and the conclusion word for word to obtain the confidence to begin and end the speech in a predetermined fashion.

Also, you can practice the speech ahead of time. Write the key words from the speech outline on one or two note cards to serve as reminders during your practice sessions and during the actual speech itself. Practice the entire speech five times to get a good command of the material. Too little practice will not give you content mastery and too much practice can make the speech sound memorized. Find your balance between too much and too little.

Requirements for Natural Delivery

We're all familiar with the saying "It's not what you say, but how you say it that's important." Well, in public speaking, "how you say it," or how you nonverbally communicate your message to the audience, is as important as what you say. As a speaker, you may use all the right words and present all the correct supporting material, but if the audience senses you are being insincere, apathetic, or manipulative, they may disregard or discount what you say.

What can you do to prevent this? It is essential that you present a topic you believe in. If you are not convinced of your message's importance and relevance for your audience, you will never convince them either. Perhaps equally important, however, is your ability to deliver your speech in a natural, genuine fashion. An enlarged conversational tone, speaker genuineness, and a desire to communicate are the three requirements for natural delivery.

Enlarged conversational tone. An enlarged conversational tone of voice is most effective in communicating speaker naturalness. An **enlarged conversational tone** means speaking with the same naturalness and qualities you use in regular conversation, only enlarged or increased to accommodate all of your audience. Talk to your audience in a conversational tone of voice that the people in the back of the room can hear.

The primary advantage to using an enlarged conversational tone is that each audience member will feel as if you are talking to him or her individually. There is a genuineness and an intimacy to this conversational style of delivery. It doesn't promote the detachment that a more rigid, exacting style of speaking might create. It doesn't foster the amusement that a more exaggerated, theatrical style of speaking could evoke. An enlarged conversational tone sounds more natural, more you.

Speaker genuineness. **Speaker genuineness** refers to your using posture, body movements, facial expressions, eye contact, and hand gestures that are familiar and comfortable for you. What does your body feel comfortable doing when you're talking with family, friends, and acquaintances? Are you animated, hands in the air, and voice full of vitality and dynamism? Are you gentler, more deliberate, and softer in voice and expression? Maybe it depends on the topic of discussion, whom you are talking with, and how you are feeling at the moment.

> *The only time you touch the hearts of your audience is when you're being yourself.*
>
> —BURL IVES

You have a range of nonverbal behaviors that feels good and right for you when speaking with others. You don't have to act or behave like someone else to be a good speaker. Be yourself when you talk to your audience.

Desire to communicate. Your **desire to communicate** gives the audience the feeling that you really want to be giving the speech. It conveys the feeling that you care about your message and the audience hearing it. When you truly convey a desire to communicate, you generate enthusiasm, conviction, and even joy. You don't have to shout, do cartwheels, and throw confetti. It's not about voice volume or body movement. It's about the feeling that you really want to talk with the audience, that you really want to be here and nowhere else.

You can create and convey this desire to communicate in two ways. First, select speech topics that you truly feel are important for your audience to hear. Speak on those topics that make you feel mad, sad, or glad. From the simple yet powerful emotions of anger, sadness, and happiness, you can select topics that have their origins deep within you. Deep speaks to deep. If you select topics that originate deep within you, you will evoke and touch deep parts of your audience. When you believe in your message, you will convey a desire to communicate with any audience.

Second, focus your attention on your audience. Look at your audience, not your notes. Make contact with individuals in the room. See them. Don't be afraid to look into their eyes. They want to hear what you have to say. If you've chosen your topic well, they need to hear what you have to say. See yourself as someone who will be presenting your audience with a gift by sharing information that will improve their lives and help make them more happy and whole. You can create an entirely different attitude by placing your audience above yourself.

Guidelines for Effective Delivery

In addition to the three requirements for natural delivery, consider the following guidelines for effective speaker delivery—dress appropriately, walk confidently to the podium, pause before speaking, look at your audience, stand and move naturally, gesture for emphasis, speak naturally, and end your speech confidently.

Dress appropriately. The clothes you wear will greatly influence the audience's perception of you, even before you speak your first words. As you walk to the podium, all eyes of the audience will be on you, so you want their initial impressions of you to be positive. This doesn't necessarily mean a suit and tie or a gown and heels. It does mean, however, that you dress appropriately for the occasion. If the speaking occasion calls for formal attire, then dress accordingly. If the setting is more casual, your clothing should be casual. Be the best-dressed person in the room. Not outlandishly so, just a notch or two above the rest. You can't go wrong with this formula.

Walk confidently to the podium. Your speech doesn't begin when you utter your first word. It really begins when you rise from your chair. The audience will observe you as you make your way to the front of the room. Walk confidently, hold your head high, and smile to the people you see along the way. Don't drag yourself up to the front of the room as if you're going to the gallows. Don't run to the podium with a wild burst of enthusiasm. Just walk confidently, remembering that your speech begins as soon as you come into the view of your listeners. You have an important message to share with them. Create a mood of expectancy.

Pause before speaking. Many times nervous speakers immediately rush into their speech even before reaching the podium. Get set physically before you begin your speech. After you have walked confidently to the front of the room, smile to individuals in the audience, glance around the room, and get accustomed to the view. Take a moment or two to pause, catch your breath, and get a feel for what you are about to do. No rushing here. Slow down. Pause. Command the attention of your audience.

Look at your audience. Before you begin your speech, establish eye contact with your audience. Look at individuals in your audience before you begin speaking. Smile to them as you see their faces. A speaker who looks at the audience is perceived as more sincere and involved than a speaker who looks down at his notes or stares above the heads of the listeners.

Establish and maintain eye contact with your audience as much as possible during your speech. Your eye contact is the most direct contact you will establish between you and your audience during the speech. Create that intimate involvement.

Stand and move naturally. Face your audience squarely, with your feet about shoulder-width apart. Don't lean on one foot more than another. Don't cross your legs. Just place your weight on both feet. If you're using a podium, don't lean on it or hide behind it. Stand one to two feet away from the podium, close enough to see your notes, yet far enough to gesture and move.

If you can, avoid using a podium altogether. It detracts from your effectiveness as a speaker. First, your audience doesn't get to see 60 to 70 percent of your body when it is hidden behind that terrible contraption. Second, it often limits hand gestures because of our tendency to lean or hold onto the podium. Finally, it hinders any body movement, because you are stuck behind the podium for the entire time you speak. Like a cage, it confines you to a space of about one square foot for the duration of your speech.

Gesture for emphasis. Use your hand and arm movements to emphasize and express important ideas and feelings during your speech. Beginning speakers often neglect to use hand gestures while speaking, preferring to clasp their hands behind their back, stuff them in their pockets, or rivet them to the podium. Rather than soothe or relax speakers, these fixed hand positions only increase their muscle tension and anxiety. By using hand gestures, you not only emphasize and express your ideas and feelings with greater effectiveness, you also relieve stress and tension.

> *Movements are as eloquent as words.*
>
> —ISADORA DUNCAN

Speak naturally. You don't have to sound like a television announcer or a professional actor to be an effective public speaker. In fact, listeners appreciate a speaker's natural voice, free of exaggeration, affect, and drama. It makes them feel that the real you is being shared. To make the most of your natural voice in public speaking, consider the following suggestions.

First, speak loud enough to be heard by all the listeners in your audience. **Volume** is how loudly or softly you speak. If you speak too softly, your audience will have a difficult time hearing you, and if you speak too loudly, your audience will be annoyed and distracted. Whether you are using a microphone or not, pay attention to those individuals in the back of audience. Are they hearing you? If in doubt, ask them. Adjust your volume so everyone can hear you. Isn't that the whole point of the speech?

Second, maintain a moderate rate of speech. **Rate** is the speed at which you talk. If your rate is too fast, your audience may experience difficulty following you and perceive it as a sign of nervousness. If your rate of speech is too slow, the audience may think you are unprepared, have lost your place, or are not interested in what you're sharing with them. Your rate of speech should be moderate, to maintain their interest and keep their minds from wandering.

Your rate of speech can be affected by pauses. Before and after important words or sentences, pause for emphasis. Silence can be a very powerful tool in highlighting important points you are trying to convey to your audience. Occasional pauses also demonstrate speaker confidence, in addition to giving your listeners a moment to consider and ponder what you have just shared.

Third, the pitch of your voice influences how an audience will perceive you. **Pitch** is the highness and lowness of your voice. You possess a natural range of pitch in which you are most comfortable speaking. For variety, you need to make full use of your pitch range by varying the highness and lowness of your voice when you speak. You don't want to sound monotone during your entire talk. Vary your pitch for emphasis and interest.

End your speech confidently. Like your introduction, your conclusion should also be delivered in a confident fashion. Many times speakers lose enthusiasm toward the end of their speech. They may rush or mumble as they close their speech. More often, speakers ramble during the conclusion, not knowing exactly how to end, or they will say "That's it" or "That's about all I have to say."

As you finish the third main point of the speech body, pause for at least three seconds as a nonverbal guidepost to your audience that the end is near. After your three second pause, summarize your three points in one sentence, and then deliver your final thought or appeal exactly as you practiced it. Don't add or delete any material now, just end your talk in a confident, natural manner. Then, smile, take a breath or two, and walk confidently back to your chair. Smile to those you see as you return to your seat. You've done a wonderful job, just as you knew you would!

Speaking Notes

When you're giving a speech, you might feel more confident having a few notes to guide you. If you do, here are some guidelines when constructing and using your speaking notes.

Use Note Cards. Use either 3 x 5" or 4 x 6" index cards when constructing your speaking notes. Don't use regular size papers, since they are more obvious and tend to make noise when handled. Index cards are easier to manage and won't fly off the podium if a breeze comes up. Number your note cards on the upper right-hand corner, so you can quickly place them in the correct order if they're ever mixed up.

Use Key Words and Phrases. Your speaking note cards should contain only key words and phrases. Unlike your formal outline, you don't need complete sentences in your speaking notes. Your preview of points can be a list of three words, rather than writing out the entire sentence.

Instead of writing out each main point transition in the body of the speech, you can just simply write "I. Define touching," "II. Relieves stress," and "III. Improves relationships." Instead of writing an entire story word for word, you can simply write, "Hugging dad story."

In the same way, each of your sub-points can be represented by one or two key words also. The review of points in the conclusion can be listed once again as three or four words and your final thought might be shortened to a couple of words or a phrase.

The purpose of the key word approach is to simply jar your memory a little so you can quickly recall the main points of your presentation without having to have all the detail of your formal outline.

You can also use your note cards to list the essential information of any evidence you'll be presenting. For instance, you need only list the documentation and the actual statistic or expert testimony you will present. Your note card can also indicate when you will be presenting any visual aids in your speech.

Use Note Cards Sparingly. Remember, this is not a manuscript speech or a formal outline you're trying to get on these speaking note cards. Just key words and phrases! One to two words for every fifteen seconds of speaking time is a good rule of thumb. So for a five-minute speech, twenty to forty key words at most ought to do it.

Place Cards On the Podium. Don't hold your note cards during your speech. Simply place your cards on the podium in chronological order from left to right and glance down at them when you need to. They're in place if you need them, but they shouldn't prevent good eye contact and directness with your audience.

PRACTICING YOUR SPEECH

Creating a skillful speech requires practice as well as thorough research and preparation. Practice is essential to success. Before you deliver your speech to an audience, you need to practice it. "We learn to do something by doing it," proclaims educator John Holt, and you learn to speak by speaking. Here are some suggestions for your practice sessions.

Practice Three Days in Advance

Do yourself a favor. Prepare your outline well in advance and give yourself the luxury of three days of practice. You'll practice your speech for only a few times each day, so you won't be investing a great deal of time. But the three days gives you the opportunity to get accustomed to your talk, make changes, and relax. This speech should be a part of you, so give yourself some time to get to know it, to become friends.

Practice Five to Ten Times

Practice your speech initially in small increments. Don't try to tackle the entire speech the first time you practice. Instead, go over the introduction a few times until you can recite it without error, then proceed to the first main point of the body and practice it until you are comfortable with the content. Continue this process with the second point, the third point, and the conclusion. Only after you have mastered each of the smaller parts of the speech should you attempt the entire speech for the first time.

> *I shall become a master of this art only after a great deal of practice.*
>
> —ERICH FROMM

Practice the entire speech two or three times during the first practice day. Practice two or three times the second day. Then practice one or two times the day before you are scheduled to give your talk. On the morning of your speech, practice delivering the entire speech only once. If you practice your speech more than ten times, you run the risk of sounding too memorized or mechanical.

Practice in a Quiet Room

Your practice room should be free from distractions, such as the phone, television, and people. Pick a quiet room in your home or apartment, during a time when everyone is gone. Shut the door. Unplug the phone. Close your eyes for a moment. Take a few breaths and block out the entire world. You're about to begin.

Practice in a Standing Position

You should stand while you practice. Many people practice their speeches at stoplights, in the grocery store checkout line, or in bed while worrying about the speech. These locations don't work. You need to feel and experience what it's going to be like when you give your speech. So standing and saying your speech out loud is the only way to accomplish this task. By the way, don't deliver your speech while standing in front of a full-length mirror. The mirror will only distract you from your practice. Concentrate on standing with your weight equally distributed on both feet, and using an enlarged conversational tone. You'll get the feel of speaking by actually speaking. You'll do well!

Time Your Practice Sessions

Using a watch with a second hand, time each of your practice sessions. Initially, time each component of your speech. If the introduction is running too long or too short, edit the content accordingly. By timing each part of your speech, you will be able to add or delete material as you go along, so that your entire speech during your final practice session should be within thirty seconds of your required time limit. Don't be afraid of the watch. It is one of your most helpful aids in speech practice.

Record Your Practice Sessions

Use an audiocassette recorder or a video camera to record your practice sessions. Both devices can provide valuable feedback on your delivery strengths and weaknesses. I know it may be difficult to get up the nerve to plug in the recorder or set up the camera to record your practice sessions. But the little time and effort you invest to record them will pay huge dividends on speech day. Fight the urge to cover up your head and hide. Plug in that equipment.

Evaluate Your Practice Sessions

Be gentle on yourself as you review the recordings of your practice sessions. Look for the strengths in your delivery. Observe the positive points of your body, gestures, face, and voice. Here is a list of items you can consider as you review your practice sessions.

Content
Was the topic appropriate and specific enough for the audience?
Was each main point developed equally and adequately?
Did your content contain human-interest stories?
Did your content contain documented research evidence?
Did you use vivid, descriptive language?

Organization
Did your introduction contain an attention getter?
Did your introduction contain a preview of main points?
Did the body contain numbered transitions before main points?
Did your conclusion contain a review of main points?
Did your conclusion contain a final thought or appeal?

Delivery
Did you get set and pause before speaking?
Did you show a clear desire to communicate?
Was your delivery natural and inviting?
Did you have straight posture?
Did you have relaxed, fluid body movements?
Did you have direct eye contact?
Did you have expressive gestures?
Was your voice loud enough?
Did you vary your voice volume, rate, and pitch?

These items are intended to focus your practice review. Don't feel as if you have to get everything perfect. The point is not to be perfect, but rather to deliver a speech that contains an important message for your audience, a speech that is a gift to your audience.

CREATING EASE IN GIVING SPEACHES: THE S.P.E.A.K. TECHNIQUE

Even after you have prepared and practiced your speech, you may feel anxious, frightened, or even terrified by the prospect of having to give your speech before an audience. Welcome to the club! Every speaker who accepts the responsibility of presenting a speech experiences some level of anxiety. It is the normal response most people have before giving a speech. Almost every novice speaker experiences some degree of stage fright—the sweaty palms, the butterfly stomach, the jumbled thoughts, and the fear of the unknown. You're not alone.

How would you feel giving a five-minute speech to five hundred people? Are you somewhat anxious just thinking about that prospect? How would you feel if the five hundred people were all speech instructors? A little bit more nervous? Most likely. Now, what would happen if those same five hundred people were all six months old—an auditorium full of baby cribs containing five hundred infants? You're probably not even a fraction as nervous as you were a moment ago when you were going to give your speech to five hundred speech instructors.

What's the difference? The difference is your perception of the possible negative evaluation of your audience. With five hundred speech instructors, the possible negative evaluation is great. Evaluating speeches is their job. With five hundred regular adults, the possibility of negative evaluation is somewhat less because evaluating speeches is not their duty. Finally, five hundred infants pose very little, if any, threat because their ability to evaluate a speech is nonexistent. Thus, the stage fright you experience in front of five hundred infants is almost nonexistent too.

You won't ever speak to an auditorium filled with infants, but you can do the next best thing. You can perceive or see the threat of negative evaluation from your audience in a very different light. Rather than viewing the audience as the enemy—as a group of people who could respond negatively to your speech—you can see them as your friends who support your speaking efforts, wish you well, and ultimately want the best for you. By changing how you perceive an audience, you can create a very different attitude and feeling within yourself.

Keep in mind the following S.P.E.A.K. Technique when you are preparing to give a speech and are concerned about stage fright. These five thoughts about speaking will enable you to deliver your speech with less fear and anxiety. In fact, they will help you welcome the opportunity to create skillful communication in your speeches.

See yourself as others do

This may be difficult for you to believe, but you appear much more relaxed to your audience than you feel when you're delivering your speech. Even though you may experience shallowness of breath, sweating palms, and a racing heart, your audience usually perceives you as being much more calm, relaxed, and confident than you feel internally. While viewing videotapes of their speeches, the vast majority of speakers are surprised by the level of composure, relaxation, and confidence they see in themselves, despite their memories of experiencing fear when speaking. Take heart; very few of your listeners will ever observe the fear you feel.

Prepare to learn about yourself

With the proper training, preparation, and attitude, giving a speech can help you learn about yourself. It can help you grow. Where else can you face one of your biggest fears, be a gift to others, and hear the applause of your audience all in one experience? Delivering an effective speech can make you happy, proud, and even inspired to experiment and experience your life more fully.

Experience reduces stress

With any physical skill or activity, the more you do it, the less anxiety you experience when repeating the behavior. As you obtain more experience speaking, you reduce your nervousness. In other words, speaking in front of an audience gets less frightening with experience.

Can you recall your first time swimming in the deep end of the pool, your first experience at the wheel of an automobile, or your first date? You probably remember your fear, anxiety, and visions of failure. But with each added experience, your fear diminished. The same holds true for public speaking. This may be your first time giving a speech. Take heart. You'll do well and with each successive experience at giving a speech, you become more confident and less anxious. The fear never leaves us completely, but experience does reduce anxiety.

Audience is your friend

Most people in an audience are attentive, supportive, and positive about you and your speech, if you give them half a chance. They are interested in what you have to say, want you to succeed, and are cheering you on. Whether it's in a public speaking class, a political rally, or an interest group, the audience is your friend. They want you to succeed. They wouldn't be there if they wished otherwise.

Keep the speech in perspective

Keep your speech in perspective. In the end, the speech you will be delivering is just a speech. It's not a life and death matter. It's only a speech that you'll be giving for a few minutes of your life. After you've concluded your speech, there will be a few moments of applause. Fifty minutes later, all the anxiety and worry will be long gone. Fifty days later, you will have a difficult time remembering what your speech was about. Fifty years later, you won't even remember you gave the speech. Maintain perspective on your speech. Do your best when delivering your speech, but in the light of eternity, it's not very significant. Be of good cheer. Create some space between you and your speech.

EXPLORING CREATIVE TASKS

1. List your fears about delivering a speech in front of an audience. Review the S.P.E.A.K. Technique regarding public speaking and see if any of the points apply to your specific fears. Which ideas were helpful in reducing your anxiety? What ideas can you suggest that will reduce or diminish your stage fright?

2. Prepare, practice, and deliver a five-minute informative speech entitled "My Future Career Goal." Your speech should contain an introduction, a body with three main points, and a conclusion.

3. Prepare, practice, and deliver a six-minute persuasive speech entitled "Three Reasons Why You Should. . . ." Select a persuasive topic you strongly believe in. Your speech should include an introduction, a body with three main points, and a conclusion.

4. Prepare, practice, and deliver a two-minute speech to entertain entitled "My Most Embarrassing Moment." Your story should contain descriptive language. Remember to deliver your speech with enthusiasm and expressive nonverbal delivery.

EXPANDING YOUR CREATIVE THINKING

1. Suppose a third-grade girl asked you to help her with a three-minute oral presentation she has to give in her class a week from now. The speech is entitled "Three Things I Love About My Life." The girl doesn't know anything about constructing a speech. What would you teach her about organizing and outlining this speech?

2. What makes you such an interesting person? What specific knowledge, experiences, and ideas do you possess that makes you different from most other people you know? What is the most important lesson or teaching you could give others from your personal life? Why would this be important to others?

3. To what kinds of careers, activities, or interests could you apply your public speaking skills? How could your public speaking skills improve your relationships with a romantic partner, children, family, and friends? What other ways could your speaking skills make your life more meaningful and rich?

4. If you could speak like any human being in the world, who would that person be? What attracts you to his or her speaking style? How could you specifically develop your speaking skills to resemble that particular speaker? How would you feel if you could speak exactly like that speaker? What would you miss about your own style of speaking?

ELEVEN

Creating Strategic Communication in Your Speeches

> Speech is power: speech is to persuade, to convert, to compel. It is to bring another out of his bad sense into your good sense.
>
> —RALPH WALDO EMERSON

Elizabeth is a college student who volunteers once a week to teach study skills at Scotts Valley High School. On any given Tuesday afternoon, you can find her in room C603 teaching study skills to a group of "at risk" students. The students like Elizabeth. She teaches in a simple, clever, and helpful style. Elizabeth tells stories that help them remember her points.

But what they really appreciate about Elizabeth are the times she gathers the group together at the beginning of each class. She sits the students in a circle and tells them how proud she is of each of them for coming to class, desiring to improve themselves, and for seeing the best in others.

At the end of class, they circle up a second time and Elizabeth briefly summarizes the day's activities and previews the skills that she'll talk about next week. But what they really love is her speech at the end. Elizabeth reminds them to choose to be better every day, to bless others, and to be gentle on themselves no matter what. "I'm here for you," she concludes her talk, "And I'm proud of you." With her words, Elizabeth creates a setting for people to learn, to be encouraged, and be blessed. And with your words, you too can teach, enlarge, and inspire others.

INFORMATIVE STRATEGIES

One of your life's most significant activities is to teach others new things, to pass on your knowledge, skills, and experience to those around you. In an individual way, you are instructing others. In a broader sense, you are passing on the culture.

Whether it's demonstrating the use of a laser printer at work, presenting a business report, leading a wildlife tour, or teaching a weekend gardening workshop, you are informing others. Elizabeth taught her students about study skills, but more important, she gave them encouragement, confidence, and inspiration. You will be given many opportunities to inform and instruct others during your lifetime, and you can do this creatively with skill and caring.

INFORMATIVE STRATEGY GOALS

There are three goals you must accomplish to be successful whenever you need to inform an audience. You must arouse the interest of your audience in your topic, assist their understanding of the material you are presenting, and help them remember what you have presented.

Arouse Audience Interest

Before your audience can understand your topic, they must be sufficiently interested in what you have to say. Without the audience's interest, you will be speaking to a group of people whose minds are wandering. Not a pleasant thought. To arouse audience interest, you should provide three kinds of information—relevant, new, and unusual.

Relevant information. First, your topic should be relevant to the audience. You are not giving this speech for your benefit. Your talk is aimed at informing or instructing the audience. As you consider possible topics to speak about, your analysis of the specific audience you will be addressing is crucial to the successful reception of your speech subject. Keep the focus on your audience. What is important to their lives? What are they interested in? How could they benefit from learning? Remember, it's about your audience, not you!

> The first goal of art is to capture the attention of the viewer.
>
> —NORMAN ROCKWELL

New information. Second, you can arouse interest in your topic by sharing new information with your audience. A topic may be relevant to an audience, but it may also be something they already know. For example, a speech about daily tooth brushing is relevant to everyone in your audience, but it is a subject that is common knowledge. We all know the benefits of daily brushing. Instead, present a speech on a new type of ultrasound toothbrush that will be on the market in the next year or a new product that effortlessly tests your teeth for plaque in only a few seconds.

Unusual information. Third, your audience's interest can be stimulated if your topic is unusual. Consider topics that are not your ordinary run-of-the-mill subjects. Consider topics and ideas in which you have interest, experience, or expertise that most other people do not. Spelunking, adjusting chronometers, coordinating hustings committees, raising spiders, and manufacturing torques are examples of unusual topics.

Help Your Audience Understand

Once you have stimulated the audience's attention and focused it on your speech topic, the second goal in your informative strategy is to help the audience understand the information you are presenting. In addition to clear speech organization (discussed in chapter 10), simple language, examples, and visual aids are three ways you can accomplish this goal.

Simple language. To help your audience understand what you have to say, it is essential that you speak in simple, clearly understood language. Although you may know more technical or complex language to communicate your ideas, use language your audience will understand.

Examples. Providing examples is one of the most concrete and effective ways you can help your audience understand the concepts and ideas you are attempting to communicate. An example provides a specific instance or incident that further illustrates the point you are attempting to make. If you are discussing the adventure a family can experience on a cross-country road trip, describe your family's trip to add depth and understanding.

Visual aids. Many concepts and ideas cannot adequately be expressed or communicated with words alone. They need to be communicated visually. Visual aids can be extremely effective in helping your audience understand your points.

The **speaker** can act as the simplest, most accessible visual aid. Your body can demonstrate how to massage a neck, block a kick, or sit in meditation in a way that words cannot. Use your body whenever you want to demonstrate a technique, emphasize a point, or act out a scene from a story.

Objects are helpful in giving the audience a look at what you are talking about. By showing the actual surfboard, guitar, or night vision scope, you leave little to misinterpretation. If possible, show any objects you will be discussing in your speech.

Drawings are the easiest visual aids to construct. Your drawing or sketch doesn't have to be a professional rendering. It simply needs to help your audience visualize what you are attempting to describe verbally. Keep your drawings simple. Stick figures, simple outlines, and basic sketches are all that are really necessary. Make certain your drawing is large enough to be seen by people in the back of the audience. Use dark colors that show contrast when used together. A picture is really worth a thousand words.

Charts and graphs can provide a wealth of information at a glance. The steps for a demonstration speech, a list of materials, word charts, color charts, flow charts, and organizational charts are just a few you can use to help your audience visualize important information. Bar graphs, line graphs, and pie graphs enable you to present a large amount of statistical information with one visual aid. Remember to make the numbers and lettering large enough for all the audience to see.

There are more elaborate yet relatively simple computer-assisted graphics programs that allow you to design professional-looking charts, graphs, and drawings for your speeches. **Microsoft PowerPoint** and **Adobe Persuasion** are two excellent software programs that can be helpful in designing and constructing visual aids for your presentations.

Electronic media such as audiocassettes, videotapes, overheads, and slides can also enhance the effectiveness of your presentations. Test any equipment you will be using ahead of time. Time the electronic presentation so it fits into the overall time limit of your speech. When you practice your speech, make certain that you include any electronic media you will be using.

Here are some guidelines to follow when using visual aids:

1. Be certain your audience can see your visual aid.
2. Talk to your audience, not your visual aid.
3. Remove your visual aid from sight when you are through with it.
4. Do not hand visual aids to the audience.
5. Use visual aids that need little or no explanation.
6. Use visual aids only to clarify or reinforce a point you are making.
7. Practice with your visual aid.

By constructing visual aids, you can put your other artistic skills, such as drawing, painting, pasting, and building, to good use. Create visual aids you'll be proud to display. Even your stick-figure visual aid says something about you, so let it convey a positive message.

Help Your Audience Remember

The final goal of creating strategic communication for an informative speech is to help your audience remember what you have shared with them. It does your audience no good if they focused attention on your speech and understood the concepts or skills you were sharing, but failed to remember anything you said.

How can you help improve your audience's memory when it comes to your specific speech? Well, much of that is out of your control. To a large extent, the retention of information is determined by each listener's level of interest, attitude, motivation, training, psychological state, and physical health. But there are some simple things you can do to create a speech that will be more memorable for your listeners. You can use creative main point structure, repetition, association, and memory objects.

> Powerful art is not
> easily forgotten,
> sometimes never.
>
> —ROBERT HENRI

Creative main point structure. One clever way you can help your audience remember your speech is to create a clever or catchy acronym that is made up of the key words from your speech. For example, "DOG" can be an acronym for *Discipline, Obedience,* and *Gentle*—the three main points or goals of your speech on training a puppy. By creating a clever acronym for the main points of your talk, you help your audience remember your speech, long after the applause has ended. What did "DOG" stand for?

Repetition. A second way you can help your audience remember your speech is by repeating key thoughts, ideas, and concepts during your presentation. Organizationally, your preview of main points in the introduction and your summary of main points in the conclusion are effective ways of repeating important ideas you want your audience to remember.

Repeat key thoughts, ideas, and statistics for emphasis by saying, "Let me repeat, the author warns us to . . . " or "I want to say that again. . . . " If you want to restate an important quotation or statistic in your own words to help your audience remember, you could add, "I think the author is telling us to . . . " or "I believe these statistics are saying that. . . . " Repetition is a powerful means of emphasizing and reminding your audience of the points that they need to remember.

Association. Having your listeners associate new information with something they are familiar with is another effective way to help your audience remember. The goal of association is to link the known with the unknown. For example, the process of blood clotting may be more easily understood and remembered by group of third-graders if you compare or associate it with mud drying or glue hardening. The concept of building an effective and satisfying relationship could be compared or associated with the process of building a beautiful and sturdy house. When you associate new information with the familiar, your audience is more likely to remember the concept, skill, or idea.

BASIC INFORMATIVE SPEECH STRUCTURES

Now that we've explored the three goals of strategic communication for informing an audience, let's examine specific informative structures or ways of arranging your information so your listeners will receive your speech most effectively.

Exposition Speeches

The primary purpose of an exposition speech is to expose or explain some object, process, or concept to an audience. Whether you are informing the audience about the structure of the human brain, the process of photosynthesis, or the concept of forgiveness, your main goal is explanation. Here are some helpful hints on presenting an exposition speech.

First, make sure that the topic is relevant to your particular audience. The topic should be useful or interesting to them. Without their interest, your efforts are doomed before you even begin researching your topic. The topic should be easily understood by your audience. The process of calculating advanced calculus formulas may interest a mathematics major, but it is way beyond the scope of algebra students. Make sure your topic can be readily understood by the audience. Finally, you should be able to cover your topic within the time limit. The creation of the universe would not be a wise topic choice for a five-minute speech. Here is a sample outline of a simple exposition speech:

> Specific purpose: To explain the process of preparing a speech.
> I. The first step is to research your speech.
> II. The second step is to outline your material.
> III. The final step is to practice your speech five times.

Description Speeches

The purpose of description speeches is to use sensory information to verbally describe something to the audience. In a sense, you use words to visually paint a picture in the minds of your listeners. In a description speech, visual language that describes size, shape, weight, and color are extremely effective in creating vivid mental images. Size can be described in terms of big and small, large and tiny. But for greater accuracy and description, exact measurements are much more effective. Shapes are geometric forms such as square, rectangle, triangle, round, and spherical. They can be used to add more specific description, such as the man "whose square, boxlike face contained an almost rectangular nose." The weight of an object can be used to describe an object. Which description is more vivid? The meteor was heavy or the meteor weighed almost fourteen tons? Finally, color is one of the most effective means of communicating description. You can even link the color to some object that is familiar to the audience, such as "blue as the sky" or "dark as night." Here is a sample outline for a simple description speech:

> Specific purpose: To describe Glacier National Park.
> I. The first attraction is the beautiful mountains.
> II. The second attraction is the pristine lakes.
> III. The third attraction is the friendly people.

Demonstration Speeches

In a demonstration speech, the speaker shows the audience how to do something. Whether you are explaining how to bake a cake, resolve an interpersonal conflict, or remove a brain tumor, the primary purpose is to demonstrate how something is done. When preparing your demonstration speech, keep these guidelines in mind:

1. Choose your topic carefully. Make certain that you have enough time to cover the basic steps of whatever process you will be demonstrating.
2. Cluster the steps of your demonstration into three or four major groups, such as "Plan-Do-Finish" or "Gather materials-Prepare-Do." Your speech will be easier for the audience to follow.
3. Use visual aids.

Here is a sample outline of a simple demonstration speech:

> Specific purpose: To demonstrate how to make a vase.
>   I. Gather your materials.
> II. Shape the clay.
> III. Heat the vase in the kiln.
> IV. Finish the vase.

Narration Speeches

Storytelling or narration can be an intimate and memorable way to make a point. A story is easier to deliver to an audience because you will often be speaking from personal experience, rather than relating facts and figures from other sources. The audience responds to stories with more interest and involvement than they do to statistics or expert testimony, and they will remember a well-told story long after they forget facts and figures. Follow these three guidelines when using a narrative:

1. Tell a story that supports the point of your speech.
2. Be familiar with your story. Don't memorize it word for word, but be familiar enough with the story to tell it without the use of notes.
3. Speak in character when telling your story. Use verbal and nonverbal behaviors that make the characters distinctive.

Here is a sample outline for a simple narration speech:

> Specific purpose: To explain the Battle of the Little Bighorn.
>   I. General Custer's campaign preparations.
> II. The actual battle with the Indians.
> III. The aftermath of Indian victory.

SAMPLE INFORMATIVE SPEECH OUTLINE

Specific Purpose: To inform the audience about taking a solo-motorcycle journey across the United States.

Introduction
Have you ever dreamed of doing something adventurous, solitary, and memorable? I had been dreaming of riding my motorcycle across the United States by myself. Well this past summer I did. I rode over 8,000 miles from Santa Cruz, Ca. to Kitty Hawk, North Carolina and back across the northern United States in 25 days and had the time of my life. Today, I'd like to tell you about the preparation, the journey, and the lessons I learned.

Body
   I. The first thing I'd like to share with you is the preparation for the trip.
      A. Dale Coyner in his book, Motorcycle Travel, says that, "The preparation for a transcontinental motorcycle trip is essential to success."
      B. Preparation of BMW R1150R motorcycle and equipment.
      C. Psychological preparation for the trip.
  II. The second thing I'd like to share with you is the journey itself.
      A. In his book, Leanings II, Peter Egan suggests that "A motorcycle is the best way to see the country, because you become part of the land you ride on and people approach you at every stop."
      B. I rode through 25 states mostly on two lane roads, staying in small towns.
      C. Story about camping near a small beach on the East Coast.
 III. The third thing I'd like to share with you is the lessons I learned.
      A. I learned to simplify my life.
      B. I learned to welcome the unexpected.
      C. I learned that this is a wonderful country.

Conclusion
Today, I told you about the preparation, the journey itself, and the lessons I learned during my solo-trip across the United States and back on a motorcycle. I hope that during your lifetime you too can take a solo-trip across the United States and discover the wonderful sights and people that make up this great nation we live in.

Bibliography
Coyner, D. 2007. *Motorcycle Travel*. Center Conway, N.H.: Whitehorse Press.
Egan, P. 2007. *Leanings II*. St. Paul, Minn.: MBI Publishing.

Suggestions for Using Visual Aids

If you decide to use any visual aids in your speech, here are some recommendations you may find helpful.

Devote Time to the Process. If you decide to use any visual aids in a speech, set aside adequate time to design, construct, and practice using whatever aids you select. Begin early in the speech process and give your visual aids the time and energy they deserve.

Make the Visual Aids Large Enough. Keep your audience in mind when designing and constructing your visual aid, especially those seated at the back of the room or auditorium. How large will your visual aid have to be so it will be seen easily by even people seated way back there?

Make the Visual Aids Simple. Visual aids should clarify or reinforce a point you are trying to make. The goal is for the audience to see and understand your visual aid within three to five seconds. Don't clutter your visual aid. Focus on what is essential and keep your visual aids simple.

Limit the Number of Visual Aids. Your visual aids should not become the primary focus of your presentation. Limit your visual aids to no more than 15 percent of your total speaking time, so in a five-minute speech, the time devoted to using visual aids should be about forty-five to sixty seconds. Don't get lost behind a mountain of visual aids.

Show Your Visual Aids Only When You're Talking About Them. Display your visual aids only when you're speaking about them. Keep your visual aids hidden from the audience you refer to them. Beginning speakers will often set up and display all their visual aids before they begin their speech, but they will be a distraction. Keep your visual aids out of sight until you need them.

Maintain Eye Contact. Don't lose eye contact with your audience by looking at your visual aids more than necessary. Talk to your audience, not the visual aid.

Don't Pass Your Visual Aids Around. Even if your audience begs you to let them handle your visual aids, DON'T! If you do, it will mark the beginning of the end for your presentation. You'll lose their attention. Maintain control and the audience's attention and don't let them touch your visual aids.

Practice With Your Visual Aids. Practice and time your speech using your visual aids. Speak to your imaginary audience and NOT to your visual aid. Keep your eyes on the imaginary audience. Whatever you do in practice is what you'll do during your real speech, so keep your eyes on the audience. As you evaluate your practice speech times, determine if you need to trim some of your visual aid segments. Often visual aids will take longer to use than you might imagine, so keep track of your practice time.

Have A Wonderful Life Anyway. No speech or speaker is perfect. Things happen to us all, so take this to heart as you use your visual aids in your speech. Don't frown, apologize, or even sigh if something goes wrong with your visual aids when you deliver your speech. Charts fall off of easels, the six-pound meatloaf will slip from the pan, and your motorcycle magazines will slide to the floor. When things like this happen, pause, take a breath, and smile. Pick up the chart, scrape up the meatloaf, or just kick the magazines out of your way. Audiences will appreciate your calm, smiling response to these minor mishaps. Remember, it's only a speech and you'll have a wonderful life anyway.

PERSUASIVE STRATEGIES

Whereas the primary goal of the informative speech is to educate, the primary goal of **persuasive speaking** is to change the beliefs and/or behaviors of others. A sales presentation, a campaign speech, an appeal for contributions to a charitable cause, and closing arguments at the conclusion of a trial are all examples of persuasive speeches.

PERSUASIVE STRATEGY GOALS

Whenever you attempt to persuade others, there are three basic goals you are trying to accomplish—to reinforce an already-held belief, change a belief, and/or motivate to action. Writer Henry Wadsworth Longfellow believed, "Art is power." As an artist of communication, you can powerfully influence and motivate your audience with the persuasive speeches you create.

Reinforce a Belief

The first persuasive strategy goal is to reinforce or strengthen an already-held audience belief. Often, the audience shares a belief with the speaker who delivers a speech that will strengthen their resolve or raise their spirits. That would be the goal of the speakers who presented speeches entitled, "Education Is Important for Our Children," "We Need to Lower Taxes," and "A Cure for Cancer Must Be Discovered Now."

Change a Belief

The second persuasive strategy goal is to change an audience belief. This is the desired outcome of a speaker who is addressing a group of listeners who do not hold her belief. Examples of speeches aimed at changing audience beliefs are "The Drunk Driving Blood Alcohol Level Should Be Raised in the State of California" or "The Minimum Age for Receiving Social Security Benefits Should Be Raised to 70 Years of Age."

Motivate to Action

The final persuasive strategy goal is to motivate the audience to action. "You should donate blood four times annually" and "I want you to invest 5 percent of your monthly income in Fujishin Mutual Funds" are two examples of speeches aimed at motivating the audience to action. The primary goal is to get the audience to physically do something.

THE PROPOSITION

Like the specific purpose of the informative speech, the **proposition** specifies exactly what you want to accomplish with your persuasive speech. Are you attempting to reinforce a belief, change a belief, or motivate your audience to action? Your proposition will state the desired outcome of your presentation. Every proposition should be limited to one sentence and should contain the goal of your talk. When constructing a proposition for your persuasive speech, keep three guidelines in mind:

1. Your proposition should meet an audience need.
2. Your proposition should be reasonable.
3. Your proposition should be specific.

Here are some examples of propositions:

> To reinforce the belief that there should be separation of religion and government.
> To convince that audience that income tax rates for the rich should be lowered.
> To persuade the audience to take a tuberculosis test.

THREE MEANS OF PERSUASION

More than two thousand years ago, the Greek philosopher Aristotle identified three means of persuasion—ethos, logos, and pathos. Ethos is the speaker's credibility, logos is the logical appeal of the message, and pathos is the emotional appeals presented during the speech. These three categories constitute the basis for your persuasive speeches.

Ethos (Source Credibility)

Ethos is the perceived credibility of the speaker. Aristotle believed that a speaker must be judged not only as competent by the audience, but also as an individual of good character. He further believed that a speaker's ethos or source credibility was the single, most important component of persuasion. Without the audience's trust and faith in a speaker, very little he says or does will have any persuasive effect or impact. The credibility of the speaker is made up of competence, character, and goodwill.

A speaker's **competence** is the expertise, knowledge, and experience she communicates to the audience. The audience will generally listen to and believe a speaker who knows what she is talking about. You can increase your source credibility by selecting speech topics in which you have previous experience, knowledge, and training.

Character is the overall collection of personal attributes a speaker possesses. Is he perceived as being honest and trustworthy? Is he an individual of integrity? Is he worthy of our respect? You can enhance character by dressing up for the speaking occasion, establishing common ground in the introduction of your speech, using appropriate language (don't swear or use slang), and always telling the truth.

The final component of ethos or source credibility is **goodwill.** We like and believe those speakers we feel have our best interests at heart. We also like speakers who are warm, friendly, and approachable. You can show goodwill by smiling, being enthusiastic, using direct eye contact, and observing the speaking time limits.

Logos (Logical Appeal)

The second category of persuasion is **logos,** or the logical appeal of your message. Reasoning, evidence, and organization are the three primary areas that your audience will consider when evaluating the logical appeal of your speech.

Reasoning. The logical appeal of your speech will provide your audience with statements that lead to the conclusion you are trying to make. In other words, your proposition is the conclusion you want your audience to reach after you have presented a series of statements or reasons for them to consider. **Reasoning** is the process of drawing a conclusion based on evidence. The two most common forms of logical reasoning are deduction and induction.

With **deductive reasoning,** you begin with a generally accepted fact or belief and connect it to a specific issue to draw a specific conclusion. For instance, the generally accepted belief that "Education is essential to a democratic society" can be applied to a specific conclusion, "We should educate immigrant children." In this case, we move from the general to the specific.

Deductive reasoning follows a pattern called the **syllogism.** There are three components to any syllogism. The **major premise** is the generally accepted fact or belief on which your argument rests. The **minor premise** focuses on the specific issue you are discussing and relates it to the major premise. Finally, once the minor premise is established by evidence and its connection to the major premise has been defended, the eventual **conclusion** can be drawn by your audience. You've probably heard the famous syllogism:

     I. All humans are mortal.
     II. Socrates is human.
     III. Therefore, Socrates is mortal.

This is an example of deductive reasoning: you begin with a general premise ("All humans are mortal"), move to a minor premise ("Socrates is human"), and then reach the specific conclusion ("Socrates is mortal").

Deductive reasoning works well when you are certain that your audience collectively holds a common belief or accepts a certain fact. When you are using deductive reasoning in a persuasive speech, keep these two suggestions in mind. First, be certain your audience believes or will accept your major premise. If you are uncertain your audience believes the major premise, you will have to present a substantial amount of evidence to convince them of its validity. Only when you have persuaded your audience of the major premise can you move on to convince them of the minor premise. Second, once you have established your major premise, focus your attention on the relationship between the major and minor premises. Statistics and expert testimony should clearly prove this relationship.

The second form of reasoning is **inductive reasoning,** which moves from specific cases to a general conclusion—from the small to the large. With inductive reasoning, we observe that something is true for a specific number of cases or instances and draw the conclusion based on those observations.

For example, suppose you have completed three courses at a certain university and found that all three of the professors were poor instructors. From this experience, you conclude that all the professors at that college are terrible. Or maybe you've owned three Chevrolet pickups and found each to be excellent in overall performance and durability. Therefore, you conclude that all Chevrolet pickups are wonderful. Here is sample outline of a persuasive speech that uses inductive reasoning:

> I. Enrolling in a communications course was beneficial for me.
> II. Enrolling in a communications course was beneficial for my sister.
> III. Enrolling in a communications course was beneficial for my brother.
> Conclusion: Enrolling in a communications course is beneficial for everyone.

If you are using inductive reasoning in your persuasive speech, consider the following guidelines:

1. Provide an adequate number of specific instances to prove your point.
2. Reinforce your argument with documented evidence.
3. Include examples that are not isolated, but represent a general trend and demonstrate widespread occurrence.

The reasoning you use—deductive, inductive, or a combination of both—to structure your persuasive speech will help you plan, test, and strengthen any proposal you may wish to present to your audience.

Evidence. The second component of logical appeal is the evidence you present to support and strengthen your reasoning. **Evidence** is any statistic, fact, or expert testimony that supports your assertions, and your effective use of evidence will persuade your audience. The use of statistics and expert opinion was addressed in chapter 10; some specific suggestions for their use in persuasive speeches are presented here.

First, you need to have an adequate **quantity** of evidence for the purposes of your speech. One extreme is to provide no evidence for your speech. The other extreme is to give too much evidence, forcing the audience to wade through a mountain of facts and figures. The answer to how much evidence is necessary lies somewhere in between the two extremes. For a simple persuasive speech, present at least one or two pieces of evidence to support each of your main points.

Second, the **quality** of your evidence needs to be credible. Do the authors have expertise, education, and experience that is credible? Are the books, magazines, and newspapers reputable? Your evidence needs to come from sources that are respected and acknowledged if your evidence is to be persuasive.

> *To be memorable, art must touch our emotions and move our hearts.*
>
> —SHIRLEY LEHNER-RHOADES

Third, your evidence should be **relevant**. Make certain that your evidence actually relates and supports the point you are attempting to make. The relevance of your evidence should be clearly apparent and applicable to your point. "So what?" should not be the response of your listeners after you have given a statistic, fact, or expert opinion.

Fourth, the evidence, you present should be **recent**. The more recent your evidence, the more effective it will be in persuading your audience. If possible, your evidence, should be taken from current periodicals, magazines, and newspapers. Interviews with experts should be as recent as possible. Books, guides, and pamphlets should be no older than five years.

Fifth, **document the author and source before you present your evidence**. "Dr. Albert Ellis in his book *A New Guide to Rational Living* warns us . . ." and "In a recent interview with Dr. Jeanne Yamada, director of mental health services at our college medical center, she encourages us to . . ." are examples of documenting your evidence before you present the statistic or expert opinion. By citing the author and source of your information first, you establish the credibility of your evidence for maximum impact.

Sixth, **restate evidence in your own words**. Nothing can confuse and discourage an audience more quickly than being unable to understand what you're saying.

This is especially true for complicated statistics and technically advanced expert opinion. You can create greater understanding by restating the evidence in your own words. "What the author is telling us is . . . ," "I think the author is telling us that . . . ," and "The results of the study show us . . ." are a few ways to begin your restatement of confusing or complicated evidence.

Research your topic thoroughly and use only the most impressive and significant evidence you can find. The evidence you use will determine how the listeners will receive your arguments. Your skillful selection and effective use of evidence will also add to your credibility as a speaker.

Organization. The final component of logical appeal is the **organization** of the speech itself. Although the basic structure of a speech was discussed earlier, there are few points I would like make about persuasive speeches. First, if your speech is clearly organized, your audience will more likely follow your arguments to their logical conclusion. Second, by previewing points in the introduction and reviewing them in the conclusion, you are helping the audience prepare to receive and remember your arguments. Third, by recapping each main point before moving to the next point, you further reinforce the proposition you are presenting. "Now that I've told you the health benefits of purchasing a health club membership, let's move on to the third reason why you should consider joining a gym. . ." Finally, when you are clearly organized in your speech presentation, you'll be perceived as being more credible to the audience.

Pathos (Emotional Appeal)

The final proof of persuasion Aristotle identified was **pathos,** or emotional appeal. Pathos appeals to the audience's emotional needs and desires. Many of our decisions are influenced to a great extent by our emotions and feelings, our gut reactions to things. Whereas logos appeals to our heads and ethos to our assessment of a person's character, pathos appeals to our hearts. Emotional appeal can have a very memorable and powerful impact on an audience.

Emotions to evoke. Emotions such as fear, compassion, anger, sadness, pride, sympathy, and reverence are just a few of the emotions you can attempt to evoke in your audience. To persuade an audience, you must involve their emotions as well as their minds. Although there are hundreds of emotions to consider, a few are especially effective in persuasive appeals.

Fear is one of the most powerful emotions you can appeal to in your audience. Our fears of serious illness, death, personal rejection, poverty, not realizing our potential, and public speaking are just a few of the hundreds of things we fear.

Anger can evoke strong responses from your audience. What makes your audience angry? Sexual predators, vandals, corrupt politicians, unfair professors, marital infidelity, kidnappers, and terrorists can make your audience feel anger.

Another emotion you can appeal to is **compassion.** Make your audience feel sympathy and caring for the physically disabled, orphans, battered women, the hungry, the homeless, the unemployed, and abused children. By raising these issues, you can have your audience feel compassion for others.

You can appeal to **pride** in one's nation, ethnic heritage, personal achievements, and family to stir emotion.

You can arouse **shame** to make your audience feel guilty for not helping others, for being too materialistic, for not being politically active, for not helping the less fortunate, and for not living up to one's full potential.

Happiness is one of the most sought-after emotions in our culture. So, in your emotional appeals, you can focus your attention on things that could bring your audience happiness: financial security, physical health, advanced education, loving relationships, caring families, artistic expression, religious practice, and expertise in public speaking.

These emotions are just a partial list of the hundreds of emotions you can consider. But they give you a feeling for the kinds of emotional material you can draw on to enhance your persuasive speeches. Follow these suggestions for using emotional appeals in your presentations:

1. **Select appropriate emotional appeals.** Consider your proposition and audience carefully before deciding on the emotional appeals you want to use. Select emotional appeals that support your proposition.
2. **Use emotional appeals toward the end of your speech.** If you begin with emotional appeals, you run the risk of having the audience feel that you think they are gullible. Make a logical appeal first, then focus on their emotions.
3. **Tell your story with emotion.** This is not the time to be monotone, lifeless, and detached. Get involved in the story. Speak in character. Use your body, face, and voice to make the characters come alive and the story to take on dimension.
4. **Use visual aids.** One picture can make us feel emotions that words cannot elicit. One graph or chart depicting the shocking distribution of wealth in the United States can haunt your audience long after the speech has been delivered. One marble sculpture can leave a lasting imprint in the minds of your listeners.

Computer Generated Visual Aids

If you decide to use visual aids delivered by a computer-generated presentational program, such as PowerPoint, keep these suggestions in mind:

Keep It Short. Your computer-generated presentational programs should be used to enhance your speech, not replace it. Limit your computerized presentation time to no more than 15 percent of your total speaking time. A helpful rule of thumb is to present one slide for every two minutes of speaking time.

Be Simple. Try to keep your presentations simple. Allow your program's design wizards to help you select the designs, colors, and print type. Don't reinvent the wheel each time you speak.

Be Consistent. Use consistent lettering, transitions, and bullets throughout your presentation. Too much variety can be distracting to the audience.

Keep It Focused. Remember to use only one to three words per bullet. Don't use more than five or six bullets per slide or you'll lose your audience. Limit each slide to one thought or idea. You don't want your audience to spend their entire time reading.

Be Flexible. When you practice your presentation, be flexible enough to edit your presentations if it's running too long or too short. Omit certain slides if you feel they're unnecessary or don't contribute to the presentation. Change the font, font size, color, or background patterns if they're distracting or unsatisfactory. Keep your design and lettering simple.

Test Equipment. Set up any equipment you'll need well before your speaking time. Test the computer program, check the room lighting, and test anything else you might be using for your speech.

Be Able To Speak Without Electricity. In the event of computer or electrical failure, be prepared to give your speech without your computerized visual aids. Unlike poster boards, computer programs depend upon properly working computer and electrical sources, so be forewarned that electrical disasters occasionally happen. People have been delivering speeches for thousands of years without plugging things into walls. You should always be prepared to do the same.

BASIC PERSUASIVE SPEECH STRUCTURES

By using the three means of persuasion—ethos, logos, and pathos—you can create an effective persuasive speech that appeals to the logic and emotions of your listeners. How you structure your persuasive speech depends on the attitude of your prospective audience. Often, novice speakers are reluctant to deliver persuasive speeches because they fear "stepping on someone's toes" or they "don't feel qualified to tell others what to believe or do."

But there are times when you need to take a stand, propose a solution, or argue a case. So approach persuasion with enthusiasm! Stand for something! Tell others how they can improve their lives!

There are four basic persuasive speech structures you can use for different audiences to proclaim your art with enthusiasm!

Speech of Reasons

When your audience has no opinion, is neutral, or is mildly in favor or mildly opposed to your proposition, consider using the speech-of-reasons approach. This straightforward, inductive reasoning structure works well for these audiences. Here is a sample outline of a simple speech of reasons:

> Proposition: To motivate the audience to watch public television.
> I.   Pubic television has no commercials.
> II. Public television is educational.
> III. Public television encourages personal growth.

Problem-Solution Speech

If your goal is to have your audience adopt a specific solution to a problem or implement a specific plan, consider using the problem-solution approach. Keep in mind that this structure works best with an audience that has no opinion, is neutral, or is only mildly in favor or mildly opposed to your proposition. Here is a sample outline of a simple problem-resolution speech.

> Proposition: To persuade college freshmen to enroll in a relationships course (solution).
> I.   College freshmen do not possess adequate relational skills (problem).
> II. The proposed relationships course will teach freshmen basic communication skills (support for solution).
> III. The proposed relationships course will enable freshmen to make new friends (support for solution).

Criteria-Satisfaction Speech

By utilizing a yes response and establishing common ground with your audience, you increase your chances of persuading a mildly hostile or hostile audience who oppose your proposition. If you first establish criteria for a workable solution to a problem, you are more likely to convince your audience that your proposition should be adopted. The important difference in this approach is that you spend approximately one-half of your speaking time trying to establish common ground with your audience during the discussion of criteria. Here is a sample outline of a simple criteria-satisfaction speech:

> Proposition: To motivate the audience to vacation at a monastery.
> I.   You want your vacation to meet these criteria.
>   A. It must be relaxing.
>   B. It must be affordable.

      C. It must be rejuvenating.
   II. A vacation to a monastery meets these criteria.
      A. It offers a relaxed, serene setting.
      B. It costs only 30% of a regular vacation.
      C. It offers spiritually rejuvenating experiences.

Negative Method

In the negative speech structure, you eliminate competing options or solutions to the problem, leaving only your proposition to be accepted by the audience. This structure of persuasive speaking is particularly effective with hostile audiences. Here is a sample outline of a simple negative speech:

> Proposition: To convince couples to seek professional counseling when experiencing serious marital difficulties.
>   I. Your present difficulties will only increase if left untreated.
>   II. Self-help books do not provide professional guidance and encouragement.
> III. Single-spouse counseling can alienate and distance the other spouse.
> IV. The only solution is to seek professional couples counseling.

Depending on the audience's attitude toward your proposition, you can use the various speech structures to create a successful persuasive presentation. No one method of main point arrangement will meet all the needs of a particular audience, but it will provide you with the most effective approach for your persuasive goals.

CREATING SUCCESSFUL SPEECHES: THE F.O.C.U.S. TECHNIQUE

The process of creating an effective speech can be a little overwhelming, especially when you take into account all the numerous components and variables involved. But take heart. Here are five simple reminders that will keep you focused when you have to prepare an informative or persuasive presentation. I call it the F.O.C.U.S. Technique for creating successful speeches.

Friend of the audience

See yourself as a friend of the audience and them as friends of yours. Using this frame of reference, you will begin to feel differently about the entire process of speaking and move from stage fright to delight! You can begin this process by seeing your audience as people who want the best for you, who are interested in what you have to say. They want you to be successful in your speaking. They look forward to benefiting from your speech. They will love you. In other words, they are not the enemy, they are your friends. And you are their friend.

SAMPLE PERSUASIVE SPEECH OUTLINE

Proposition: To motivate the audience to turn off their cell phone for one day.

Introduction
Story about addiction to the cell phone. Today, I want you to invite you to turn off your cell phone for one day, because it will decrease stress, make you less self-absorbed, and increase your free time.

Body
I. The first reason you should turn off your cell phone for one day is that it will decrease stress.
    A. List ways cell phone use increases our daily stress.
    B. *Journal of Marriage and Family*, Dec. 2005, states that, "Cell phone use negatively affects one's level of stress and family satisfaction."
    C. Story of Sarah who turns off her cell phone to reduce stress.
II. The second reason you should turn off your cell phone for one day is that it will make you less self-absorbed.
    A. The cell phone increases our focus on ourselves.
    B. *The New York Times*, Dec. 2, 2007, warns that, "Cell phone use has become a primary manifestation of self-centeredness and causes a lack of consideration for others."
    C. Story about woman who gave up her cell phone to do more charity work.
III. The third reason you should turn off your cell phone for one day is that it will increase your free time.
    A. Tamara Gaffney of Telephia Customer Matrix reports that, "The average 18–24 year old uses 900 minutes of cell phone time per month."
    B. List other things an individual can do with those 1,200 minutes (15 hours).
    C. Story about my giving up my cell phone for one day and the things I did.

Conclusion
Today I've invited you to give up your cell phone for just one day, because it will decrease your level of stress, make you less self-centered, and increase your free time. So, if you've been feeling stressed and frustrated that you don't have enough time for fun activities or just for yourself anymore, then turn off your cell phone for just one day—24 hours. Take out the battery to your phone right now and enjoy the peaceful experience of silence and reclaiming your life.

Bibliography
Chesley, Nancy. *Journal of Marriage and Family*, December 2005; vol. 67: p.1237.
Richtel, Matt. *The New York Times*, December 2, 2007.
Gaffney, Tamara. Telephia Customer Matrix, May 2006.

Organize your speech simply

Often, we confuse and fatigue our audience with too much information and too many points in our speeches. Rather than choose simplicity, we choose complexity, believing that more and longer is better. But the opposite is true. Keep your speeches simple in structure—an introduction, a body with three or four points, and a conclusion. Keep them shorter than longer. Leave your audience wanting more, not less. Simple is best.

Critical thinking

Use critical thinking skills when brainstorming topics, researching, testing evidence, and structuring your speech. Evaluate the material for your speeches critically to ensure that it comes from qualified, reliable sources. Test your evidence to ensure that it supports the main points of your speech. Evidence will increase the logical appeal of your presentation and boost your credibility as a speaker. Your documented information also will give you a sense of confidence.

It's just not you standing up there alone, but in a way, every expert, researcher, and author you cite is standing next to you, at least in spirit. It's no longer just you, but a group of you now saying the same thing to the audience. So the next time you are alone in the library or on the computer researching a speech, think of your efforts as gathering a team of experts who will stand beside you when you share your speech with the audience.

Uplift your audience

The purpose of your speech is to inform or persuade the audience. Your listeners are the reason you are investing a portion of your life researching, creating, practicing, and delivering your speech. Make your presentation worth their time. Consider the audience first and foremost. Will your speech benefit them? Will it improve or enhance their lives in some way? Will they become better people because of what you are going to share with them? The primary goal of any speech you give is for the benefit of your audience. Will your gift—your speech—be uplifting?

Stories to develop your points

Whether you are giving an informative or persuasive speech, stories will add depth and dimension to your presentation. As we discussed earlier, the stories you include in your speech will be remembered long after facts and figures are forgotten. Stories are the things of which our lives are made. Add to the lives of your listeners by sharing stories that support or develop your points. Your audience will love you for it.

Maybe you'll never be a study skills teacher, but you will be required to speak in front of groups of people many times during your life. Your audience may be the city council, prospective business clients, family members at a reunion, or parents at a PTA meeting. No matter what audience you address, the knowledge and skill to create strategic speeches—speeches structured for specific informative and persuasive purposes—are powerful assets.

EXPLORING CREATIVE TASKS

1. Select and research one specific topic of interest to you. Use the library, experts in the field, and the Internet to gather information about your topic. Was it difficult to find information? How do you feel about knowing more about your topic? Would you ever consider using this topic for a speech?

2. Research, prepare, practice, and deliver a four-minute informative speech entitled "My Most Important Life Lesson." Focus on something you have learned from an experience, an individual, or a class. Each of your three main points should explain some aspect of your lesson, such as what is was, what you learned, and how you apply it in your life now. Include one piece of documented evidence to support a point. Your speech should include an introduction, a body, and a conclusion.

3. Research, prepare, practice, and deliver a six-minute informative speech entitled "What It's Like to . . ." Your topic should focus on something that reflects who you are, something you did, or something you learned. For instance, what is like to be a museum tour guide, an only child, or a graduate of an Outward Bound School. Each of your three main points should explain some aspect of your speech topic. Include three pieces of documented evidence to support your points. Your speech should include an introduction, a body, and a conclusion.

4. Research, prepare, practice, and deliver a seven-minute persuasive speech entitled "I Want You to . . ." Your proposition should focus on a topic for which you have strong conviction. For instance, "I want you to invest in mutual funds," "I want you to enroll in a first aid course," and "I want you to volunteer for Big Brothers/Big Sisters." Each of your three main points should contain a separate reason supporting your proposition. Include three pieces of documented evidence (one per main point) and share an emotional appeal story in your third point. Your speech should include an introduction, a body, and a conclusion.

EXPANDING YOUR CREATIVE THINKING

1. If you taught a college-level course, what ten things would you do or create to make your class enjoyable, beneficial, and practical for students? How do you think your students would respond to your ten ideas or activities? What are the disadvantages of those ideas or activities? What would you enjoy about being an instructor?

2. Professions such as education, law, the clergy, and sales can require a great deal of public speaking. How would your speaking skills develop if your professional responsibilities required you to give speeches daily? How would your anxiety about speaking change over the years? What encouraging advice would you give about stage fright to someone starting in your career after you have been in the field speaking for twenty years?

3. What are some activities, clubs, or organizations that you could become involved with that would improve your speaking skills? How do you think they would benefit your speech improvement? What would it take to become active in one of those activities or organizations? What is preventing you from becoming involved right now?

4. Is there anything you would sacrifice your life for? Are there any individuals, organizations, groups, beliefs, or ideals for which you would risk your life? Why? How can you convince others that they should do the same? What specific reasons could you provide to persuade an audience of your peers?

TWELVE

Creating Successful Communication During an Interview

> I don't have a lot of respect for talent.
> Talent is genetic. It's what you do with it
> that counts.
>
> —MARTIN RITT

It was 8:40 in the morning when Todd Forbes rushed through the front doors of Aztech Computers and blurted to the receptionist, "I'm late for my interview with Terri Houghton in Personnel. Please tell her I'm here."

"Take a seat and I'll ring Ms. Houghton," the receptionist said.

A few moments later Ms. Houghton entered the waiting room. "Welcome to Aztech Computers, Mr. Forbes. I'm Terri Houghton."

"I know I'm late, but this place isn't easy to find," complained Todd.

"It is a little out of the way. Have a seat," said Terri as they entered her office. "Let's begin. I've reviewed your résumé and I was impressed with your grades in college. How did you get interested in Aztech Computers?"

"I read your ad in the newspaper."

"What position are you most interested in?"

"I could probably do a good job in any position you assigned to me."

"What skills do you have to offer our company?"

"I learn things really fast and I got straight As in college," boasted Todd. "Plus, two of my friends work in computers and they say it's pretty easy to learn."

"Are you familiar with our laptop computer line?" Terri inquired.

"Not really. I haven't had time to research your company. I've spent the past week interviewing with ski resorts at Lake Tahoe."

"What specific experience have you had in the computer industry?"

"I haven't had any jobs working with computers. I did take a few classes in computer programming, but they weren't that exciting."

"Can you think of any college courses you took that were related to business?"

"No, but I never received lower than an A."

"Well, Todd," Terri sighed, "your grades are something to be proud of. I'm interviewing five other applicants. I'll get back to you in a week or so."

Needless to say, Todd didn't get the job.

INTERVIEWING

One of the most important communication skills you can learn is your interviewing skills—both as the interviewer and the interviewee. An **interview** is a communication transaction in which an interviewer engages in questioning and discussion with an interviewee to gather information. Every interview involves an **interviewer,** who is responsible for conducting and guiding the interview process and the **interviewee,** who is the subject of the interview.

> *There is an art to interviewing, no less significant or mysterious than painting, sculpture, or music.*
>
> —NANETTE VIDALES

In reality, much of your daily communication consists of interviews—you ask questions of others to gather information. You ask questions about a product in a store to decide if you will buy the item. You inquire about the requirements for a course from a current student before enrolling in that class next semester. You even ask a friend about the personality traits of a mutual friend for a possible date (not all interviewing is professional or academic!).

This chapter examines two kinds of interviewing—information gathering interviewing and employment interviewing.

THE INFORMATION-GATHERING INTERVIEW

The most common type of interview is the information-gathering interview, such as an interview with an expert for a report, term paper, or speech. Other types of information-gathering interviews include those conducted by journalists for publication, product survey researchers who interview shoppers in your local mall, and organizational researchers who interview employees to collect data on management effectiveness and production methods.

As a student, you will most likely be required to interview experts for a term paper, a speech, a group presentation, or a newspaper article. The inclusion of expert testimony provides valuable information and adds credibility to your report. You may cringe at the thought of interviewing an expert. It's too much work, you tell yourself. You don't know what to ask. You're afraid that the person you want to interview will refuse your request. But don't worry. You can create a successful interview without having to suffer much. In fact, you may discover that your interview was much more valuable and enjoyable than you first imagined! There are four steps you can take to create a successful information-gathering interview.

Locating an Expert to Interview

First you need to find a potential expert to interview. Brainstorm individuals in the community who may have training in or experience with the subject you are investigating. For instance, on the topic of housing costs in your area, you could contact a real-estate agent, a building contractor, or a bank loan officer.

Colleges are also a good source for experts in many fields. Call the appropriate department and ask for an expert in the subject area you are researching. You can also consult the course catalog or class schedule to find out which instructors teach related or relevant courses.

Finally, you may already know an expert. Think about all the people you know—family, friends, colleagues, coworkers, classmates, and neighbors—who may qualify as experts in the subject you are researching. You'll be surprised at whom you come up with if you think hard enough.

Preparing for the Interview

An effective interview just doesn't happen by chance or accident. It has to be created. You need to research and plan for the interview. Follow these suggestions to make your information-gathering interview more successful.

Request an interview well in advance. Once you have decided on an individual to interview, request the interview at least one or two weeks in advance. Don't expect the person to drop everything and clear his calendar with only a day's notice. Identify yourself and your purpose for the interview. Ask for a date, time, and location that is convenient for the interviewee (not you). Be respectful of the interviewee's schedule. Request a thirty-minute interview. Less than thirty minutes doesn't provide enough time for most interviews and more than thirty minutes can cut into the interviewee's schedule too much. Also ask if you can record the interview if you prefer not to take notes.

Research the subject. It is important that you are informed about the subject. Read at least one current book and any periodical or magazine articles on the topic. This will provide a basis for writing interview questions and will enable you to discuss the subject with some fundamental knowledge of the topic.

Prepare a question list. Prepare a list of at least ten to fifteen open-ended questions that will encourage the interviewee to talk. Begin with general questions and continue to more specific and focused questions relevant to your report. Be prepared to probe the interviewee's responses to your questions. You may not use all the questions you prepare, but having enough questions ensures that you won't have to make up questions as you go along.

Prepare for a positive experience. Most beginning interviewers feel some degree of apprehension or anxiety before talking with an expert. Yet after the interview, they are usually pleased with the experience. Most individuals you interview will be happy to share their knowledge and experience. Rather than dread being interviewed, they look forward to the time they will spend with you. It's their way of passing on what they know to others. So be of good cheer as you anticipate the interview.

During the Interview

Now that you have researched the subject and prepared your list of questions, you are ready for the interview. Here are some suggestions for creating a successful interview.

Dress up. Show respect for the expert by dressing up for the interview. Nothing too fancy—no suit or evening gown is required. But wear something more formal than jeans and a T-shirt. Look nice. Your appearance should make a positive impression, showing respect for the interviewee.

Check your materials. Make sure you have the interviewee's address and phone number in case you need to contact her if traffic is heavy or you have a flat tire. Also remember to bring your list of questions, pen, note pad, or tape recorder.

> *Asking the right questions and listening carefully during an interview requires concentration, skill, and creativity. It's as much an art as it is a science.*
>
> —TERESA GRUBER

Arrive fifteen minutes early. You may think fifteen minutes is too early, but you never know about traffic or finding the place. Even if you arrive early, you can sit in your car and review your questions. By arriving early, you are creating enough space in your schedule to relax and collect yourself before the meeting. You also show respect for the expert's time by not charging into his office late, like Todd.

Begin the interview with general questions. Follow the list of questions you have prepared. Begin with open-ended general questions and use more specific follow-up questions when appropriate.

Listen carefully. Remember, the purpose of this interview is to gather information from the expert. Let the expert do most of the talking—about 80 to 90 percent of the total time, which means that you speak only 10 to 20 percent. In a thirty-minute interview, that means you have three to six minutes to ask questions and offer comments. Use your paraphrasing skills if you are unclear or confused about anything the interviewee says.

Take notes. You can't possibly remember everything that is shared during your thirty-minute interview, so some form of note taking or recording is necessary. If you get permission, record the interview. If not, take notes on the important points. Don't try to get every sentence down on paper. Spend time being attentive also. Create an interview that is focused yet relaxed. There is more to this interview than simply gathering information. You're in the presence of a human being who has agreed to help you, so be present, pleasant, and appreciative.

Inquire about contacts or leads. Ask the interviewee if she can direct you to any additional information or experts. You may be surprised by her willingness to share books, articles, and names of other individuals who have expertise in the subject matter.

Ask for additional information. Toward the end of the interview, ask the interviewee if there is anything you didn't inquire about or wasn't covered that you should know. This gives the interviewee an opportunity to address any information that was overlooked.

Show your appreciation. Tell the interviewee how thankful you were to be given the opportunity to spend time with him. Offer to send a copy of your report or paper.

After the Interview

Congratulations! You have just conducted a successful information-gathering interview! But don't start celebrating just yet. There are a few more things you have to do before you bring out the party hats and streamers.

Review your notes. Go over your interview notes while the experience is still fresh in your mind. Make any additional comments or notes as they come to mind. Do this as soon as you return home from the interview. One or two days later is too late. You'll forget much of what took place.

Write a thank-you note. As long as you are at your desk, write a thank-you note to the interviewee. It's amazing how many times interviewers forget to send a thank-you note. Show your appreciation. Be courteous and send that note!

Follow up leads or contacts. In the next few days, look up the experts, books, or journal articles the interviewee suggested for further information.

THE EMPLOYMENT INTERVIEW

Some of the most important interviews you will ever participate in will be employment interviews. During the course of your career, you most likely will change jobs several times, and each job change will require a minimum of one employment interview. Your primary goal in an employment interview is to sell yourself, your accomplishments, and your skills. You will also be seeing if the organization will meet your goals and needs. During an employment interview, you have only one chance to make a good impression, so the preparation and skill you bring to the interview will determine your overall success. Here are five necessary steps for a successful employment interview.

Examining Yourself

Before you begin applying for employment, there are some preliminary steps you can take to ensure that you desire and are qualified for the position. You'd be surprised at how often individuals will apply for a job without really considering whether or not they want the job, or if they are even qualified. Remember Todd? He was not qualified for the job, nor did he really appear to want the job. Todd may have been better off investing his time interviewing at some additional ski lodges. Ask yourself the following questions to check your interest and qualifications.

Do you want to work? If you are just graduating from college, ask yourself if this is the time to begin your career. Not every graduate has to begin a career immediately after graduation. If you are between jobs, ask yourself the same question. Are you in a financial position to take a few months off, travel or relax at home instead of applying for jobs right now? Sometimes we need a break from the grind of working or school. If you are not burdened by student loans, a mortgage, or hungry mouths to feed, why not give yourself a break for a while? To work now, if you don't need or want a job, could do more harm than good in the long run.

If you do want to work or need the job, continue to the next question. I know you would rather be playing on the warm beaches on Hawaii or Greece, but keep reading.

Do you want this particular job? After reading the job announcement or newspaper ad, ask yourself if you want this particular job. Entire books and career guidance classes are devoted to this subject of job choice. It is not the intent of this book to discuss job choice other than to remind you that you are the one who must spend a significant portion of your life at your job. In the end, it is you who must ultimately answer the question, "Do I really want this particular job?" Give this question serious consideration.

Are you qualified for this job? Once you have decided that you want a particular job, ask yourself if you are qualified. Be certain that your education, training, and experience meet the minimal requirements for the job. Be realistic. Although enthusiasm may score some points, experience selling magazines in high school may not qualify you for a marketing position if you have no college training or professional experience in that field.

Complete a personal assessment sheet. In most employment interviews, you will be asked questions focusing on your education, work-related experiences, accomplishments, skills, interests, strengths, weaknesses, and career goals. To give yourself an idea of your strengths, list three or four responses to each of the following categories. On one sheet of paper, list these headings—education, work-related experiences, accomplishments, skills, interests, strengths, weaknesses, and career goals—and under each heading brainstorm three or four appropriate responses. Whenever possible, list specific examples from your life. These examples will be helpful in developing your responses to the interviewer's questions.

When you are asked about a weakness or past mistake, talk about something that is not directly related to the job for which you are interviewing. Then speak about the weakness or mistake as a growth opportunity or how you learned a valuable lesson from it. For instance, you could relate a time when you did not delegate job responsibilities and worked longer hours than was expected of you. Now, however, you have learned to appropriately delegate duties to others, so you can lead a balanced life.

Getting the Interview

Once you have decided on a particular job, met the minimum job requirements, and completed your personal assessment sheet, you can begin the second step of the employment interview process—contacting the organization that is hiring. This step involves a cover letter and a résumé.

The cover letter. A **cover letter** is a brief letter stating your interest in the position for which the company is advertising. Address the cover letter to the person with the authority to hire you. Do not address it to the "Human Resource Department" or "Personnel." You may have to call the company to get the name (and the correct spelling) of the person responsible for hiring.

In the cover letter, you should include how you found out about the position, your primary reasons for being interested in the position, and how your specific qualifications (education, training, work-related experiences, and skills) meet the needs of the organization.

Your cover letter should be brief—one page. Never use a form letter. Your letter should look neat, well organized, and free of any spelling or grammatical errors. Print your letter on high-quality paper and leave adequate margins on all sides. Overall, your cover letter should be professional and pleasing to the eye. It is the first piece of information an employer sees from you. Make it your best.

The résumé. A **résumé** is a one- or two-page summary of your training, skills, and accomplishments. Entire books devoted to the art of writing resumes. Here, we highlight the eight most common components.

1. **Contact information.** Provide your name, address, and telephone number(s).
2. **Job objective.** Describe the type of employment you are seeking.

3. **Education.** Begin with your highest degree and continue in reverse order.
4. **Training.** List any specialized training, courses, and so on.
5. **Employment history.** List both paid and unpaid work experience, beginning with the most recent. Include employment dates, primary job responsibilities, and accomplishments and awards.
6. **Professional affiliations.** List professional groups to which you belong and any offices you have held.
7. **Special interests and skills.** List interests and skills that are related to the job for which you are applying.
8. **References.** These are individuals who know your work, your abilities, and your character. Do not include their names, but simply state, "References furnished upon request."

As you construct your résumé, think in terms of how your education, training, skills, and work experience can fit the requirements of the advertised job. Present only those skills and accomplishments that show you can do the job. Emphasize your strengths throughout the résumé, but always be truthful. Do not exaggerate or lie about anything. Above all, your résumé should be written with the company in mind—how can you satisfy the company's employment needs?

Preparing for the Interview

Once you have been asked for an interview, you can begin the third step in the interviewing process—preparing for the interview. This step involves researching the company, reviewing possible interview questions, and role-playing the interviewing.

Researching the company. Very few applicants ever research a company before an interview. You will make a strong impression if you show familiarity with the organization you are attempting to join. Researching the company will also help you anticipate questions the interviewer might ask and enhance your responses.

The artist should research and study the subject before painting. Let the spirit of the subject become your spirit.

—LEE FLEMMING

When you research a company, try to learn as much as possible about its history, its products and services, its corporate culture, its major competition, and the department you are hoping to join. Review its annual report, corporate pamphlets, relevant journal articles, or related local newspaper articles. If you know any employees of the company, interview them for important information.

Reviewing possible interview questions. Although you can never be totally certain about the exact questions you will be asked, there are some fairly common topics that are addressed in almost every interview. Here is a list of commonly asked questions during an interview:

1. Why did you choose your undergraduate major in college?
2. Explain how you schedule your time during an average day.
3. How do you prioritize tasks when you have a great deal to do?
4. Why did you select our company for employment?
5. What training, skills, abilities, and experiences can you contribute to our company?
6. As a worker, what are your strengths?
7. As a worker, what are your weaknesses? (Remember to present them as challenges for your growth or lessons you have learned.)
8. Have you ever worked in a job that did not match your skills, likes, or abilities? How did you handle this situation?
9. Tell me about a time when you had to demonstrate leadership. How did others respond to you? How did the situation turn out?
10. What leadership traits do you possess?
11. Tell me about an instance when you had to work overtime to complete a project. How did you feel about this?
12. If you knew that this job would require you to work fifty hours a week for the next two months, would you still be interested in it? Why or why not?
13. Describe the kind of people you work best with. Why?
14. Describe the kind of people you prefer not working with. Why?
15. Tell me about a time when you felt pressured by colleagues or coworkers to do something you felt was wrong, unfair, or unethical. What did you do?
16. Tell me about a time when you had to stand up for a decision you made, even if it made you unpopular. How did you react? How did you feel?
17. Tell me about a time when you experienced interpersonal conflict with a coworker or colleague. What did you do? How did it turn out? How did you feel?
18. Describe some of your communication strengths. How have you used or implemented any of these skills or abilities recently?
19. How many days were you absent from work or school in the past year? What were the reasons for your absence?
20. What kinds of barriers or obstacles have you had to overcome to get where you are today?
21. Do you consider yourself a "self-starter"? If so, give a recent example of a project you initiated.
22. Let's assume you made a decision that was unpopular, although you sincerely believed it was right. Then two weeks later you received information that made you question your original decision. What would you do?

23. Tell me about some of your leisure activities. What do you do for fun or relaxation?
24. Where do you see yourself ten years from now?
25. What are some things you would like to accomplish in your lifetime?

These are just a few of the questions that may be asked during an employment interview. Don't try to memorize your answers to each one. Instead, use them to stimulate your thinking as you prepare.

Interview role-play. Writer Leo Tolstoy once observed that "Everyone thinks of changing the world, but no one thinks about changing themselves." One of the most beneficial activities you can do as you prepare for your interview is to change yourself—to improve your communication skills by videotaping an interview role-playing situation.

For this, you will need a friend, a video camera, and a playback unit. Set up a table or desk with a chair on either side. One chair is for you, the interviewee, and the other is for your friend, the interviewer. Position the video camera to record only you, the interviewee. Set it up behind the "interviewer," making sure your friend's head doesn't block the picture. The picture should include everything from your face to your hands. It isn't necessary to include the "interviewer" in the picture because we are concerned only with your communication behaviors.

Once everything is set, punch the record button and role-play about three minutes of interviewing. Have your friend ask a question from the interview list we just looked at and respond as fully as possible to the question. During the three minutes, you should be able to get through about two or three questions if you develop your responses adequately.

After this first taping, review the three-minute video *without* sound. On a note pad, write down specific nonverbal behaviors you liked and behaviors you felt could be improved. Did you look enthusiastic? Did you smile? Did you have direct eye contact? Were your facial expressions pleasant, warm, and friendly? Did you fidget or play with your hair or jewelry? Did you avoid eye contact? Discuss your list of behaviors with your friend. Remember to look for what you did well first. Be generous with the compliments. Then look for one or two things you might want to change or improve. Be nice to yourself.

Next, review the *same* three-minute video *with* sound. On your note pad, write down specific verbal behaviors and responses you liked and others that you could improve. Was your voice loud enough? Did you speak too fast or slow? Did you pause before responding to questions? Did you have vocal variety or was your voice monotone and lifeless? What were your verbal responses like? Did you answer the questions fully? Did you provide specific examples to support your points? Discuss your list of behaviors and responses with your friend.

After noting some things you want to improve, record a second role-playing interview for three minutes, modifying or changing those specific behaviors or response patterns. Review this second three-minute tape *without* sound, noting nonverbal behavior strengths and weaknesses. Then review it again *with* sound, checking for improvement in your vocal behavior and answers to questions.

This videotaped role-playing exercise will be one of the most important and beneficial activities you will do as you prepare for your interview. One picture is worth a thousand words. As you view yourself on screen, be gentle on yourself. No one is perfect. We're all doing the best we can. So, emphasize what's good and identify one or two behaviors you want to improve each session.

> *There is no such thing as an insignificant improvement.*
> —TOM PETERS

Don't overwhelm yourself. The point is to improve your interviewing skills, not to be perfect.

During the Interview

Well, you've come a long way! You have secured an employment interview, researched the company, and prepared for the interview. Now you are set to actually interview. It is perfectly natural to be nervous as the day draws near. It would be unusual not to be a little anxious. Nervousness can also be viewed as a sign that you are taking this process seriously, eager to do well, and maybe even excited about being hired. Here are some specific suggestions on how you can put all this positive energy to use on interview day.

Bring interview materials. It's a good idea to bring a copy of your résumé to the interview, even though the interviewer suppposedly has one. Also bring any additional materials you feel could be of interest to the interviewer—a pamphlet you designed, an article you authored, and so on. Carry whatever can fit easily into your briefcase. Remember to bring the address, phone number, and name of the interviewer.

Dress professionally. This is the occasion to wear your best clothes. Men should dress in a suit or sports coat, dress shirt, and tie; women in a tailored dress or skirted suit. Make sure your clothes are cleaned and pressed. Wear dress shoes and shine them before leaving the house. Don't wear excessive jewelry and keep your perfume or aftershave to a minimum. Dress professionally for the occasion. It not only shows respect for the interviewer and the company, it also communicates respect for yourself.

Arrive fifteen minutes early. This is not the time to be late. Don't make a poor impression as Todd did with his interviewer by showing up ten minutes late. Leave earlier than necessary. Take those extra minutes to sit in your car and collect yourself before walking into the building. Those few minutes of silence will help to focus and calm you.

Notify the receptionist five to ten minutes before your appointment that you have arrived and whom you are scheduled to see. Make sure you smile and sound friendly, because the interview is beginning now with the receptionist. He may be asked for his impressions of you after the interview.

Greet the interviewer. Greet your interviewer with a firm handshake, direct eye contact, a smile, and a friendly hello. Confirm the pronunciation of the interviewer's last name if you're uncertain. Address the interviewer as Mr., Ms., Mrs., or Dr. during the interview. Don't use the interviewer's first name.

Speak and act in a pleasant manner. Much of the interviewer's impressions of you will be based on your voice and how you come across nonverbally. Is your voice pleasant to listen to? Is your voice warm and conversational in tone? Are you speaking at a comfortable rate? Don't rush your words. Don't force your sentences. Avoid slang and expressions that are not familiar to the interviewer or appropriate for the occasion. Sit in a relaxed, comfortable manner, without appearing sloppy or lazy.

Use direct eye contact when responding to questions, but don't stare at the interviewer for the entire time. Be direct, yet natural. Remember to smile. Your smile will communicate friendliness and a positive attitude. Overall, speak and act like the kind of individual you would want to hire if the roles were reversed.

Thoughtfully consider each question. There's often a tendency to respond to each question immediately, without really considering the response. Give yourself permission to pause a moment or two before beginning your answer. If you don't understand a question, paraphrase what you thought you were asked to check its accuracy. If you still don't understand, ask the interviewer to repeat the question.

Answer each question thoroughly. Avoid brief answers of a word or two. Develop your responses as best you can, citing examples to support your points. Don't ramble on and on, however. Look for feedback from the interviewer's face. Often, nonverbal behavior can signal when you have adequately answered the question. If you are uncertain, ask the interviewer if she would like you to provide another example to develop your point. If you don't know the answer to a question, admit it. Don't pretend you know the answer or exaggerate a response. Your honesty will be appreciated.

Listen effectively. During the interview, remember to use your listening skills. Don't interrupt the interviewer. Listen to the questions or comments until you hear that pause that signals that it is your turn to speak. Nod your head occasionally as a sign that you are understanding the question. Smile as you listen. As mentioned earlier, if you don't understand a question, paraphrase it before you attempt to answer.

Be positive. Emphasize the positive in all your responses. Even if the interviewer asks a question about a weakness, frame your response in a positive fashion—as an area of growth or a learning experience. Never say anything bad or negative about anyone, especially former coworkers or bosses. Communicate the positive in every word that comes from your mouth.

Demonstrate an enthusiastic attitude. Your attitude is vitally important. Create a positive impression by demonstrating enthusiasm during the interview. Be enthusiastic in the way you speak, move, and interact. This doesn't mean that you have to shout and do cartwheels. But it does mean that you communicate that you are happy to be there and will work hard if hired. The interviewer will reason that if you aren't enthusiastic in the interview, you'll never be energetic on the job. Communicate your interest, commitment, and enthusiasm!

> *Give me a museum and I'll fill it.*
>
> —PABLO PICASSO

Limit your discussion of salary and benefits. At the conclusion of most employment interviews, you will be asked if you have any questions. This is not the time to ask about salary, getting a spacious office with a view, or the company's benefits package. Those discussions will come *if* you are offered the job. It would be more advantageous to ask a question or two about the position your are applying for or the company in general. Also ask when you will receive a decision on the position. Remember, you are still being evaluated by the interviewer. Avoid sounding self-centered or greedy. Make a positive, enthusiastic impression all the way to the end of the interview.

Thank the interviewer. Thank the interviewer for the opportunity to interview. Smile and shake the interviewer's hand firmly. Congratulations! You should have made a favorable impression on the interviewer if you followed these suggestions. You have done a great job! Now, relax, sit in your car for a moment, and go treat yourself to a milkshake.

After the Interview

Well, how was the milkshake? I hope you had some time to unwind and relax. But don't relax too much; there are still a couple of things yet to do.

Write a thank-you letter. Before you go to bed tonight, write a thank-you letter to the interviewer. Thank the interviewer for the opportunity to interview and briefly allude to a few of the important points raised during the session. Keep the letter brief, appreciative, and positive. End by saying that you are looking forward to hearing from him or her.

Follow up. If you needed to send additional information or materials to the interviewer, make certain that you do it as soon as possible. It is most effective if you include any follow-up material with your thank-you letter.

Call in two weeks. If you haven't received any communication from the interviewer or the company for two weeks or in the timeframe specified by the interviewer, call the company's personnel department (not your interviewer) and ask for the status of the hiring process. Don't make a nuisance of yourself. You just don't want to be forgotten.

Either way it's good. If you get hired, congratulations a second time! May your new job be everything you hoped it would be and more.

If you didn't get the job, congratulations also! You prepared, practiced, and participated well. It was an honor to be selected for an interview in the first place. Everyone who applies is not asked for an interview. And everyone who interviews is not offered a job. Be gentle on yourself. You are much more experienced and skilled in the interviewing process and this will pay off during your next interview. And there will be a next time.

CREATING A SUCCESSFUL INTERVIEW: THE W.I.N. TECHNIQUE

You will be much more successful interviewing for a job if you have the right attitude. Possessing a healthy attitude toward the work required for interviewing; investing in your mental, physical, and emotional health; and navigating your own career path are the aspects of the W.I.N. Technique to interviewing.

Work

This chapter described the necessary steps required in successful employment interviewing. Examining your motivations and qualifications for a particular job, role-playing the interview, and writing the thank-you letter involve a tremendous amount of work. Hours of research, preparation, planning, and practice are necessary for any successful employment interview. It's not easy. It's not for the merely interested inquirer or casual seeker. It's for the individual who is sincerely committed to doing his or her best—to be willing to work long hours to get a job.

Invest

Successful interviewing depends on your willingness to invest in yourself. Most of this investment occurs long before you begin searching the want ads for employment: your investment of time, money, and effort during your college, graduate school, or professional training.

Workshops, seminars, extension classes, refresher courses, and professional reading are an additional investment in yourself and your skills that will enable you to qualify for positions. Participating in professional organizations and related volunteer organizations is an investment of your time and energy that will help you become a more well-rounded and valuable individual.

In addition to the mental and technical investments, it is beneficial to invest in your physical well-being. Getting regular exercise, staying within a normal weight range, eating a healthy diet, getting plenty of sleep, and laughing a lot with good friends are things that will not only make a favorable impression during a interview, they will increase the odds that you'll be a pleasant, productive, and happy employee.

Finally, emotional investments in yourself will ultimately determine whether or not an interviewer hires you. You may be the most skillfully qualified and physically healthy applicant for a job, but a negative attitude can prevent you from being hired. With increasing frequency, companies both large and small are using psychological testing in the interview process. A candidate's emotional stability, maturity, and general health are vital considerations.

Navigate

You are the one who determines the path you will follow. Whether selecting your major in college or deciding on a particular job, you are the one most responsible for saying yes or no. Often your decisions involve other people, but ultimately you should navigate the waters of your career.

Remember the first step of the interviewing process outlined in this chapter: "Do I want this particular job?" It's very important that you consider this question before applying for a job. You'll be spending one-half of your waking life working there if you get the job, so "there" better be a place you want to work. Decide early on, before you send the cover letter.

If you are offered the job, take some time to consider if you still want to work at that company. You've most likely had a few weeks to consider this question between the interview and the moment the company calls you. Take into consideration the attitude of the interviewer, the corporate culture you picked up on before and after the interview, and your intuitive heart response to the whole situation. You don't have to accept a job, simply because it is offered to you. You could respond by saying, "Thank you for your kind offer, but I'm no longer interested in the job." Wow! Wouldn't that be a mouthful?

There many times you will be presented with choices that only you can decide. Should I supervise this group? Should I submit my proposal? Should I make this suggestion? Should I work weekends? Should I ask for a raise? Should I accept this promotion? Should I look for another job? In these and many other decisions related to your job, you should be the one to decide. Not others. Navigate the waters of your own career.

To a great extent you determine, in word and behavior, the success or failure of any interview. Todd's poor communication behavior prevented him from creating a positive impression on his interviewer. Had Todd arrived on time, responded more effectively to the questions, and demonstrated an eagerness and enthusiasm for the position, the outcome of the interview may have been much different. By your attitude, words, and behavior, you help create the quality of your life.

EXPLORING CREATIVE TASKS

1. List ten questions you would like to be asked by a good friend that would provide information about who you are, what you believe, and how you feel. The questions can be about any topic you feel comfortable sharing. Meet with a friend and have him or her interview you, using your list of ten questions. How did the interview go? How did it feel sharing questions you wrote? What was the response of your friend to this activity? What did you learn about yourself?

2. Make an appointment for an information-gathering interview with an individual who is currently employed in a profession you are interested in pursuing. Construct a list of ten to fifteen questions for the interview. What was the interview like? What specific job benefits and liabilities did you learn about? How do you feel about this job now that you have conducted the interview? Why? Did you write a thank-you note?

3. Make an appointment for an employment interview. This interview can be for a full-time, part-time, or temporary position. Review the employment interviewing guidelines before you begin the interviewing process. What was your interview like? What were your interviewing strengths? What were your interviewing weaknesses? What did you learn about yourself during this activity? Did you get the job?

4. Write a one-page job description of your "ideal" job. Describe your job duties and responsibilities as specifically as possible. Remember, this is your "ideal" job so be good to yourself and create duties and activities that you would love doing every workday. What an assignment—to create a job for yourself! How do you feel about your job? What did you especially like about the job you created? Did anything you listed in your job description surprise you? Why? What job or career most closely resembles the "ideal" job? What would your life be like if you pursued that job? Why?

EXPANDING YOUR CREATIVE THINKING

1. What questions could you ask loved ones that would invite or encourage self-disclosure? What topics could you inquire about that would deepen your relationships with others? How could you modify or improve the manner in which you ask and respond to questions that would create more supportive relationships?

2. What kind of overall first impression do you make with those you meet? Are you satisfied with the way you interact with those you first meet? Why? How could you improve the first impressions you make when you are introduced to someone? Do you wish you were more extroverted or introverted? Why? Do you wish you asked more provocative questions? What questions have you been asked that have made an impression on you? Which of these questions would you feel comfortable asking when you first meet someone?

3. How could you communicate or interact differently during an employment interview for a job or position you didn't need? Suppose you have already

successfully interviewed for two other positions and you've received job offers from both companies, but you thought you would still go to an interview at a third company. Knowing you have two other job offers, how do you think you would feel during this third interview? What thoughts would you have? How would your communication behavior change if you know you didn't have to succeed in this interview? Could this changed perspective or attitude benefit you if this were the first of three job interviews? How?

4. What kinds of things would you do as an employment interviewer to create a supportive, friendly, and effective interview? How would you arrange the physical environment, what questions would you ask, and how would you interact with the interviewee to ensure a successful interview?

Afterword

> *Art is a fruit that grows in man,*
> *like a fruit on a plant, or a child*
> *in its mother's womb.*
>
> —JEAN ARP

Whether you realize it or not, you are an artist, and your life is the canvas on which you will create your greatest work. Your most important creation will not be a painting, a sculpture, or a book. Rather, it will be the person you become during this lifetime, every day of your life.

In this book, you have learned many ways to explore and expand your communication skills. I hope that you will choose to be more creative in the ways you think, speak, listen, and interact with others. It is my sincere wish that you develop your skills and talents as an artist of communication and create a masterpiece during this lifetime.

References

Chapter 1. Creating Effective Communication in Your Life

Carnegie, D. 2008. *Lifetime Plan for Success.* Edison, N.J.: BBS Publishers.

Fujishin, R. 2003. *Gifts from the Heart.* Lanham, Md.: Rowman & Littlefield.

Kinkade, T. 1996. *Simpler Times.* Eugene, Ore.: Harvest House Publishing.

————. 2000. *Lightposts for Living.* New York: Warner Publishing.

Knapp, M., and Vangelisti, A. 1996. *Interpersonal Communication and Human Relationships* (third ed.). Boston: Allyn and Bacon.

Littlejohn, S.W. 1996. *Theories of Human Communication.* Belmont, Calif.: Wadsworth.

Meyerson, M. 1999. *Six Keys to Creating the Life You Desire.* Oakland, Calif.: New Harbinger.

Moran, V. 1999. *Creating a Charmed Life.* San Francisco: Harper San Francisco.

Osborn, S., and Motley, M. 1999. *Improving Communication.* Boston: Houghton Mifflin.

Satir, V. 1993. *Peoplemaking.* Palo Alto, Calif.: Science and Behavior Books.

Stewart, J., and Logan, C. 1998. *Together: Communicating Interpersonally.* Boston: McGraw-Hill.

Suzuki, S. 1994. *Zen Mind, Beginners Mind.* New York: Weatherhill.

Wood, J., ed. 1996. *Gendered Relationships.* Mountain View, Calif.: Mayfield.

Chapter 2. Creating Positive Communication with Yourself

Cooley, C. 1902. *Human Nature and the Social Order* (rev. ed., 1922). New York: Charles Scribner's Sons.

Ellis, A. 1987. *New Guide to Rational Living.* North Hollywood, Calif.: Wilshire Book Company.

Fanning, P. 2002. *Self Esteem.* Alcoa, Tenn.: Fine Communications.

Helmstetter, S. 1992. *What to Say When You Talk to Yourself.* New York: MJF Books.

McKay, M. 2000. *Self-Esteem.* Oakland, Calif.: New Harbinger.

Moore, T. 1992. *Care of the Soul.* New York: HarperCollins.

Osborn, S., and Motley, M. 1999. *Improving Communication.* Boston: Houghton Mifflin.

Storr, A. 1988. *Solitude.* New York: Free Press.

Thoele, S. 2001. *The Courage to be Yourself.* Newburyport, Mass.: Red Wheel/Weiser.

Trenholm, S., and Jensen, A. 1995. *Interpersonal Communication* (third ed.). Belmont, Calif.: Wadsworth.

Chapter 3. Creating Expressive Verbal Communication

Adler, R. 2007. *Looking Out, Looking In.* Belmont, Calif.: Wadsworth Publishing.

Ginott, H. 2003. *Between Parent and Child.* New York: Crown Publishing.

Goleman, D. 1995. *Emotional Intelligence.* New York: Bantam Books.

Gordon, T. 2000. *Parent Effectiveness Training.* New York: Crown Publishing.

Knapp, M., and Vangelisti, A. 1996. *Interpersonal Communication and Human Relationships* (third ed.). Boston: Allyn and Bacon.

Maltz, D., and Borker, R. 1982. "A Cultural Approach to Male-Female Miscommunication." *Language and Social Identity,* ed. by John Gumpert. Cambridge: Cambridge University Press.

Patterson, K. 2002. *Crucial Conversations.* Hightstown, N.J.: McGraw-Hill.

Stewart, J., and Logan, C. 1998. *Together: Communicating Interpersonally.* Boston: McGraw-Hill.

Stone, D. 1999. *Difficult Conversations.* New York: Viking.

Tannen, D. 1990. *You Just Don't Understand.* New York: Ballantine.

Trenholm, S., and Jensen, A. 1995. *Interpersonal Communication* (third ed.). Belmont, Calif.: Wadsworth.

Wood, J., ed. 1996. *Gendered Relationships.* Mountain View, Calif.: Mayfield.

CHAPTER 4. CREATING SUPPORTIVE NONVERBAL COMMUNICATION

Canary, D., and Cody, M. 1994. *Interpersonal Communication.* New York: St. Martin's.

Duck, S. 1997. *Handbook of Personal Relationships.* New York: Wiley.

Ekman, P. 2003. *Unmasking the Face.* Cambridge, Mass.: ISHK Publishing.

———. 2007. *Emotions Revealed.* New York: Holt & Co.

Godek, G. 1995. *1001 Ways to be Romantic.* Naperville, Ill.: Casablanca Press.

Hall, E. 1966. *The Hidden Dimension.* Garden City, N.Y.: Anchor Books.

Hartley, G. 2007. *I Can Read You Like a Book.* Franklin Lakes, N.J.: Career Press.

Knapp, M. L., and Hall, J. 1992. *Nonverbal Communication in Human Interaction.* New York: Harcourt Brace Jovanovich.

Leathers, D. G. 1992. *Successful Nonverbal Communication: Principles and Applications.* New York: Macmillan.

Mehrabian, A. 2007. *Nonverbal Communication.* Piscataway, N.J.: Transaction Publishers.

Montagu, A. 1986. *Touching: The Human Significance of the Skin.* New York: HarperCollins.

Reiman, T. 2007. *Power of Body Language.* New York: Simon & Schuster.

Seiler, W., and Beall, M. 1999. *Communication: Making Connections.* Boston: Allyn and Bacon.

CHAPTER 5. CREATING SPACIOUS COMMUNICATION WITH ANOTHER CULTURE

Almaney, A. J., and Alwan, A. J. 1982. *Communicating with Arabs.* Prospect Heights, Ill.: Waveland Press.

Chaney, L. 2005. *Intercultural Business Communication.* Upper Saddle River, N.J.: Prentice-Hall.

Eckert, S. 2005. *Intercultural Communication.* Nashville: South-Western.

Friedman, T. 2007. *The World is Flat.* London: Picador Publishers.

Hall, E. 1976. *Beyond Culture.* Garden City, N.Y.: Anchor Books.

Lustig, M. W., and Koester, J. 1993. *Intercultural Competence.* New York: HarperCollins.

Samovar, L. 2006. *Communication Between Cultures.* Belmont, Calif.: Wadsworth.

Seiler, W. 1999. *Communication: Making Connections.* Boston: Allyn and Bacon.

Storey, J. 1996. *Cultural Studies and the Study of Popular Culture.* Athens: University of Georgia Press.

CHAPTER 6. CREATING RECEPTIVE COMMUNICATION AS A LISTENER

Barker, L. 1981. "An Investigation of Proportional Time Spend in Various Communication Activities by College Students." *Journal of Applied Communication Research.*
Canary, D., and Cody, M. 1994. *Interpersonal Communication.* New York: St. Martin's.
Duck, S. 1997. *Handbook of Personal Relationships.* New York: Wiley.
Fine, D. 2005. *The Fine Art of Small Talk.* New York: Hyperion.
Hamlin, S. 1988. *How to Talk So People Will Listen.* New York: Harper Row.
Hocker, J., and Wilmot, W. 1995. *Interpersonal Conflict* (fourth ed.). Madison, Wis.: Brown and Benchmark.
Knapp, M., and Vangelisti, A. 1996. *Interpersonal Communication and Human Relationships* (third ed.). Boston: Allyn and Bacon.
May, S. 2007. *How to Argue So Your Spouse Will Listen.* Nashville: Thomas Nelson.
Nichols, R. 1959. *Are You Listening?* New York: McGraw-Hill.
Pease, A. 2001. *Why Men Don't Listen and Women Can't Read Maps.* New York: Broadway Books.
Shelby, J. 2007. *Listen with Empathy.* Charlottesville, Va.: Hampton Roads Publishing.
Wolvin, A. D. 1991. "A Survey of the Status of Listening Training in Some Fortune 500 Corporations." *Communication Education* (40).
Wolvin, A. D., and Robick, C. G. 1996. *Listening* (fifth ed.). Dubuque, Iowa: Brown and Benchmark.

CHAPTER 7. CREATING HEALTHY COMMUNICATION IN RELATIONSHIPS

Chapman, G. 1992. *The Five Love Languages.* Northfield, Vt.: Northfield Publishing.
———. 2006. *Everybody Wins.* Carol Stream, Ill.: Tyndale House Publisher.
Duck, S. 1997. *Handbook of Personal Relationships.* New York: Wiley.
Fujishin, R. 2003. *Gifts from the Heart.* Lanham, Md.: Rowman & Littlefield.
Ginott, H. 2003. *Between Parent and Child.* New York: Crown Publishing.
Hendrix, H. 2007. *Getting the Love You Want: A Guide for Couples.* New York: Henry Holt & Co.
Knapp, M., and Vangelisti, A. 1996. *Interpersonal Communication and Human Relationships* (third ed.). Boston: Allyn and Bacon.
Moore, T. 1994. *Soul Mates.* New York: HarperPerennial.
Osborn, S., and Motley, M. 1999. *Improving Communication.* Boston: Houghton Mifflin.
Sherman, R. 1984. *Handbook of Structured Techniques in Marriage and Family Therapy.* New York: Brunner/Mazel.
Wood, J., ed. 1996. *Gendered Relationships.* Mountain View, Calif.: Mayfield.

CHAPTER 8. CREATING COOPERATIVE COMMUNICATION IN GROUPS

Dewey, J. 1910. *How People Think.* Boston: D.C. Heath.
Ellis, D., and B. A. Fisher. 1993. *Small Group Decision Making: Communication and the Group Process.* New York: McGraw-Hill.
Fujishin, R. 1996. *Discovering the Leader Within.* San Francisco: Acada Books.

———. 2007. *Creating Effective Groups.* Lanham, Md.: Rowman & Littlefield.

Greenleaf, R. 1998. *The Power of Servant Leadership.* San Francisco: Berrett-Koehler Publishers.

Guffey, M. 2006. *Business Communication.* Nashville: South-Western.

Harris, J. 1996. *Getting Employees to Fall in Love with Your Company.* New York: Amacon.

Hocker, J., and Wilmot, W. 1995. *Interpersonal Conflict* (fourth ed.). Madison, Wis.: Brown and Benchmark.

Rothwell, D. 2007. *In Mixed Company.* Belmont, Calif.: Wadsworth.

Scot, Ober. 1998. *Contemporary Business Communication* (third ed.). Boston: Houghton Mifflin.

Whetten, D. A., and Cameron, K. S. 1995. *Developing Management Skills* (third ed.). New York: HarperCollins.

Wright, D. 2003. *Communication in Small Groups.* Belmont, Calif.: Wadsworth.

CHAPTER 9. CREATING GUIDING COMMUNICATION AS A LEADER

Beebe, S. 1995. *Communicating in Small Groups.* New York: HarperCollins.

Clarke, B. 2002. *The Leader's Voice.* New York: Select Books.

Drucker, P. 1999. *Management Challenges for the 21st Century.* New York: Harper-Business.

Fujishin, R. 1996. *Discovering the Leader Within.* San Francisco: Acada Books.

———. 2007. *Creating Effective Groups.* Lanham, Md.: Rowman & Littlefield.

Greenleaf, R. 2002. *Servant Leadership.* Mahwah, N.J.: Paulist Press.

Keyton, J. 1999. *Group Communication.* Mountain View, Calif.: Mayfield.

Lencioni, P. 2007. *Death by Meeting.* New York: John Wiley & Co.

Maxwell, J. 2002. *Leadership 101.* Nashville: Thomas Nelson.

Schultz, B. 1996. *Communicating in Groups.* New York: HarperCollins.

Wood, J., et al. 1986. *Group Discussion: A Practical Guide to Participation and Leadership.* New York: HarperCollins.

CHAPTER 10 CREATING SKILLFUL COMMUNICATION IN A SPEECH

Carnegie, D. 2006. *Public Speaking for Success.* New York: Penguin Group.

Fujishin, R. 2008. *The Natural Speaker* (sixth ed.). Needham Heights, Mass.: Allyn and Bacon.

Kearney, P., and Plax, T. 1999. *Public Speaking in a Diverse Society.* Mountain View, Calif.: Mayfield.

Kushner, M. 2004. *Public Speaking for Dummies.* New York: John Wiley & Sons.

Lucas, S. 2007. *The Art of Public Speaking.* Hightstown, N.J.: McGraw-Hill.

Motley, M. 1997. *Overcoming Your Fear of Public Speaking.* Boston: Houghton Mifflin.

Osborn, S., and Motley, M. 1999. *Improving Communication.* Boston: Houghton Mifflin.

Van Ekeren, G. 1994. *Speaker's Handbook II.* Paramus, N.J.: Prentice Hall.

CHAPTER 11. CREATING STRATEGIC COMMUNICATION IN YOUR SPEECHES

Fujishin, R. 2008. *The Natural Speaker* (sixth ed.). Needham Heights, Mass.: Allyn and Bacon.

Hamlin, S. 2005. *How to Talk So People Listen.* New York: HarperCollins.

Kearney, P., and Plax, T. 1999. *Public Speaking in a Diverse Society.* Mountain View, Calif.:
    Mayfield.
Lucas, S. 1998. *The Art of Public Speaking.* Boston: McGraw-Hill.
Monarth, H. 2007. *The Confident Speaker.* Hightstown, N.J.: McGraw-Hill.
O'Hair, D., and Stewart, R. 1999. *Public Speaking.* Boston: Bedford/St. Martin's.
Osborn, S., and Motley, M. 1999. *Improving Communication.* Boston: Houghton Mifflin.
Rogers, W. 2006. *Persuasion.* Lanham, Md.: Rowman & Littlefield.
Verderber, R. 2005. *The Challenge of Effective Speaking.* Belmont, Calif.: Wadsworth.

CHAPTER 12. CREATING SUCCESSFUL COMMUNICATION DURING AN INTERVIEW

Anderson, B., and Ross, V. 1998. *Questions of Communication.* New York: St. Martin's.
Bolles, R. 2007. *What Color Is Your Parachute?* Berkeley, Calif.: Ten Speed Press.
Bozell, J. 1999. *Anatomy of a Job Search.* Springhouse, Pa.: Springhouse Press.
Hawley, C. *Job-Winning Answers to the Hardest Interview Questions.* New York: Barnes &
    Noble Books.
Kessler, R. 2006. *Competency-Based Interviews.* Franklin Lakes, N.J.: Career Press.
Medley, H. *Sweaty Palms.* Dublin: Business Plus Publishing.
Scott, M., and Brydon, S. 1997. *Dimensions of Communication.* Mountain View, Calif.:
    Mayfield.
Verderber, R., and Verderber, K. 1998. *Inter-act.* Belmont, Calif.: Wadsworth.
Whitcomb, S. 2005. *Interview Magic.* St. Paul, Minn.: JIST Publishing.

Index

Other Books by Randy Fujishin

Gifts from the Heart:
10 Communication Skills for Developing More Loving Relationships

From the Preface:

Deep in our hearts we all desire relationships that are loving, healthy, and meaningful. We want relationships that nurture our spirit, encourage our growth, and even make us laugh in the quiet of the night. We yearn for this. Yet many times, this is not our experience.

Because no one is born with the communication skills that bring us closer to those we love, they must be learned. As a relationship communications instructor and a marriage and family therapist, I have had the privilege of helping men and women, just like you, learn, practice, and improve ten fundamental communication skills necessary for any long-term relationship. I encourage my students and clients to view each skill as a gift they can share rather than simply a behavior they can implement. This perspective empowers them to participate more fully in their relationships by giving these gifts of communication instead of waiting to receive what the other person might offer. These gifts, whether intended for a spouse, parent, family member, lover, or friend, can greatly enhance and strengthen any relationship.

Discovering the Leader Within:
Running Small Groups Successfully

From the Preface:

Working in groups is part of your life. Whether you're the chairperson of a committee, a volunteer in a fund-raising group, a member of an assembly team, or the head of a family reunion planning committee, you will be working with others in small groups to solve problems.

The purpose of this book is to provide you with a basic understanding of solving problems in a small group setting and the skills necessary to participate in and lead effective group discussion. Unlike other books dealing with group problem solving, this book emphasizes your personal growth and development as you work with others in the group process. Furthermore, the knowledge and skills you gain from this book will enable you to discover the leader within you—that part of you that helps the group achieve its goals.